D167452

# STUDENT'S GUIDE TO
# LANDMARK
# CONGRESSIONAL LAWS
# ON SOCIAL SECURITY
# AND
# WELFARE

**Recent Titles in**
**Student's Guide to Landmark Congressional Laws**

Student's Guide to Landmark Congressional Laws on Education
*David Carleton*

Student's Guide to Landmark Congressional Laws on the First Amendment
*Clyde E. Willis*

Student's Guide to Landmark Congressional Laws on Youth
*Kathleen Uradnik*

# STUDENT'S GUIDE TO LANDMARK CONGRESSIONAL LAWS

# ON SOCIAL SECURITY AND WELFARE

## STEVEN G. LIVINGSTON

STUDENT'S GUIDE TO
LANDMARK CONGRESSIONAL LAWS
John R. Vile, Series Editor

**Greenwood Press**
Westport, Connecticut • London

**Library of Congress Cataloging-in-Publication Data**

Livingston, Steven (Steven Greene)
    Student's guide to landmark congressional laws on social security and welfare /
Steven Livingston.
        p.   cm.—(Student's guide to landmark congressional laws, ISSN 1537–3150)
    Includes bibliographical references and index.
    ISBN 0–313–31343–1 (alk. paper)
    1. Social security—Law and legislation—United States.   2. Medicare—United
States.   3. Public welfare—Law and legislation—United States   I. Title.   II. Series.
KF3600 .L58   2002
344.73'023—dc21        2002016610

British Library Cataloguing in Publication Data is available.

Library of Congress Catalog Card Number: 2002016610
ISBN:   0–313–31343–1
ISSN: 1537–3150

First published in 2002

Greenwood Press, 88 Post Road West, Westport, CT 06881
An imprint of Greenwood Publishing Group, Inc.
www.greenwood.com

Printed in the United States of America

The paper used in this book complies with the
Permanent Paper Standard issued by the National
Information Standards Organization (Z39.48–1984).

10 9 8 7 6 5 4 3 2 1

# Contents

# Series Foreword

Most of the Founding Fathers who met at the Constitutional Convention in Philadelphia in the summer of 1787 probably anticipated that the legislative branch would be the most powerful of the three branches of the national government that they created. For all practical purposes, this was the only branch of government with which the onetime colonists had experience under the Articles of Confederation. Moreover, the delegates discussed this branch first and at greatest length at the convention, the dispute over representation in this body was one of the convention's most contentious issues, and the Founding Fathers made it the subject of the first and longest article of the new Constitution.

With the president elected indirectly through an electoral college and the members of the Supreme Court appointed by the president with the advice and consent of the Senate and serving for life terms, the framers of the Constitution had little doubt that Congress—and especially the House of Representatives, whose members were directly elected by the people for short two-year terms—would be closest to the people. As a consequence, they invested Congress with the awesome "power of the purse" that had been at issue in the revolutionary dispute with Great Britain, where the colonists' position had been encapsulated in the phrase "no taxation without representation." The framers also entrusted Congress with the more general right to adopt laws to carry out a variety of enumerated powers and other laws "necessary and proper" to the implementation of these powers—the basis for the doctrine of implied powers.

Wars and the threats of wars have sometimes tilted the modern balance of power toward the president, who has gained in a media age from his position as a single individual. Still, Congress has arguably been the most powerful branch of government over the long haul, and one might expect its power to increase with the demise of the Cold War. Especially in the aftermath of President Franklin D. Roosevelt's New Deal and President Lyndon B. Johnson's Great Society program, the number and complexity of laws have increased with the complexity of modern society and the multitude of demands that citizens have placed on modern governments. Courts have upheld expansive interpretations of federal powers under the commerce clause, the war-powers provisions, and the power to tax and spend for the general welfare, and in recent elections Democratic and Republican candidates alike have often called for expansive new federal programs.

It has been noted that there are 297 words in the Ten Commandments, 463 in the Bill of Rights, 266 in the Gettysburg Address, and more than 26,000 in a federal directive regulating the price of cabbage. Although the U.S. Constitution can be carried in one's pocket, the compilation of federal laws in the *U.S. Code* and the *U.S. Code Annotated* requires many volumes, not generally available in high-school and public libraries. Perhaps because of this modern prolixity and complexity, students often consider the analysis of laws to be the arcane domain of lawyers and law reviewers. Ironically, scholars, like this author, who focus on law, and especially constitutional law, tend to devote more attention to the language of judicial decisions interpreting laws than to the laws themselves.

Because knowledge of laws and their impact needs to be made more widely accessible, this series on Landmark Congressional Laws presents and examines laws relating to a number of important topics. These currently include education, First Amendment rights, civil rights, the environment, the rights of young people, women's rights, and health and social security. Each subject is a matter of importance that should be of key interest to high-school and college students. A college professor experienced in communicating ideas to undergraduates has compiled each of these volumes. Each author has selected major laws in his or her subject area and has described the politics of these laws, considering such aspects as their adoption, their interpretation, and their impact.

The laws in each volume are arranged chronologically. The entry on each law features an introduction that explains the law, its significance, and its place within the larger tapestry of legislation on the issues. A selection from the actual text of the law itself follows the introduction. This arrangement thus provides ready access to texts that are often difficult for students to find while highlighting major provisions, often taken from literally hundreds of pages, that students and scholars might spend hours to distill on their own.

These volumes are designed to be profitable to high-school and college students who are examining various public policy issues. They should also help interested citizens, scholars, and legal practitioners needing a quick, but thorough and accurate, introduction to a specific area of public policy-making. Although each book is designed to cover highlights of the entire history of federal legislation within a given subject area, the authors of these volumes have also designed them so that individuals who simply need to know the background and major provisions of a single law (the Civil Rights Act of 1964, for example) can quickly do so.

The Founding Fathers of the United States devised a system of federalism dividing power between the state and national governments. Thus, in many areas of legislation, even a complete overview of national laws will prove inadequate unless it is supplemented with knowledge of state and even local laws. This is duly noted in entries on laws where national legislation is necessarily incomplete and where powers are shared among the three layers of government. The U.S. system utilizes a system of separation of powers that divides authority among three branches of the national government. Thus, while these volumes keep the focus on legislation, they also note major judicial decisions and presidential initiatives relating to the laws covered.

Although the subjects of this series are worthy objects of study in their own right, they are especially appropriate topics for students and scholars in a system of representative democracy like the United States where citizens who are at least eighteen years of age have the right to choose those who will represent them in public office. In government, those individuals, like James Madison, Abraham Lincoln, and Woodrow Wilson, who have acquired the longest and clearest view of the past are frequently those who can also see the farthest into the future. This series is presented in the hope that it will help students both to understand the past and to equip themselves for future lives of good citizenship.

This editor wishes to thank his friends at Greenwood Press, his colleagues both at his own university and at other institutions of higher learning who have done such an able job of highlighting and explaining the laws that are the focus of this series, and those students, scholars, and citizens who have responded by reading and utilizing these volumes. When the Founding Fathers drew up a constitution, they depended not only on a set of structures and rights but also on the public-spiritedness and education of future citizens. When Benjamin Franklin was asked what form of government the Founding Fathers had created, he reportedly responded, "A republic, if you can keep it." When we inform ourselves and think deeply about the government's role in major areas of public policy, we honor the faith and foresight of those who bequeathed this government to us.

John R. Vile
Middle Tennessee State University

# Timeline of Social Security and Welfare Laws

1862  **Homestead Act of 1862**
America's first "welfare" policy, the Homestead Act allowed any American over the age of 21 or the head of a household, to settle on government-owned land and, upon working the land for five years, take title of it. This was claimed as a solution to urban unemployment and low wages.

1879  **The Pension Arrears Act**
Liberalized the pension program for disabled Civil War veterans, in effect, creating America's first mass government pension system.

1890  **Disability Pension Act**
A second liberalization of the Civil War pension system that allowed virtually every Union veteran to obtain a government pension. Created a large-scale federal old-age program that covered two-thirds of aged, nonimmigrant Northern white males and their families.

1909  **National Conference on the Care of Dependent Children**
A White House-sponsored meeting that led to among the first calls for federal welfare programs for children and mothers.

1912  **Creation of the Children's Bureau**
The United States' first federal social welfare agency. It was charged with investigating matters pertaining to the welfare of children. The agency today resides in the Department of Health and Human Services.

1921  **The Infancy and Maternity Protection Act**
Better known as the Sheppard-Towner Act, this was the first federal bill to improve America's health via the provision of funds to assist local maternal and child health care services. It is also the first program to employ the concept of matching funds, the form of financing that would be used for many future social welfare programs.

1929        **Repeal of the Infancy and Maternity Protection Act**

1929–41     **The Great Depression**
            America's worst economic crisis created the political conditions for the
            creation of a social insurance system.

1932        **Election of Franklin D. Roosevelt**
            Roosevelt wanted a national system of social insurance, and developed
            the Social Security Act.

1935        **The Social Security Act**
            America's most important piece of social legislation, the Social Security
            Act created a joint federal-state unemployment compensation program,
            a federal old-age insurance program, and a series of joint federal-state
            public assistance programs, the best known being the Aid for Depend-
            ent Children program.

1937        ***Stewart Machine Co. v. Davis* and *Helvering v. Davis***
            The Supreme Court rules the Social Security Act of 1935 to be consti-
            tutional.

1939        **Social Security Act Amendments of 1939**
            The Social Security Act was revised to include survivor's benefits for the
            spouse or dependent children of an eligible deceased worker, and to
            include a supplemental benefit for a nonworking spouse of a benefici-
            ary. The calculation of social security benefits was liberalized and the
            first steps were taken in shifting the program from being an annuity
            plan to a "pay-as-you-go" plan.

1944        **President Roosevelt asks for an "Economic Bill of Rights"**
            FDR asked Congress for federal health care and disability programs, as
            well as an expansion of Social Security. Congress never acted on his
            requests, but the speech introduced the issues that would dominate the
            American social insurance debate for the next 20 years.

1944        **The Servicemen's Readjustment Act (G.I. Bill)**
            The first social legislation after World War II, the G.I. Bill subsidized
            the cost of higher education, and home and business purchases, for
            veterans. It also provided limited job training and unemployment assis-
            tance.

1949        **President Truman proposes a National Health Care plan**
            The plan would have provided comprehensive health benefits to all
            Americans. The first presidential effort to create such a program, it was
            defeated in Congress.

1950        **The Social Security Amendments of 1950**
            The Amendments extended social security coverage to an additional ten
            million Americans, finally bringing the vast majority of workers into the
            program. It also raised benefits by 77.5 percent, the largest benefit in-
            crease in program history. This brought social security benefits close to
            the level of a "livable pension."

1956    **The Social Security Amendments of 1956**
The Amendments added a federal disability program to Social Security.

1962    **The Public Welfare Amendments of 1962**
The Amendments recreated Title IV of the Social Security Act to focus on poor families as much as poor children. The rechristened Aid for Families with Dependent Children program focused upon rehabilitation services, and providing families with the skills to improve their life circumstances. Two-parent families became eligible for AFDC assistance.

1964    **The Economic Opportunity Act**
The EOA launched President Johnson's "War on Poverty." It consisted of a series of job training and work experience programs, together with federal grants for community-centered antipoverty programs. The Office of Economic Opportunity was created to coordinate this, and other welfare efforts.

1964    **The Food Stamp Act of 1964**
This act created food stamps, perhaps America's best known antipoverty program.

1965    **The Social Security Amendments of 1965**
The Amendments created Medicare and Medicaid. Medicare is the primary health care program for Americans over the age of 65. Medicaid, operated by the states, is the health care program for indigent Americans.

1969    **President Nixon proposes the "Family Assistance Plan"**
Nixon attempted to replace the Aid to Families with Dependent Children program with a federal guaranteed annual income plan, supplemented with work incentives. His program was rejected by Congress, but it did lead to the Supplemental Security Assistance program, and, indirectly, the Earned Income Tax Credit.

1972    **Cost-of-Living Adjustment added to Social Security**
As part of a bill raising the debt ceiling, future social security benefits were made to rise automatically at the rate of the Consumer Price Index.

1972    **The Special Supplemental Nutrition Program for Women, Infants, and Children**
As part of the Children's Nutrition Act of 1966, Congress established a temporary program to provide funds to the states to enable them to provide supplemental nutritious foods to pregnant women and young children. The program was made permanent in 1975.

1972    **Supplemental Security Assistance**
The Social Security Amendments of 1972 replaced Titles I, X, and XIV of the Social Security Act (the programs for the needy aged, the disabled, and the blind, respectively) with Supplemental Security Assistance, a federally managed guaranteed income program.

1974    **The Office of Economic Opportunity is terminated**

1975     **The Earned Income Tax Credit**
Low-income workers were given a tax credit that would reduce their income taxes. The EITC was expanded in 1978, 1986, 1990, and 1993.

1977     **The Food Stamp Act of 1977**
The Food Stamp Act of 1964 was completely rewritten to drop the requirement that food stamps must be purchased. It also incorporated earlier revisions that liberalized benefits, and made the program mandatory upon the states.

1977     **President Carter proposes the "Program for Better Jobs and Income"**
The program would have guaranteed jobs to the poor who could work, and guaranteed an income to those who could not. The PBJI died in Congress.

1981     **The National Commission for Social Security Reform established**
Also known as the "Greenspan Committee," the commission recommended social security reforms that were incorporated in the Social Security Amendments of 1983.

1983     **The Social Security Amendments of 1983**
To resolve a financing crisis, Congress enacted reforms that included additional workers, raised the retirement age, and, for certain individuals, reduced social security benefits or raised the FICA tax.

1988     **The Family Support Act of 1988**
The Family Support Act redirected welfare policy towards maintaining the nuclear family and encouraging welfare recipients to enter the workforce.

1996     **The Personal Responsibility and Work Opportunity Reconciliation Act of 1996**
The PRWORA, the most extensive overhaul of welfare policy in 60 years, eliminated the AFDC program in favor of "Temporary Assistance to Needy Families" grants to operate state-run programs. The act imposed lifetime limits on how long an individual can obtain public assistance and made it mandatory to work to receive that assistance.

2001     **The Senior Citizen's Freedom to Work Act of 2001**
This act repealed the "earnings test" for all social security beneficiaries who do not take early (age 62) retirement.

# Introduction

America is a welfare state. When two-fifths of Americans receive income transfers from the government, and federal spending on retirement pensions, health care, and income security programs approaches one trillion dollars a year, one can hardly argue otherwise. In fact, over one half of the United States budget is expended on social insurance. Yet many commentators focus upon the relative backwardness of America in this regard. The U.S. system of social insurance is piecemeal, and far less comprehensive in coverage than most European systems. America appears the laggard in providing universal, comprehensive social care for its citizens. There is something to this claim, but one could as easily argue the real puzzle is actually quite the reverse. Faced with seemingly insuperable cultural, political, and constitutional obstacles, how did a welfare state come to be constructed in this country? The laws in this volume provide an answer to this question.

Presented in the following chapters are the laws that created the American system of social insurance. These laws are introduced chronologically. Each chapter develops the background and motivation for one of these laws, and the political actions and debates that surrounded its passage. The chapter then contains an explanation of the content of the law as actually enacted, and its contribution to the creation of the American welfare state. Edited excerpts from the laws follow each explanation. In several cases, where two laws were intimately connected, they are considered together. The 23 laws included in this volume constitute the most important pieces of American national social insurance legislation, whether defined by historical interest, administrative development, financial impact, the numbers of Americans affected, or simply by their symbolism. Together they are responsible for virtually the entirety of this nation's present social insurance regime. Their politics is the politics of its construction. They are the key episodes in the creation of a web of social policies that today envelops the life of every American.

What do we mean, precisely, by social insurance, or by calling the United States a welfare state? Simply put, social insurance is the set of programs that provide family income security for all Americans. And a welfare state is one that finances and administers these programs. Life is risky. Insurance is a means to protect ourselves against those risks. Most risks are handled through private insurance. A few argue that all risks ought to be handled in this manner. But in practice this has proved difficult. Some risks are not very amenable to private insurance contracts. Income security is one such risk. How would one protect oneself from a systemic economic collapse, such as the Great Depression, or from the costs of fighting in World War II? Some individuals would be unable to purchase the policies they would need. Children and aged retirees are two examples. Other individuals would fail to purchase a policy, and, through their failure, impose costs on the rest of society. For the same reasons we must buy "uninsured motorist" coverage for our own cars, we would face having to cover the social costs of other people's failure to buy their insurance. These social costs might include increased crime, lower national income, or even the stability of the social order itself. Or, alternatively, we would have to allow the uninsured to pay the full costs of their failure, whether that be grinding poverty, a degraded life, or even early death. Few wealthy societies have willingly chosen the latter. They have instead developed social insurance, and it depends on government action.

The social insurance needed for family income security varies by circumstance. For someone in the workforce, the risks to income are losing one's job or losing the ability to work altogether. Hence the need for unemployment and disability insurance. For someone who has retired from the workforce, the threat is not having, or losing, the savings on which to live. Hence the need for an old-age assistance program. For a person unable to enter the workforce, the problem is lack of access to a sufficient income. For someone not old enough to join the workforce, the threat is the failure to gain the skills that would enable the person to gain employment when he or she attained majority. Against these latter risks, the government provides what is loosely termed "welfare," a set of policies to inculcate necessary skills while providing financial assistance in the interim. Finally, for all groups, catastrophic expenses also constitute a serious risk to income security. In modern societies, health care has proved the likely source of such catastrophe, and has led to government-supported health programs.

Which risks will be covered through government action, how they will be covered, and to what extent, are all political questions. They are answered, in our case, through the workings of the American political system; that is, through the interaction of popular opinion, interest group pressure, elections, presidential initiative, congressional action, and tests of constitutionality. Because it is the result of politics, the shape of our social insurance system has changed dramatically over the course of our history.

The change has not been random. Over the last two centuries, a rural, agricultural society became urban and industrial (and today, postindustrial). This evolution logically produced ever greater demands for government-led social insurance. As Americans left the farm, they encountered risks not previously known. They might lose their job, or never find one. They needed job skills far beyond those of their grandparents. And, though being unable to work or being too aged to work were not new problems, separation from the extended family meant there may be no one to take care of them. In each case, government assistance was an answer. The expansion of the welfare state was the result.

But here is where the United States has differed. Compared to other industrialized nations, the U.S. system of social insurance is narrow in scope and was late in coming. The economic impetus was the same, but the response was different. It turns out there is no one "rational" response to a society's need for social insurance. What accounts for the uniqueness of the American welfare state?

Let's begin with the American political culture. Polling data suggest the U.S. public has a rather complicated set of expectations of government action. It is neither pro- nor antigovernment. However, it has long held a set of definite prejudices about whom the government should help. Americans believe that, in the first instance, individuals must help themselves. They must work hard, obey the law, and "play by the rules." Towards these individuals, should they find themselves in trouble, Americans will countenance government help. Thus, assistance for senior citizens, the disabled, or the "deserving poor" is widely supported. But this support dissolves when the programs are thought to be directed at individuals who are shirking their responsibilities, lazy, or taking advantage of the public largesse. This set of beliefs has anchored U.S. social insurance policy in the work ethic, creating a unique twist to the American welfare state. We have no public employment program, no guaranteed income, no permanent "dole." The American social insurance system is the product of a continuing fight over exactly who deserves assistance, and how much they should get.

To this, we add our federal system of government. The American Constitution is one of enumerated powers. For most of our history, social insurance was believed to be a matter for the states, not the federal government. Indeed, President Roosevelt and his advisors developed the Social Security Act of 1935 in the shadow of the very real threat it would be declared unconstitutional, an illegal intrusion into the powers reserved for the states. Until recently, most social insurance policy was a patchwork quilt of state policies. When it came to social insurance, the difference between living in, say, Wisconsin or Arkansas, may have been as great as if one lived in different countries. Federalism braked the development of a unified, American system of social insurance, and limited the scope of the system that did eventually develop. The American welfare state was built over the opposition of those who believed the states could, and should, be responsible for these policies. The struggle over this issue has framed every major social insurance initiative of the last century.

Then, we must consider the role of Congress itself. The fulcrum of Washington politics, the rules and norms of congressional behavior profoundly affect the fate of the legislation it considers. Congress is a highly parochial body. It reflects the ambitions, and the power, of members who are each elected not by America, but by their particular states or districts. The committee system, the seniority system, and the special powers of the speaker of the House and other leaders, have all made difficult the development of a rational, coherent social insurance program. Powerful individuals have their own agendas, and, in the U.S. Congress, not infrequently the ability to achieve them. In this volume we will see many instances of major legislation powered or blocked by individual members of Congress who happened to reside at key points in the legislative process. In particular, for most of the twentieth century, the most important congressional committees were disproportionately held by members from the region most opposed to the expansion of social insurance, the South. The United States does not elect political parties to govern it, nor does it vote for political manifestos then ratified by a compliant assembly. It elects several hundred individuals, loosely linked by party, ideology, or region. Legislation only emerges through the pulling and hauling of those individuals, along with whatever outside pressure may be exerted upon them. To expect anything other than deeply compromised, hastily redrafted, and piecemeal legislation as the result of this process is to miss this essential feature of our political system. No other industrialized state has a legislative body like the U.S. Congress, and this explains much of why America has never produced a social insurance system that looks much like that of any other nation.

Each of these characteristics can be seen as a conservative force. They make difficult the passage of ambitious, expansive federal legislation. Only under favorable political circumstances are such bills passed. This has given the development of U.S. social insurance policy an episodic quality. A political opening, such as that provided by the Great Depression or the Great Society, enables a flurry of legislation, but it is then followed by a long period of retrenchment and consolidation. The American welfare state is the cumulation of such episodes.

## THE DEVELOPMENT OF AMERICA'S SOCIAL INSURANCE POLICY

The American constitution mentions neither income security nor any of its components. It comes no closer than the preamble's vague admonition to "promote the general Welfare." Neither the founders nor America's early citizens desired or anticipated significant federal social insurance programs. To the extent citizens looked for such help, they looked to their states. And what the states provided was minimal. Orphanages and poor houses about sum up the "safety net" of nineteenth-century America. The two great exceptions were both because of unusual historical circumstances. Each could be argued to have merely proved the larger rule. The first exception was the Homestead Act (1862). It offered the American frontier as a safety valve for the landless and the unemployed. But only someone with the initiative and ability to relocate and then work the land could take advantage of the act. The second exception was the pension system provided for Civil

War veterans. By 1890 the family of virtually every northern veteran was eligible. The generosity of this system rivaled its more famous European social welfare programs. But once again, it was not for everyone. It was a onetime program for the meritorious, those who had saved the republic. Each of these acts were isolates: one-shot policies rather than the foundation for a larger social insurance system. And each reflected a deep cultural belief that government social action should be restricted to those who "deserved" it, whether that be through service to the country or through their own labor.

The pressure for the government provision of social insurance only began with the Progressive movement at the turn of the last century. With industrialization and urbanization well under way, demands for social insurance began in earnest. But these demands were addressed at the state level. As a result, very little significant federal social legislation was passed in this era. The Children's Bureau (1912) established the first federal "welfare agency." And the Infant and Maternity Protection Act of 1921 (the Sheppard-Towner Act) was the United States' first foray into health care. The latter is equally significant for introducing the idea of federal matching grants-in-aid for state programs, a form of financing that has become the backbone of the U.S. social insurance system.

By 1929, even these limited efforts were under attack, and Sheppard-Towner was repealed. A volume on landmark social insurance legislation authored in 1930 might very well have concluded there would never be any! But the Great Depression came, and, as in so many other areas of American life, it changed everything. With a farm crisis and a quarter of the working population unemployed, the deserving poor suddenly seemed to include millions upon millions of Americans. As the Depression dragged on, and states were shown to be wholly unable to protect their citizens from its effects, unprecedented demands for federal action were made. Franklin Roosevelt, the political product of the Depression, attempted to meet those demands. The groundwork had been laid by the Progressives. A series of state social insurance laws were available for models, as were the experts who had developed and supervised them. The overwhelming Democrat majorities in Congress then made federal action possible. For tactical reasons, Roosevelt decided to build a federal system of social insurance all at once. This was the Social Security Act, enacted in 1935. Social Security has been termed the "big bang" that began the American welfare state. It contains nine different social insurance programs, as well as the means to finance them. Roosevelt didn't get everything he wanted, but he did begin major programs for the aged, the unemployed, and the poor. In 1939, amendments to the Social Security Act expanded the program for the aged to include benefits for the spouse and survivors of a pensioned worker.

Roosevelt's strategy to enact this legislation, and the uncertainty over its constitutionality, produced several significant peculiarities of the American welfare state. First, because the constitutionality of state programs seemed much less in doubt, most of the social security programs were given to the states to administer, under their own rules, subject to limited federal mandates. This system persists to the present. Much social insurance, while mostly paid for by the federal government, is actually provided by the states. The two big exceptions are Medicare and the Old-Age and Survivors (OASI) program of Social Security, which, because of the mobility of Americans, are extremely difficult to operate at the state level. Then, second, to ensure continuing political support for his program, Roosevelt developed the old-age benefits program to look like a private pension program. Workers would contribute money every month, and then receive a pension calibrated to their lifetime payments when they retired. As countless experts have noted, this is not an accurate summation of how the program actually works. In reality, it is a system where workers pay into a pool (the Social Security Trust Fund) and then receive stipulated benefits from this pool when they retire. There is no necessary link between contributions and benefits. This tactic has served to make this program one of America's most popular politically. Indeed, today to almost all Americans, "social security" means the OASI, not any of the other programs in the same bill. But it also produced the grand division in American social insurance policy: between "entitlements" and "means-tested" programs. The former are programs that all Americans can receive once they have met eligibility requirements, usually that they have been in the labor force for a minimum length of time. The latter are programs were eligibility is determined based on income level. Entitlements are somehow believed deserved, a right adhering to the eligible person. Means-tested programs have become known as "welfare" and are generally unpopular, unsupported, and in constant danger of reduction or elimination.

Social Security passed constitutional muster in 1937, the high-water mark of the "big bang" of social welfare programs. By World War II, this era of social activism had passed, and a more conservative era of consolidation had begun. Nothing shows the change in times better than the Serviceman's Readjustment Act of 1944, better known as the G.I. Bill. The first major social policy of the postwar era, it did not reflect the ideals of the Social Security Act at all. Though it arguably extended American social insurance through its provision of job training, education benefits, and subsidized home and business mortgages, it did so only for veterans. This appears to be a return to the nineteenth-century view of restricting social insurance to meritorious citizens, and this is the reason why Roosevelt himself initially opposed the bill. By the same token, President Truman's attempt to add a national health care component to Social Security led to a crushing political defeat.

However, in an important respect the postwar era was not like the 1920s. The enactment of Social Security had created an administrative apparatus, and a very large clientele, Americans over age 65. These, along with an American labor movement, then at the height of its power, served to protect Social Security from its opponents. In fact, in 1950 proponents were able to amend Social Security to include many more workers and substantially raise benefits (the Social Security Amendments of 1950), and in 1956 they were able to add disability benefits to the OASI program (the Social Security Amendments of 1956). If there was any question, President Eisenhower's 1953 public declaration of support for Social Security was also a declaration that the American welfare state was here to stay.

If the 1930s saw the big bang of that state, the 1960s saw its unparalleled expansion. Numerous new programs were added to the U.S. social insurance system, and older programs were increasingly federalized. No one has a decisive explanation for the 1960s, but as with the Great Depression, everything seemed to change. Previously excluded individuals and groups were now seen as among the "deserving" poor, and the rightful objects of federal action. Perhaps due to increasing wealth, a more risk-averse America demanded more social insurance. Social Security benefits were repeatedly increased, until in 1972 they were linked to the Consumer Price Index and made automatic. And, in a striking shift, Americans assigned the government the duty not just of minimally protecting its citizens, but of preventive and remedial action to reduce the number of people who found themselves needing government support. The Public Welfare Amendments of 1962 was the herald of these changes, though it did not itself initiate major programs. That was left to the two bills of 1964, the Food Stamp Act and the Economic Opportunity Act ("The War on Poverty") and, especially, the Social Security Amendments of 1965 that created Medicare and Medicaid. The present political division between the entitlements of Social Security and welfare is nowhere more apparent than in the fate of these bills. Medicare is today all but politically untouchable, while the EOA has been rescinded, Medicaid all but abandoned to the states, and the food stamp program, after some early expansions, substantially restricted.

President Richard Nixon responded to the growing unpopularity of welfare with a plan to replace the largest welfare program, the Aid to Families with Dependent Children, with a guaranteed income. His "Family Assistance Plan" was defeated in Congress. But Nixon's activity, the dying embers of the 1960s, led to a last burst of social insurance legislation. The Supplemental Security Assistance program (the Social Security Amendments of 1972) essentially combined the three smaller Social Security Act public assistance programs (for the needy aged, the disabled, and the blind) into one new program, complete with the guaranteed income. Why did these groups alone attain a guaranteed income? They alone were now considered the deserving poor. The WIC program (the Special Supplemental Nutrition Program for Women, Infants, and Children) was also created in 1972. To assist the working poor, the Earned Income Tax Credit was established in 1975.

As at previous times, this period eventually came to a close, and a more conservative period of consolidation began. President Jimmy Carter's failure to get any part of his desired welfare reform (the 1977 Program for Better Jobs and Income) through Congress signals the start of this era. As the number of its recipients rose relentlessly, the social insurance programs directed at income security for the poor became deeply unpopular. Demands increased to reduce the numbers on the welfare rolls.

President Ronald Reagan made substantial eligibility cuts in his first year of office. Social welfare experts turned their attention towards rehabilitating family life itself, if antipoverty programs were to work. This led to the Family Support Act of 1988, which added more work requirements for welfare recipients, and included measures to foster family life, discourage illegitimate births, and mandate determination of paternity. This was followed by an even more drastic reform, the Personal Responsibility and Work Opportunity Reconciliation Act of 1996. This act ended the AFDC program, replaced it with state grants, and mandated lifetime limits on how long an individual could draw welfare benefits. A fall in caseloads at the end of the century at least temporarily quieted this "side" of social insurance.

Instead, it is the entitlement portion of the social insurance system, in this same time of consolidation, that is perhaps now poised to attract the controversy. Massive increases in government outlays on Social Security and Medicare have been, and will become, central budgeting issues. A near collapse of the Social Security system led to a presidential commission, and through the Social Security Amendments of 1983, legislation that quietly narrowed the benefits of the program. Similar commissions have been established to consider reforms for Medicare, and, again in 2001, Social Security, though significant legislation has yet to issue.

The last legislation of this volume, the Senior Citizen's Freedom to Work Act of 2001, is not its most momentous. Its significance lies in the continuity it reveals in America's social insurance policy. The desire to reward work, the generosity accorded entitlements, and the vagaries of the congressional attention that led to its passage, remain continuing themes in the construction of the American welfare state.

A glance at the past shows an immense change over the preceding 200 years. Americans today live in a society that affords them protections against loss of income and poverty that would astonish earlier generations. The benefit is a series of laws that enable Americans to live with vastly reduced fears of a life of dire poverty. The cost is a far more intrusive government, and the distaste of seeing lifestyles and behaviors to which one objects supported with federal dollars. So far, though they grumble, Americans have accepted this cost. But because the definition of social insurance changes through time, because the financial resources with which to provide this insurance varies, and because the politics of the social insurance system is so indeterminate, reflecting momentary shifts in power and personality, the construction of the American welfare state, and of the American system of social insurance, will never be completed. It will always be a contested area of government action.

# 1

# The Homestead Act of 1862

"Go West, young man, go forth into the Country." Horace Greeley's words must rank among the most famous, and by now the most hackneyed, in American history. When written they were not merely an exhortation to the adventurous, they summed up one of the nation's first ideas for public assistance. It was the idea embodied in the Homestead Act of 1862, one of the United States' most celebrated pieces of legislation.

By the time of the act's repeal, in 1976, over 500,000 Americans had settled on over 80 million acres of public land under its provisions. It is central to the history of the American West. But its importance stretches further. Support for the act was an essential cement for the emerging Republican party in the 1850s, and the politics of its passage have been credited by both contemporaries and historians for the election of Abraham Lincoln.

The origins of the Homestead Act reach back to the Jacksonian era. Cheap public land always had a natural constituency: residents on the western frontier and all Americans who endorsed the Jeffersonian ideal of a country of sturdy yeomen working their own farms. America's original policy had been to offer its public lands for sale. But many farmers, and even state legislatures, began petitioning for "preemption," the right to occupy the land first and pay for it later. Thomas Hart Benton, the Missouri senator and ally of Andrew Jackson, led the federal fight for such a policy, and finally obtained the Petition Act of 1841. This allowed a squatter (one who occupied a piece of land without having purchased it) to purchase the occupied land at the minimum government price. The politics of passage evoked a sectional conflict that would return with the Homestead Act. Most congressmen from the eastern states saw little benefit to their region from easing the purchase of public lands, and therefore voted against programs that, as they saw it, would only reduce government revenues. (Before the Civil War, public land sales ranked with tariffs as the major sources of these revenues.)

The boom-and-bust economy of the 1830s that culminated in the Panic of 1837 served to turn interest from easing the purchase of land to providing it simply as a means to lessen economic hardship. This view was first articulated by America's young labor movement. Its leaders, located almost entirely on the eastern seaboard, were convinced that western migration would reduce unemployment in the east, and, by the same token, raise the wage rates for the working people who stayed behind. The National Reform Association and its founder, the labor leader George Henry Evans, introduced the call for free western land for those who would settle upon it. Listening was Horace Greeley. A well-known newspaperman and reformer, Greeley came to agree with Evans, and issued his famous slogan in 1837, the year of the Panic. Eleven years later, after he was elected to the House of Representatives from New York City, he introduced a homestead act. Westerners were surprised, and his fellow easterners aghast. But his reasoning, he explained to the House, was simple: He represented more landless men than any other member on the floor.[1] Greeley and Evans were actually indifferent to whether the land was free or merely cheap enough that the indigent could afford it. The point was to provide a way for the unemployed to support themselves.

Greeley's bill was greeted most warmly by the representatives of the states on the southwestern frontier. Andrew Johnson of Tennessee led this group, and he had sponsored his own homestead bill, as had members from Alabama and Kentucky. Sam Houston of Texas would soon join Johnson as being among the most fervent supporters of homesteading. Johnson's bill would have offered public land to any head of a family "without money and without price." By 1848, the many advocates had reached consensus that the appropriate homestead grant was one quarter (160 acres) of a section of America's least expensive public lands.[2]

Labor advocates, social reformers, and frontier congressmen may have been enthusiastic about homesteading, but, though they argued for homesteading "not as a political, but as a philanthropic measure," they encountered a determined opposition.[3] Though much of it had a sectional basis, opponents made several telling arguments. First, they questioned the constitutionality of the plan. Was it not an unconstitutional taking of property to give away land that was jointly owned by all the citizens of America? Second, they claimed that the loss of land-sales revenue would put the country in a financial crisis. Whigs, in particular, saw a plot to defeat any future plan of national improvements through the elimination of the revenues that would make it possible. Finally, nativists worried that a right to homestead would produce a flood of immigrants from Europe's worst slums. For these reasons, opponents initially kept the homestead bills bottled in committee.

But then a signally important event occurred, not only in the history of this act, but in the political history of the United States. The homesteading movement linked with the antislavery movement. The same northern proponents of homesteading also became leaders in the free-soil movement. Labor leaders, and the factions of both the Democrat and Whig parties that wished to stop the territorial expansion of slavery, briefly joined forces to create a political party under the motto "free soil, free speech, free labor, free men." As the motto suggests, the free-soil movement saw the problems of poverty, urban unemployment, and slavery as having one and the same root, the inability to own one's labor. Homesteading became a key part of the free-soil movement, for it spoke to the belief that the only legitimate title to a piece of land came from a person's labor upon it. Once seen in this context, the battle for homestead legislation could not help but be drawn into the far larger battle over slavery in America. And indeed, homestead proposals began appearing as part of broader antislavery bills, and, in several instances, were drawn to include enslaved African-Americans.

Once this occurred, the sectional battle over homesteading was redrawn. While the midwest and western frontier were by now all but unanimously in favor of an act, the slave states of the South became violently opposed. Among major political figures, only Sam Houston and Andrew Johnson continued to support the idea in the South (and Houston would finally abandon it shortly before the Civil War).

Consequently, the Democratic party divided bitterly over homesteading. Senator Stephen A. Douglas, its western leader, had sponsored a homestead bill in the Senate in 1850. Proslavery Democrats responded by eventually removing him from his chair of the Committee on Territories. The Democrat split enabled its opponents in the Whig, and later Republican, parties to make the issue their own. Homesteading became a focusing issue around which the Republican party organized. Though the soul of the new party was in the slavery issue, homesteading was the issue upon which broad popular support could be built. For, as noted by an early Minnesota Republican, "This Homestead Measure overshadows everything with us, and through the West."[4] Through homesteading, and its principle of "free soil, free labor," western Democrats indifferent to slavery could be brought into the party, as could the laboring classes of the east, where slavery was also for many a secondary concern.

However, Republican unity still hid a continued lack of enthusiasm for the bill in much of the eastern seaboard. In 1854, eastern senators added a requirement that homesteaders must work their land for at least five years and pay 25 cents an acre before they could obtain title to it. Even then many voted against the bill. Combined with westerners who thought such a bill too compromised, the legislation again died. However, the notion stuck that a homesteader must work the land for five years.

In 1856, a new Republican, Galusha A. Grow, later called the "father of the Homestead Act," opened in earnest a legislative campaign that finally succeeded in producing the law. Grow was then chair of both the House Committee on Territories and the Committee on Agriculture and later became the Speaker of the House. He was aided by one of America's worst economic crises, the Panic of 1857. The economic depression raised anew the issue of public assistance for the destitute. As historian Eric Foner has noted, by then "the basic Republican answer to the problem of urban poverty was neither charity, public works, nor strikes, but westward migration of the poor, aided by a homestead act."[5] As the Depression deepened, eastern Republican opposition to the Homestead Act melted away.

By the late 1850s, the larger population of the North ensured that proponents of homesteading could push a bill through the House of Representatives. The Senate was the problem. There were still enough southern senators to stop the consideration of a bill. But they could not breach the coalition of northern supporters, and advocates of a bill inched toward victory. When the elections of 1858 returned more Republicans, southern senators fell to their last line of defense: the sympathetic Buchanan administration. In 1859 panicked antihomesteaders informed the administration that they did not have the votes to force postponement. Only when Buchanan's officials were able to find several absentee antihomestead senators and whisk them to the Senate was even a tie vote obtained (Vice President Breckinridge was then able to cast the deciding vote to postpone debate).

This effort to stop homestead legislation all but exhausted the Senate's Democrats. Stephen A. Douglas, believing that his presidential ambitions were at stake, refused to bow to southern wishes and unite the party against a bill. Andrew Johnson, now in the Senate, also ignored the pleas of fellow southerners and continued his long fight. In 1860, the party finally shattered over this issue. In that year, after the House had again passed a bill, Johnson, in the Committee on Public Lands, crafted a substitute homestead bill that would make homesteaders pay 25 cents an acre for their land, and would restrict the right of homesteading to heads of families. He hoped that the provision on payment would end Buchanan's announced opposition to the bill on constitutional grounds. At first, Republicans attacked Johnson's bill, but then realizing it was the best on offer, they shifted to support. With Democrats irreconcilably divided, the bill easily passed, and opponents could only rely on the veto of President Buchanan. Buchanan, rewarding his southern supporters, obliged. His veto message specifically referred to the inflammatory effect of the bill on the slavery issue.

For Republicans, Buchanan's veto was a godsend. Their 1860 election platform featured a prominent homestead plank, authored by none other than Horace Greeley. Abraham Lincoln made the veto a major campaign issue, arguing that only a Republican victory would ever ensure a Homestead Act. Lincoln, of course, won. The new speaker, Rep. Grow, indicated that enacting the Republican homestead plank would be one of the new Congress' first orders of business. Yet, when Congress returned following the election, it was still not clear whether supporters had the votes in the Senate. Only the secession of the South guaranteed its success.

In 1861, Rep. Cyrus Aldrich of Minnesota was given the honor of introducing the Homestead Act. But supporters bungled their chance. Procedural irregularities stalled the bill, while the coming war was bringing new questions to the fore. Easterners, who had muted their criticism of homesteading after the Panic of 1857, now worried again about the loss of revenue entailed by the bill. Could this be afforded in time of war? The war also opened the problem of soldiers' bounties. In previous wars, America had rewarded its veterans with land grants. But wouldn't a homestead act undercut this reward? Some members of Congress felt that so important a piece of legislation should be delayed until after the end of the war. So when Justin Morrill of Vermont motioned to postpone consideration of the bill, it carried by a surprisingly easy vote of 88 to 50.

Speaker Grow and other supporters were shocked. Grow took personal charge of the bill. He obtained statistics to show that revenues from public lands had already all but ceased. An amendment was added specifically to set aside lands for soldiers' bounties. The cost to the GOP of campaigning in the 1862 elections without having enacted the bill was clearly spelled out. And Grow put his own authority on the line. Breaking precedent, he stepped down from the Speaker's dais and spoke from the floor in favor of the bill. Thanks to his efforts, the bill was passed with only 16 votes opposed. The Senate then followed with its own 33 to 7 vote in favor. With the exception of Oregon's proslavery Senator Lane, all the nays came from the border states. On May 20, 1862 President Lincoln signed the Homestead Act.

As passed, the Homestead Act offered up to 160 acres of the government's cheapest land (that valued at $1.25 acre), or up to 80 acres of land valued at $2.50, to any person who would work that land for five years. The effect was instant. Even before the Civil War had ended, over 25,000 Americans made use of the act.

The Homestead Act of 1862 has attained an almost mythical status, making a determination of its true impact difficult. Land speculators and railroads, not individual farmers, continued to gain title to most western lands. Nor did the act end unemployment and poverty in the east. Nevertheless, the impact of an act that led to over a half a million Americans obtaining new land can hardly be gainsaid. As aspiration or inspiration, few other acts in American history can compare. Wrapping a real and growing need for public assistance within widely held notions of an ideal mode of life, the Homestead Act of 1862 can truly be called the nation's first welfare policy, one that, whatever its success, was rooted in America's deepest ideological beliefs.

# 1. The Homestead Act of 1862

An act to Secure Homesteads to Actual Settlers on the Public
Domain

*Be it enacted by the Senate and House of Representatives of the United States of America in Congress assembled,* That any person who is the head of a family, or who has arrived at the age of twenty-one years, and is a citizen of the United States, or who shall have filed his declaration of intention to become such, . . . and who has never borne arms against the United States Government or given aid and comfort to its enemies, shall, from and after the first of January, eighteen hundred and sixty-three, be entitled to enter one quarter section or a less quantity of unappropriated public lands, upon which said person may have filed a preemption claim *[a claim giving the settler the right to purchase a tract of land, to the exclusion of all other persons]*, or which may . . . be subject to preemption at one dollar and twenty-five cents, or less, per acre; or eighty acres or less of such unappropriated lands, at two dollars and fifty cents per acre, to be located in a body, in conformity to the legal subdivisions of the public lands, and after the same shall have been surveyed. . . .

Section 2. And be it further enacted, That the person applying for the benefit of this act shall, upon application to the register of the land office in which he or she is about to make such entry, make affidavit before the said register or receiver that he or she is the head of a family, or is twenty-one years or more of age, or shall have performed service in the army or navy of the United States, and that he has never borne arms against the Government of the United States or given aid and comfort to its enemies, and that such application is made for his or her exclusive use and benefit, and that said entry is made for the purpose of actual settlement and cultivation, and not either directly or indirectly for the use or benefit of any other person or persons whomsoever; and upon filing the said affidavit with the register or receiver, and on payment of ten dollars, he or she shall thereupon be permitted to enter the quantity of land specified: Provided, however, That no certificate shall be given or patent *[a government deed granting property]* issued therefor until the expiration of five years from the date of such entry. . . .

Section 3. And be it further enacted, That the register of the land office shall note all such applications on the tract books and plats *[maps that shows property boundaries]* of his office, and keep a register of all such entries, and make return thereof to the General Land Office, together with the proof upon which they have been founded.

Section 4. And be it further enacted, That no lands acquired under the provisions of this act shall in any event become liable to the satisfaction of any debt or debts contracted prior to the issuing of the patent therefor.

Section 5. And be it further enacted, That if . . . before the expiration of the five years aforesaid, it shall be proven, after due notice to the settler, to the satisfaction of the register of the land office, that the person having filed such affidavit shall have actually changed his or her residence, or abandoned the said land for more than six months at any time, then and in that event the land so entered shall revert to the government.

Section 6. And be it further enacted, That no individual shall be permitted to acquire title to more than one quarter section under the provisions of this act. . . .

May 20, 1962

## NOTES

1. Lurton D. Ingersoll, *Life of Horace Greeley: American Newspaperman* (New York: Beekman Publishers, 1974 [originally 1873]), p. 206.

2. U.S. public lands were at that time "graduated." Different prices were charged depending upon how valuable the land was thought to be.

3. As reported in the New York City newspaper, *The Courier and Enquirer.* Benjamin Hibbard, *A History of the Public Land Policies* (New York: Peter Smith, 1939), p. 366.

4. James T. Du Bois and Gertrude S. Matthews, *Galusha A. Grow: Father of the Homestead Law* (New York: Houghton Mifflin, 1917).

5. Eric Foner, *Free Soil, Free Labor, Free Men: The Ideology of the Republican Party Before the Civil War* (New York: Oxford University Press, 1970), p. 27.

# 2

## The Civil War Pension System

Few people realize that, long before the creation of Social Security, America had once had one of the most liberal old-age pension systems in the world. This system paid out more than five billion dollars in pensions between 1866 and the arrival of Social Security. In the last years of the nineteenth century, it consumed more than a quarter of the entire U.S. budget. Experts have claimed it was every bit as generous as the more heralded program of Bismarck's Germany. The origins and disappearance of this gigantic program are important to understanding the development of America's modern social welfare programs.

This first old-age pension system grew out of the Civil War. As in previous wars, Congress was quick to enact a program pensioning soldiers who incurred permanent disability in direct consequence of their military duty. Dependent widows and orphans would also receive pensions in cases of death. The Pension Act of 1862 was only novel in its inclusion of mothers and orphan sisters as potential dependents. Most expected the 1862 act to offer modest support for those most harmed by the war, and then, like the pension systems for the Mexican and 1812 wars, to quietly fade away. They had not reckoned on the numbers of men who would fight, or on the new politics of postwar era.

The numbers of disabled soldiers was far higher than anyone could have imagined when the Civil War began. The huge number of cases swamped the rickety pension process, forcing passage of the Consolidation Act of 1873 to revamp and revise the entire system. The huge number of cases also led to an explosion of pension lawyers, who assisted veterans, or their dependents, obtain their pensions. These lawyers, called claims or pension agents, became alarmed after the Act of 1873 took hold and the number of soldiers filing new claims began to drop. They realized that only new legislation would encourage the new claims they needed to stay in business. After all, 10 years after the war, if a soldier had still not made a claim for a pension, why should he suddenly do so?

The claims agents recognized the legislation they would need. They desired a revised pension act that would give a disabled Civil War veteran a lump sum payment equal to all pension payments he would have received had he filed at the date of his discharge. Then he would begin his regular pension. The agents made use of the fact that existing law required elaborate proof of the disability, and of its origin in the Civil War, for a veteran to obtain his pension. They argued that that this payment of "arrears" was only fair, given how difficult it was to obtain this proof for veterans who had filed late. The agents began an intense lobbying campaign, including developing pro-arrears newspapers that were mailed to veterans.

The claims agents could make use of an additional argument as well: The large U.S. budget surpluses of the 1870s made an arrears program appear quite affordable for the country. Even so, they were initially unsuccessful. A series of arrears bills were introduced in Congress, but none was passed. Opposition from southern and border state congressmen was to be expected, as their constituents would receive almost nothing from such a bill. More interesting was the conflicted sentiment of the veterans themselves. After the war, northern veterans had organized the Grand Army of the Republic. The size and prestige of the G.A.R. gave it tremendous political power and moral authority, but it took no stance on the arrears legislation. Most veterans had not been disabled by the war, and were unaffected by the legislation.

Nevertheless, claims agents continued to press their case. And it is at this point that the changed political landscape of post-Civil War America became decisive. In the late 1870s, America was divided almost evenly between the two political parties. The 1876 presidential election had been virtually a tie, with Rutherford B. Hayes declared the winner only as a result of the decision of a special electoral commission and a secret deal between the parties. In this environment, members of both parties understood that every vote would be needed to win in the next closely fought election. Liberalizing the pension law was one way of attracting some of these votes. In this context, Republicans in the House of Representatives offered an arrears bill in April 1878. This bill stipulated that all Civil War pensions would commence from the date of death or discharge of the soldier. By a vote of 164 to 61, it passed on the last day of Congress. Those voting against were entirely Democrats from the South or from border states. The opposition from the areas of the former confederacy may have been critical in rousing the G.A.R. to announce itself in support of the bill in June 1878. It became an issue of patriotism for the veterans' organization. The bill was then reintroduced in the Senate early in 1879. As elections neared, even southern democrats saw the political costs of blocking the bill, and it passed 44 to 4, with 28 abstaining. Interestingly, the Hayes administration had opposed the bill because of the role of the claims agents in securing its passage. But President Hayes signed the Arrears Act of 1879 on January 25, 1879.

As a result of the Arrears Act, the average first pension payment rose to $1,000 at a time when the average nonfarmer earned $400 a year.[1] Not surprisingly, enactment of the law led to a fivefold increase in the number of disability pension claims filed. More importantly, the act mobilized the G.A.R. The veterans group recognized what the new law signified politically: Organized pressure could win more generous pensions. At their 1882 annual encampment, the Grand Army took the radical step of demanding pensions for all disabled veterans, whether or not they could prove their disability to be war related. In part, this was due to a large increase in the number of claims rejected due to the need for such proof. But, more generally, the Grand Army argued that the pensions were owed simply due to patriotism, the fulfillment of the "contract" between the soldiers and the state they had protected.

There was opposition, mostly from the South, although some in the G.A.R. thought these demands sullied the purity of the northern cause and the soldiers who had sacrificed so much on its behalf. The potential cost of the bill also frightened many Democrats. Democrats were fighting to reduce American tariffs, then the major source of government revenues, and, with the election of Grover Cleveland in 1884, they appeared near to achieving their goal. The increase in federal expenditures necessitated by a liberalized pension system would make this impossible. (Some Democrats argued that the pension plan was nothing but a GOP plot to prevent tariff reform.) Still, in January, 1887, a bill to so liberalize the pension system passed in the House and Senate. President Cleveland, however, vetoed it on grounds of cost. G.A.R. pressure only intensified with the defeat. With Cleveland publicly opposed, the Republicans saw their opportunity, and moved to endorse an even more liberal pension system. Their 1888 election platform included the promise of a universal pension system. Every single honorably discharged veteran should be eligible for an old-age pension! This pledge may have been decisive in electing their candidate, Benjamin Harrison, himself a prominent veteran, to the presidency.

Shortly thereafter, the new Republican-controlled Congress introduced several bills to further liberalize the pension system. Each endorsed this radical idea that a veteran, or his survivors, should receive a pension simply because he had served in the war. The House went the furthest, passing a bill offering an eight-dollar-a-month pension to each veteran who had served at least 90 days and had reached 62 years of age. The Senate remained more modest, desiring to keep the test of disability, defined as inability to earn a living at manual labor, but it wanted a pension for every such disabled veteran no matter what the source of the disability. Southerners continued their opposition, and were now joined by many northern manufacturers who became alarmed at the potential cost of giving pensions to every aged veteran.

These manufacturers were key members in the GOP coalition and probably influenced Harrison to announce his support, in December 1889, of the more moderate Senate bill. Called the Disability Pension Act of 1890, it sailed through the Congress. This law has also been called the Dependent Pension Act of 1890. "The most costly pension law ever enacted," the Disability Pension Act of 1890, created pensions for every veteran over the age of 62 who could show his inability to earn a living at manual labor and for every veteran's widow who relied on daily labor for her support.[2] The law doubled the annual cost of pensions paid by the federal government.

After 1890 virtually all veterans could obtain a pension at the age of 62. Further expansions of the pension system merely codified this fact. In 1904, Teddy Roosevelt signed Presidential Order 78, declaring old age itself to be a disability if it decreased a veteran's physical abilities by one half. In 1912, President Taft signed the final liberalization, formally recognizing pensions for all veterans who had served 90 days and were over 62. Note these were also in election years.

Coverage under the Civil War pension laws was surprisingly large. By the turn of the century 997,735 pensioners had enrolled under the provisions of the 1890 act. Two-thirds of the nonimmigrant northern white males over age 65 were drawing pensions, indeed 35 percent of *all* northern males over 65 were receiving them.[3] This is roughly in the same range as the pension programs being then enacted in continental Europe, but with much more generous payments. The Civil War pension laws introduced Americans to the idea of a large-scale federal old-age program, and thus created the precedent for the social welfare programs to come. As I. M. Rubinow, one of America's first social insurance experts concluded, "the system of war pensions represents a very important entering wedge for a national system of old-age pensions."[4]

But it is also a fact that the system ended with the last Civil War veteran. And here we confront a second precedent, or more accurately, obstacle, for future American social welfare policy. In no way were these pensions intended to be truly universal or available to every aged citizen. The Civil War pension system was always justified as one of modest support earned solely by our nation's war veterans. Veterans deserved federal pensions because of their sacrifice. The pension program was seen more in political and moral than in socioeconomic terms. Pensions were an acknowledgment of services rendered, not a method of ameliorating poverty or the difficulties of old age generally. This limited the scope and development of the system. There was not a way, on its own principles, to expand the pension program to other categories of citizens. The Civil War system could not make the leap to embrace all Americans, or all aged Americans, because it was embedded in a different moral sensibility, one of special recognition of meritious service, not of a general federal obligation to the welfare of the citizens of the United States. Thus, it was that the Civil War pension system expired with the veterans it supported, and the construction of a permanent old-age system was left to the following generation.

## 2a. The Arrears Act of 1879

An Act to provide that all pensions on account of death, or wounds received, or disease contracted in the service of the United States during the late war of the rebellion, which have been granted, or which shall hereafter be granted, shall commence from the date of death or discharge from the service of the United States; for the payment of arrears of pensions; and other purposes.

*Be it enacted by the Senate and the House of Representatives of the United States of America in Congress assembled,* That all pensions which have been granted under the general laws regulating pensions, or may hereafter be granted, in consequence of death from a cause which originated in the United States service during the continuance of the late war of the rebellion, or in consequence of wounds, injuries, or disease received or contracted in said service during said war of the rebellion, shall commence from the date of the death or discharge from said service of the person on whose account the claim has been or shall hereafter be granted, or from the termination of the right of the party having prior title to such pension. . . .

Sec. 2. That the Commissioner of Pensions is hereby authorized and directed to adopt such rules and regulations for the payment of the arrears of pensions hereby granted as will be necessary to cause to be paid to such pensioners, or, if the pensioners shall have died, to the person or persons entitled to the same, all such arrears of pensions as the pensioner may be, or would have been, entitled to under this act.

Sec. 3. That section forty-seven hundred and seventeen of the Revised Statutes of the United States . . . be, and the same is hereby, repealed. . . .
*[This section had stipulated that, in order to receive a pension, the would-be pensioner had to provide evidence from armed service or other records that he or she suffered injury or disease while in the line of duty.]*

January 25, 1879

## 2b. The Disability Pension Act of 1890

An Act granting pensions to soldiers and sailors who are
incapacitated for the performance of manual labor, and
providing for pensions to widows, minor children, and
dependent parents.

*Be it enacted by the Senate and House of Representatives of the United States of America in Congress assembled,* That in considering the pension claims of dependent parents, the fact of the soldier's death by reason of any wound, injury, casualty, or disease which . . . would have entitled him to an invalid pension, and the fact that the soldier left no widow or minor children . . . it shall be necessary only to show by competent and sufficient evidence that such parent or parents are without other present means of support than their own manual labor or the contributions of others not legally bound for their support . . . *[to receive the soldier's pension].*

Sec. 2. That all persons who served ninety days or more in the military or naval service of the United States during the late war of the rebellion and who have been honorably discharged therefrom, and who are now or who may hereafter be suffering from a mental or physical disability of a permanent character, not the result of their own vicious habits, which incapacitates them from the performance of manual labor in such a degree as to render them unable to earn a support, shall, upon making due proof of the fact . . . be placed upon the list of invalid pensioners of the United States, and be entitled to receive a pension not exceeding twelve dollars per month, and not less than six dollars per month. . . .

Sec. 3. That if any officer or enlisted man who served ninety days or more in the Army or Navy of the United States during the late war of the rebellion, and who was honorably discharged has died, or shall hereafter die, leaving a widow without other means of support than her daily labor, or minor children under the age of sixteen years, such widow shall, upon due proof of her husband's death, without proving his death to be the result of his army service, be placed on the pension-roll from the date of the application under this act. . . .

June 27, 1890

## NOTES

1. William H. Glasson, *Federal Military Pensions in the United States* (Oxford: Oxford University Press, 1918), p. 164.

2. Glasson, p. 233.

3. Jill Quadagno, *The Transformation of Old-Age Security: Class and Politics in the American Welfare State* (Chicago: University of Chicago Press, 1988), p. 47, and Theda Skocpol, *Protecting Soldiers and Mothers* (Cambridge: Harvard University Press, 1992), p. 132.

4. I. M. Rubinow, *Social Insurance* (New York: Arno Press, 1969 [Henry Holt, 1913]), p. 407.

# 3

# The Children's Bureau (1912)

As late as during the presidency of Teddy Roosevelt, the United States did not have a single federal agency concerned with any aspect of the social welfare of Americans. This changed on April 9, 1912, when Congress created the Children's Bureau. This was an historic change, not only because it was a significant institutional innovation for the United States, but because the Bureau went on to become a forceful advocate for additional federal welfare programs.

The creation of the Children's Bureau occurred from the intersection of two major currents of early-twentieth-century politics in the United States: the Progressive movement and the woman's movement. The Progressive movement, a reaction to the political corruption and unregulated industrial practices so apparent by the first decade of the century, included significant demands for greater government protection of workers and the "deserving" poor. The latter were those who had become impoverished solely as a result of their life circumstances, for example, individuals who were blind, physically disabled, or too old to work. Foremost in this group were thought to be widowed and indigent mothers. Poor mothers were being placed in the position of either giving up their children or neglecting them, as they needed to work long hours at low pay to obtain the money needed to keep their family together. Mothers too poor to care for their children had either to move into county or charitable "poor houses," or to see their children taken from them and placed in orphanages.

This "solution," so natural to earlier generations, increasingly distressed Americans, who, more and more, were coming to believe that home life was central to the formation of character, and that no other social institution could substitute for the nuclear family. In this context, Progressives took up the call for the provision of public assistance to help indigent mothers keep their families together. The equally new and growing woman's movement joined in exerting political pressure for this assistance. Organizations such as the National Congress of Mothers, parent-teacher organizations, and state Women's Federations pressed for Mother's Aid bills to provide pensions for poor mothers. Women's magazines and yellow journalists contributed a steady stream of heart-rending stories of broken and destitute families.

These efforts were generally at the state level, for this was still the age when almost all domestic policies were undertaken by states, not the federal government. Eventually, 44 states passed mothers' aid laws. But a key moment in the effort came in 1909, when supporters were able to convince Teddy Roosevelt to call for a National Conference on the Care of Dependent Children. Some two hundred activists attended. Under the auspices of the White House, the issue was "federalized." Nationally provided assistance to the children of mothers without a "normal breadwinner" was proposed, as well as a federal children's bureau to oversee it. These activists faced a huge political obstacle: While Americans sympathized overwhelmingly with widows or disabled mothers, there was as yet little support for assisting mothers merely because they were indigent. Roosevelt too recognized this problem, and so did not even attempt to forward the proposal for mothers' assistance to Congress, instead calling only for a children's bureau that would be limited to gathering information on child welfare in the United States.

While this today may seem the most innocuous of initiatives, it aroused fierce opposition at the time. Many Progressives were themselves torn by the proposal. Progressivism, after all, was in many quarters more attracted to weakening and controlling the government than to expanding it. But more vociferous opposition came from industrial interests and some charities. The concern among many industrialists was that the Bureau might open the door to more onerous and better enforced child labor laws. Opposition from charities might seem odd, but grew from the fear of their being displaced by the government. The theme tying all these opponents together was opposition to a more powerful government. Otis Bannard, representing the New York Charity Organization Society, summed up this view in complaining that mothers' pensions were "an entering wedge towards state socialism."[1]

As a result of this opposition, the legislation to create the Children's Bureau took three years to get through Congress. The need to overcome arguments that the Bureau would intrude into family life led proponents to include a proviso barring Bureau investigators from entering any private house if the head of family forbade it. Finally, in 1912, after a week of debate, the Senate passed the bill and the House later followed suit. President Taft, a reluctant supporter, signed the bill, in part to improve his standing with Progressives before the coming presidential election.

The Children's Bureau, intended as an information-gathering agency, instead became a major governmental lobbyist for additional federal welfare programs. Future social legislation, including portions of the Social Security Act, would first be developed in the Bureau. It was the first federal agency to be headed by a woman, Julia Lathrop, a tireless advocate for child welfare expenditures. Today the Children's Bureau is part of the U.S. Department of Health and Human Services and has a budget of over $4 billion. It is responsible for issues of child abuse and neglect, child protective services, family preservation and support, adoption, foster care, and independent living.

## 3. An Act to Establish in the Department of Commerce and Labor a Bureau to be Known as the Children's Bureau

*Be it enacted by the Senate and House of Representatives of the United States in Congress assembled.* That there shall be established in the Department of Commerce and Labor a Bureau to be Known as the Children's Bureau.

Sec. 2. That the said bureau shall be under the direction of a chief, to be appointed by the President, by and with the advice of consent of the Senate . . . The said bureau shall investigate and report to said department upon all matters pertaining to the welfare of children and child life among all classes of our people, and shall especially investigate the questions of infant mortality, the birth rate, orphanage, juvenile courts, desertion, dangerous occupations, accidents and diseases of children, employment, legislation affecting children in the several States and Territories. But no official, or agent, or representative of said bureau shall, over the objection of the head of the family, enter any house used exclusively as a family residence. . . .

April 9, 1912

**NOTE**

1. Quoted in Marvin Olasky, *The Tragedy of American Compassion* (Lanham, MD: Regnery Gateway, 1992), p. 140.

# 4

# The Infancy and Maternity Protection Act of 1921 (Sheppard-Towner Act)

The Sheppard Towner Act, the most significant social insurance policy between the Progressive era and the New Deal, has been called the "the first major dividend of the full enfranchisement of women."[1] It was the greatest legislative success of the new Children's Bureau. Although it only lasted eight years, it remains an important piece of legislation for two reasons. It was the first federal bill aimed at improving health care for any group of American civilians, and it introduced the concept of matching grants to the area of social policy. Matching grants are a form of funding where the federal government offers states or local communities money to carry out a policy on the condition that the latter match the federal monies with their own contributions. This has since become the form of financing for many social programs.

The Sheppard-Towner Act owes its origins to the Progressives as well as the rising women's movement. By the time of World War I, many Progressives were pushing for compulsory health insurance for workers. Though part of Teddy Roosevelt's national platform in 1912, most efforts were at the state level. None, however, came even close to success. Yet, the issue of government-mandated health assistance had been raised, and it was quickly seized by proponents in the women's movement and their allies in the new Children's Bureau.

In 1917, acting under the Bureau's investigative authority, its director, Julia Lathrop, proposed a program to offer federal funds to local maternal and child health care services. The funds would be used to help provide confinement care for pregnant women, medical exams for children, and an increased number of public health nurses. The Children's Bureau argued for the program based on its findings of a direct correlation between poverty and infant mortality, and of the failure of many pregnant women to receive any prenatal advice or care. Local health care services, as noted above, would be expected to equal the federal expenditures.

Congress was unenthusiastic. Not until 1920 did Senator Morris Sheppard (Dem., Texas) and Congressman Horace Towner (Rep., Iowa) combine to sponsor a bill containing Lathrop's ideas along with an appropriation for $4 million in matching funds to carry them out. The Sheppard-Towner bill passed the Senate, but died in the House.

The opponents of the bill were many. Fiscal conservatives complained of its costs, and states rights advocates of its federal intrusion. Supporters of alternative medicine decried its privileging of physicians in health care. Antisuffragists (such as the chair of the House Interstate Commerce Committee, which had authority over the bill) saw the bill as yet one more baneful effect of women in politics. The act was even caught up in the postwar "red scare," the wave of fear over communism that followed the Russian Revolution. Anti-Bolshevik groups rallied to oppose the act, one accusing a leading proponent of being "the ablest legislative general Communism has produced."[2]

But these opponents soon encountered a tidal wave of pressure. In 1920 the women's suffrage movement had succeeded in obtaining the ratification of the Nineteenth Amendment, giving women the vote. Mobilized, and ready for a new cause, the movement turned to the Sheppard-Towner Act. The National League of Women Voters and virtually every other major women's organization made the act their new priority. *Good Housekeeping* and other "women's magazines" focused on the issue. The effect was overwhelming. According to the *Journal of the American Medical Association*, "the women's lobby supporting [Sheppard-Towner] was one of the strongest ever seen in Washington."[3] Politicians became very nervous. With women newly enfranchised, no one knew how or on what basis they would vote. Would the fate of this bill sway millions of women voters?

The Democratic party announced its support, and so did the new president, Republican Warren Harding. When Harding called for a special session of Congress, in 1921, he explicitly included Sheppard-Towner. He pressured antisuffragist congressional Republicans to drop their opposition. The result was an overwhelming vote for the bill in both houses, and it was enacted into law November 23, 1921. An indication of the power of the lobbying efforts is that many believed the bill would have failed were the vote secret. However, as a result of the remaining opposition, the amount of the appropriations for the law was reduced to $1.48 million for the first fiscal year and $1.27 for the five years thereafter.

The Sheppard-Towner Act was largely administered by the Children's Bureau. By 1926 the act made possible the employment of 812 public nurses and had created some 3,000 Sheppard-Towner prenatal clinics across the country.[4] In some states, it was the first publicly offered maternity and infant care of any kind. On its own terms, the act appeared a success. Yet, when it came time to reenact the program, the Senate refused to do so (although it did allow a further two years of appropriations).

The program died because fiscal conservatives, never fully reconciled to the policy, were joined by a powerful new opponent: the American Medical Association. The AMA, newly organized, was gathering strength as the decade progressed, and it did not like Sheppard-Towner. Doctors were opposed, not because of anything in the act itself, but because the organization believed that any publicly provided medical services threatened the private, fee-for-service relationship between doctors and their patients. Sheppard-Towner was a symbol of the path doctors did not wish to travel. The growing political strength of doctors was matched by the decline of the suffrage movement. With several postenfranchisement elections under their belt, fears of a united bloc of women voters receded, and legislative opponents found they had the political strength to end the program.

For the next several years efforts were made to revive the program, but opposed by the U.S. Public Health Service and lacking support from President Hoover, they were without success. It was left to the New Deal to revive and complete the ideals of the Sheppard-Towner Act.

## 4. An Act for the Promotion of the Welfare and Hygiene of Maternity and Infancy, and for other Purposes [Sheppard-Towner Act]

*Be it enacted by the Senate and the House of Representatives of the United States of America in Congress assembled,* That there is hereby authorized to be appropriated annually . . . the sums specified in section 2 of the Act, to be paid to the several states for the purpose of cooperating with them in promoting the welfare and hygiene of maternity and infancy as hereinafter provided.

Sec. 2. For the purpose of carrying out the provisions of this Act, there is authorized to be appropriated . . . , for the current fiscal year of $480,000 to be equally apportioned among the several States, and for each subsequent year, for the period of five years, $240,000, to be equally apportioned among the several States in the manner hereinafter provided . . . *[and]* . . . for the use of the States, subject to the provisions of this Act . . . an additional sum of $1,000,000, and annually thereafter, for the period of five years, and additional sum not to exceed $1,000,000 . . . And provided further, That no payment out of the additional appropriation herein authorized shall be made in any year to any State until an equal sum has been appropriated for that year by the legislature of such State for the maintenance of the services and facilities provided for in this Act. . . .

Sec. 4. In order to secure the benefits of the appropriations authorized in section 2 of this Act, any State shall . . . accept the provisions of this Act and designate or authorize the creation of a State agency with which the Children's Bureau shall have all necessary powers to cooperate as herein provided in the administration of the provisions of this Act. . . .

Sec. 8. Any State desiring to receive the benefits of this Act shall, by its agency described in section 4, submit to the Children's Bureau detailed plans for carrying out the provisions of this Act within such State, which plans shall be subject to the approval of the board. . . .

Sec. 9. No official, agent, or representative of the Children's Bureau shall by virtue of this Act have any right to enter any home over the objection of the owner thereof, or take charge of any child over the objection of the parents, or either of them, or the person standing in loco parentis or having custody of such child. Nothing in this Act shall be construed as limiting the power of a parent or guardian or person standing in loco parentis to determine what treatment or correction shall be provided for a child or the agency or agencies to be employed for such purpose. . . .

November 23, 1921

## NOTES

1. J. Stanley Lemons, *The Woman Citizen: Social Feminism in the 1920s* (Urbana: University of Illinois Press, 1973), p. 153.

2. James Johnson, "The Role of Women in the Founding of the United States' Children's Bureau," in *Remember the Ladies: New Perspectives on Women in American History: Essays in Honor of Nelson Manfred Blake,* edited by Carol V. R. George (Syracuse: Syracuse University Press, 1975), p. 192.

3. *Ibid.,* p. 189.

4. Sheila Rotham, *Woman's Proper Place: A History of Changing Ideals and Practices, 1870 to the Present* (New York: Basic Books, 1978), p. 102.

# 5

## The Social Security Act of 1935

The Social Security Act is arguably the most significant piece of legislation of the twentieth century. At one stroke, the social welfare of Americans became an explicit, and central, purpose of the United States government. Overturning a history of isolated, narrow, and state-led social insurance policies, the Social Security Act profoundly changed the federal structure of the United States. The Social Security Act brought the federal government directly into the life of almost every American. Washington now took the lead in developing, controlling, and bankrolling social policies in the United States, producing a vast transfer of power and policy from the states to the federal government. Finally, the Social Security Act served as the backbone for a massive expansion in social insurance programs that would ensue over the coming decades.

The Social Security Act was a sudden and dramatic break from America's earlier approach to social welfare. As we have seen, for the first 140 years of our history, there had been little government activity in this era. Although the Progressive movement had raised social insurance issues at the state level, legislative victories had been slim. Before the Social Security Act only one state (Wisconsin) had completed enaction of a law to protect unemployed workers.[1] Only 17 states had pension laws for needy senior citizens, and just three, California, Massachusetts, and New York, were of any size. Each was extremely restrictive. Combined, these laws covered but 3 percent of the elderly, and averaged just 65 cents a day in benefits. No state had a law offering a retirement pension to private sector workers. (Only 5 percent of workers had access to any pension plan.) In fact, the percentage of state budgets devoted to social welfare programs was actually going down during the first three decades of the twentieth century.[2] Compared to other industrialized nations, America's social policies could only be termed primitive. Faith abounded in the market's ability to handle unemployment and poverty.

What, then, explains the remarkable change that occurred in 1935? Three factors stand out. First, by the late 1920s America had largely industrialized. Americans had left the farm for jobs in the booming manufacturing and service sectors. This movement had vastly increased the wealth of America, but it had also created new social problems. Traditionally, farmers had neither "retired" nor been fired or laid off. A farmer worked the farm from childhood until death. But this was not the case in the industrial sectors. Here a worker could finally become too old to continue working, or could lose his or her job because of economic forces outside of the worker's control. One could now speak of someone "leaving" the workforce. What did America, or at least America's employers, owe these individuals?

This rather abstract question became all too real following the collapse of the American economy in 1929. The Great Depression was unlike anything anyone had ever seen. As banks failed and the economy contracted, both jobs and life savings were wiped out. By 1932, 38 percent of the nonfarm workforce was jobless. Starvation was reported in the press. And unlike earlier economic crashes, America did not quickly recover. Poverty, unemployment, and the dire circumstances of the aged could no longer be argued to be temporary aberrations. Indeed, the question now asked was, how long could they be endured? To make matters worse, the Depression had led to the bankruptcy or failure of many of the local poverty relief agencies that had served as the safety net in earlier times. Several states attempted to step in and finance relief to their unemployed workers, but they soon exhausted their budgets and had to beg Washington for help.

President Herbert Hoover's efforts to bring America out of the Depression did not encompass the federal government's expansion into the area of social welfare. But Hoover, blamed for the Depression, had become deeply unpopular, and, in 1932, Americans elected a new president, Franklin Delano Roosevelt. President Roosevelt's philosophy was virtually the opposite of Hoover's. FDR believed in an active government, one that would willingly intervene and experiment with new policies to end the Depression and the social problems it had produced. His election was the third factor necessary for the development of Social Security.

By the time Roosevelt took office, America was in its fourth year of the Depression. Political pressures for comprehensive government action were building. FDR responded by initiating the large number of policies that became known as the New Deal. Programs such as the National Recovery Act, the Civilian Conservation Corps, the Works Progress Administration, and others, were offered to revive the American economy and support its jobless citizens. Roosevelt also created the Federal Emergency Relief Administration to take over the collapsing state relief plans. But some of these programs, such as the NRA, were later declared unconstitutional, while others, however effective in their own terms, did not appear to be producing an economic recovery.

So other leaders came to the fore with ideas of how to solve poverty and unemployment. Senator Huey Long of Louisiana offered his Share the Wealth Plan. Claiming it would make "every man a king," Long proposed that all Americans should receive $5,000 a year to keep them out of poverty. Everyone over 60 should receive a government pension. To pay for this, Long suggested taxing and confiscating much of the fortunes of America's millionaires. In the House of Representatives, Earnest Lundeen of Minnesota introduced a bill that would compensate all unemployed or disabled workers, as well as the aged, by paying them an amount equal to the average local wage. A wealth tax would again be used to support the program. The most politically potent idea came from a retired California doctor, Francis Townsend. In 1933 Townsend published a plan to give all retired persons over the age of sixty $200 a month, on the condition that they spend the money within 30 days (criminals were excluded). These "Old-Age Revolving Pensions" would be financed by a 2 percent national sales tax. Townsend's plan offered a perfect combination of goals: The money would not only support needy senior citizens, but would also revive the economy as they spent it. Twenty-five million Americans signed petitions supporting the plan, and Townsend Clubs spread across the country. More modestly, a group calling itself the Association for Old-Age Security asked Congress to give grants-in-aid to the states to help them provide pensions for senior citizens. Other proposals were being made at the state level.

Many in Congress were sympathetic to these ideas. Dr. Townsend was asked to testify before the Senate in February 1935. Other New Dealers, especially Senator Robert Wagner of New York, were pressing ahead on their own. In 1934 Wagner shepherded a social insurance program for railroad workers through the Congress, only to see it declared unconstitutional by the Supreme Court. The same year he had cosponsored a plan for a national system of unemployment insurance called the Wagner-Lewis Bill. Lacking FDR's support, it died. Roosevelt had also thrown cold water on that year's Dill-Connery Bill, an attempt to enact the plan of the Association for Old-Age Security.

Roosevelt had put off both Wagner's plan and the Dill-Connery bill by saying that more study was needed. But he realized that his most loyal New Dealers were crying for action. He also could not help but note that Senator Long was a rumored presidential candidate in 1936. And, as 1934 progressed, he watched as the socialist Sinclair Lewis swept the California Democratic gubernatorial primary and nearly won the general election on a radical social platform.

## ROOSEVELT OFFERS A NEW PROGRAM

So, in June 1934, Roosevelt announced to Congress that he would undertake the study necessary to introduce a national social insurance program the following winter. To that end, he created a Committee on Economic Security to advise him. The committee was composed of five key administration officials: Henry Wallace, secretary of Agriculture, Henry Morgenthau, Jr., secretary of the Treasury, Homer Cummings, the attorney general, Harry Hopkins, the Emergency Relief administrator, and, as chair, Frances Perkins, the secretary of Labor. This committee was advised by a council of 23 business and labor leaders, and by a technical board of experts. In his direction to the committee, Roosevelt made a fundamental decision: Rather than a series of different policies or bills, he wanted *one* program that would protect every American from *every* kind of severe economic distress.

Roosevelt demanded a program that would be comprehensive, financially sound, and capable of passing Congress. FDR felt unable to endorse programs such as those of Dr. Townsend, let alone Senator Long, because he thought them fiscally irresponsible. They would saddle the American government with potentially huge financial liabilities far into the future. This led him to prefer programs funded by worker contributions rather than from the government's general revenues. He was similarly concerned that his program not come to be seen as just a welfare program, fearing political difficulties if he could not distinguish his program from the cradle-to-the-grave social welfare policies of Europe. So he demanded a program built around insurance principles rather than charitable principles. As he put it, "we must not allow this type of insurance to become a dole through mingling of insurance and relief. It is not charity. It must be financed by contributions, not taxes."[3]

A last problem, potentially the most severe, was the constitutionality of any program Roosevelt might devise. In the 1930s there were doubts about the constitutionality of any social legislation. The Supreme Court had dealt harshly with many of Roosevelt's New Deal programs. In *Schechter v. United States* (1935), the Court had ruled the National Industrial Recovery Act of 1933 unconstitutional. The Agricultural Adjustment Act (AAA) of 1933 was one of seven other programs to meet the same fate (*United States v. Butler*) and was in the midst of being rejected by lower courts as the Social Security plan was being developed. Senator Wagner's pension program for railroad workers also was voided by the Court. Court rulings narrowly interpreted both the Commerce Clause and state regulatory powers, the purported constitutional basis for the New Deal programs. The essential constitutional problem is that the Tenth Amendment appears to grant to the states all powers not given the federal government, and nowhere in the Constitution is the power to implement a social insurance program enumerated.

Roosevelt's first solution to this problem was to insist that as much of the program as possible would be jointly implemented with the states. Later, as the Committee on Economic Security considered the problem, it wavered between justifying the program either in the federal government's power to tax or in the Constitution's preamble "to provide for the general welfare." To strengthen the case for constitutionality, the tax (or contribution) portions of the program were placed in different sections of the bill from the spending provisions so that the former could be argued as the federal government's constitutional right to raise revenue. However the AAA had been drawn in an identical manner, and it was eventually to fail to pass muster. Thus, everyone knew the ultimate fate of Social Security would rest with the Supreme Court, and this certainly concentrated FDR's mind as reviewed his committee's proposals.

On January 15, 1935 the committee issued its report. Though there had been much wrangling, it unanimously proposed a legislative act composed of five parts: (1) grants for states to allow them to offer public assistance to indigent senior citizens and dependent children; (2) a joint federal-state program for unemployment insurance; (3) a federal old-age insurance program; (4) grants for states to offer expanded public health and child welfare services; and (5) a health insurance program. However, the health insurance idea was soon dropped in the face of a vociferous opposition from the medical community that made its survival in Congress unlikely. Two days later, Roosevelt forwarded the remaining four recommendations to Capitol Hill. Senator Wagner was given the honor of introducing the bill the Senate, and Rep. David J. Lewis of Maryland sponsored it in the House.

## THE POLITICS OF PASSAGE

Roosevelt was a brilliant politician, and his efforts to craft a "sellable" piece of legislation were successful. Opponents were immediately placed on the defensive. Roosevelt had neatly placed himself in the middle of his opponents, dividing those who thought he had gone too far from those who thought he had not gone far enough. The latter he knew would eventually rally behind him as it became clear his proposals were the best they could obtain.

Republicans were virtually unanimous in their opposition to the bill. Some suggested an alternative to creating an antipoverty program, funding it from the general revenues. However, such a program would have to be authorized and appropriated every year, and FDR saw through this ruse. Once opponents could finally gain enough votes in Congress, even if it were years later, they could proceed to reduce or eliminate the program. That is why the president had insisted on programs funded by worker contributions. As he bluntly explained it, "[w]e put those payroll contributions there so as to give the contributors a legal, moral, and political right to collect their pensions and unemployment benefits. With those taxes in there, no damn politician can ever scrap my social security program."[4] But the GOP was no threat to the bill. By the mid-1930s the Republicans had reached almost the nadir of their popularity.

With only 25 senators and 103 representatives in 1936, they could neither block, nor even slow the legislation on their own.

The question was whether conservative Democrats, especially those from the South, would join them in voting against the program. Business, broadly opposed to the bill, could be expected to pressure these members of Congress to kill, or at least gut, the bill. Oddly enough, labor unions could not be expected fully to counter that pressure. The American Federation of Labor (AFL) had opposed federal old-age insurance. Samuel Gompers, the hero and longtime head of the AFL, argued that federal pensions would supplant union benefits and make it more difficult to organize, while unemployment insurance would buy off idled workers and reduce their desire to organize. After his death, the AFL slowly shifted its position but never became a united force on this issue. At the time of the hearings, the then AFL president, William Green, still preferred direct subsidies to unemployment insurance for workers.

Of the four proposals contained in the bill, two, those for unemployment insurance and old-age insurance, were by far the most costly and ambitious. They became the focus of attention.

## UNEMPLOYMENT INSURANCE

Several states had been earlier battlegrounds for unemployment insurance, and Roosevelt's plan merely raised that battle to the national level. There were two major issues. First, should the United States adopt the model that was passed in Wisconsin ("the Wisconsin Plan") or the plan that was under debate in Ohio ("the Ohio Plan")? The former was essentially a reserve plan, whereby each employer was responsible for taking care of his or her own employees. Employers would be required to pay a percentage of their payroll into a fund, controlled by the government, up to a certain maximum dollar amount. When employees were laid off, they would draw a weekly check out of their employer's portion of the fund for a specified number of weeks, or until they found other work. The employer would then be required to replenish the fund.

The Ohio Plan would require employers and employees, every pay period, to contribute a percentage of their payroll into a general fund. Employees who lost their jobs would draw a check, as in the Wisconsin Plan, but it would be upon the general fund. Advocates of the Wisconsin Plan claimed that maintaining the link between employee and employer would encourage companies not to lay off workers, and would financially reward companies that kept their employees. Those supporting the Ohio Plan argued that keeping this link was a bad idea. Most unemployment was due to economic conditions outside the control of a company, and, should a company be unable to maintain its contributions or go out of business, what would happen to the employees who needed to draw upon its funds? They preferred to pool the risk among all employers, as in an insurance fund.

The second issue was who should run the program, the federal government or the states? Many reformers and a number of large businesses preferred a federal program. A federal program would discourage states from poaching businesses from one another by offering especially stingy unemployment programs. (A small program would mean lower taxes, an attractive proposition for an employer.) On the other hand, a number of states were already in the midst of developing their own unemployment programs and might oppose a federal program based on different principles. And then there was the constitutionality problem to worry about; on the face of it, states appeared to have a more solid constitutional grounding for undertaking these programs.

Roosevelt's instincts, as always, were to combine the most attractive and politically realistic elements of each issue, and, fortunately for him, a novel tax idea first used in a 1926 federal estate tax law allowed him to do so. This was the "tax offset." The United States could collect the taxes for an unemployment fund, but allow employers to credit any taxes they had paid to a state unemployment fund against the federal tax. Here is a simple example. If the federal government taxed a business one dollar for unemployment insurance, and the state taxed the business 95 cents for *its* unemployment fund, the business could credit the 95 cent tax it had paid to the state against the dollar federal tax, and thereby only have to pay the federal government a nickel. The federal government's role would simply be to collect the money and give most of it back to the states. Such a plan should encourage every state to adopt an unemployment plan with similar benefits. If a state wished to have a smaller plan, it would be giving up tax revenues in exchange for nothing. The floor provided by the restrictions of the federal tax would, at the same stroke, eliminate any temptation to attract businesses by offering a smaller unemployment policy, since the business would end up paying the same tax anyway. It would just go to the federal government instead of the state. Finally, a tax offset plan would allow the government to let each state design its own policy, for the federal role was essentially only to create this common floor under all the plans. This would solve the problem of what kind of plan to adopt, and ease any fears of its constitutionality. This idea was exactly what FDR was looking for. He vigorously endorsed it.

The plan offered to Congress, then, was one where the federal government would manage the pool of money, but each state would implement and manage its own unemployment insurance program. Once a state had enacted a program, it would receive monies from the federal pool up to 90 percent of the taxes paid by employers in that state. The tax to fund the pool was set at 3 percent of payroll, to be phased in between 1936–1938. Many, such as the sponsor, Senator Wagner, preferred a 5 percent tax, but Roosevelt bowed to business pressure in setting the 3 percent level. To avoid controversies over what type of program states should adopt, the federal program would not mandate any particular benefit standards.

The House of Representatives was not enthusiastic about the program. Business was opposed, the left wing of the Democrats disappointed, and the chair of the powerful Ways and Means Committee, Robert Doughton (Dem., NC), where the bill was first considered, was skeptical. However, the committee contented itself with stripping a provision that rewarded employers with good records, and making state programs based on Wisconsin-style plans ineligible. By the time the bill was heard in the Senate, the even more controversial old-age pension program was dominating attention, and unemployment insurance was reduced to a sideshow. However, Senator LaFollette of Wisconsin did obtain the reversal of the prohibition on Wisconsin-type plans. Indeed, bitter exchanges between social insurance experts supporting Wisconsin vs. Ohio plans generated more heat than any other aspect of the program.

## OLD-AGE INSURANCE

The greater controversy aroused by FDR's plan for an old-age insurance system eventually drew most of the attention away from the unemployment insurance debate. As early as 1930, some members of Congress had been pushing for a national pension system. The earliest proposals were for the federal government to pay a portion of the costs of state-run pension systems. But financing the program was the big obstacle. In 1930s' America only 5 percent of

Americans paid an income tax, and any program that would significantly increase this percentage was bound to be politically difficult. Business was opposed to the program because of the tax implications. Representatives from the segregated South were also opposed because of fears that their states could not afford to pay for a pension plan, and because a plan appeared to promise a level of financial support to African-Americans that they regarded as unacceptable. If these forces could coalesce, they would be enough to stop any federal pension plan.

Roosevelt, realizing he operated under these constraints, offered a program that would prevent these natural allies from joining together. Many New Dealers, the experts of the Committee on Economic Security, and those on the left wing of the labor movement wanted an old-age pension system built upon European lines. Such a system would be national, universal in coverage, generous, and well financed via use of the progressive income tax. Close associates, such as Harry Hopkins, argued with FDR for such a system. Roosevelt opposed them, for reasons of political expediency and personal belief. FDR apparently believed genuinely that it was morally wrong to create a program that might foist a deficit on future Congresses and that had even the appearance of being a dole for the aged. He told Secretary Perkins that granting federal monies to workers on the verge of retirement "bordered on immorality."[5] He wanted a pension system essentially like that of a private company. Run on insurance principles, it would pay retirees based on their contributions to the system during their working life. In this, he was supported powerfully by Henry Morgenthau and the U.S. Treasury Department.

Roosevelt unwaveringly argued for the creation of a trust fund to which employers and employees would contribute equally. Social Security benefits would be paid from the fund to the employees once they had attained retirement age. This disappointed many New Dealers, who saw this formula as a form of regressive taxation that would limit the size of pensions, especially to those with lower incomes. Roosevelt appeased this group by adding a voluntary annuity plan. Workers could buy a retirement annuity from the Treasury Department that would supplement their Social Security payments.

The easy way to appease many potential opponents, as well as minimize constitutional difficulties, would have been to follow the unemployment insurance model and allow each state to run its own program subject to this funding formula. But many people move between states over the course of their lives, and the record-keeping and program coordination among the states that this would make necessary made a series of state-run programs impractical. Federal actuaries thus insisted on a truly national program. Even at the risk of constitutional challenge, Roosevelt accepted this argument.

While business was largely opposed to the bill, the idea of a national pension system appealed to some big businessmen, who feared competition with firms located in low-tax states, should the United States move to a state-level Social Security system. The national plan thus drove a small wedge between larger businesses, that operated in many states and small businesses that operated in one. The latter were the most concerned about the Social Security tax, and the most hostile to the program. This split was to FDR's advantage. To further dampen opposition, a very large number of Americans were excluded from the program. Farm workers, domestic labor, and "casual labor" (day labor) were all exempted. Government workers and the nonprofit sector (which had vigorously opposed the system) were also left out. Thus, a considerable portion of America was not covered under the new program.

Excluding farm workers and domestic labor was also a back door method to meet the demands of segregationists. In hearings, representatives such as Howard W. Smith of Virginia made clear they wanted a program that allowed states to "differentiate between persons."[6] They opposed a national program that mandated a minimum standard of payments to Americans in every state. Their power was such that Roosevelt retreated on another front: agreeing that the federal government's efforts in the area of assistance to the indigent elderly should be limited to offering matching monies to state-run programs. The workers excluded from the Social Security system, however, constituted virtually all the rural South, and this served to diminish the strength of southern opposition to the program.

Finally, to blunt business opposition, the initial tax for the program was revised downward to begin at a low 2 percent (1 percent each for employer and employee) on the first $3,000 of earnings, and then gradually rise to no higher than 6 percent. The first payments would not begin until 1942, five years after enactment. This modest tax also meant rather modest benefits. The maximum monthly payment would be $85 (approximately $1,100 in 2001 dollars). Compare this to the $120 a month offered to retired railway workers under the Wagner bill of the previous year.

## CONGRESS ENACTS SOCIAL SECURITY

Even with these many compromises, it was unclear whether the program would pass. In the House of Representatives, friendly members of the Ways and Means Committee privately told Roosevelt that he should drop the old-age pension if he wished to the see the rest of his bill become law. At this same time, Dr. Townsend was testifying on behalf of his plan, and against Social Security, while the chair of the House Labor Committee was trying to push through a far more ambitious "Worker's Employment and Social Insurance Bill."

When FDR instead reiterated his support, the Ways and Means Committee went to work, dropping the voluntary annuity program and reorganizing the entire program under a new Social Security Administration (at some point in the proceedings "Social Security" replaced Roosevelt's preferred "economic security"). Both were successful efforts to pick up more support. (FDR had wanted the program to be distributed among existing federal agencies.) The power of the Ways and Means Committee in the House was such that, after having made these compromises, it was able to get the bill reported to the floor of the House under a rule that severely restricted amendments. This made the outcome of the House debate a foregone conclusion. The few amendments were turned back easily, and, essentially given the choice of all or nothing, the House voted for the entire Social Security package by an overwhelming 372 to 33.

The Senate was a bigger obstacle. Senator Gore of Oklahoma (Dem.) reflected the mood of many when he asked the secretary of Labor, Frances Perkins, "Now, Miss Perkins, wouldn't you agree that there is a teeny-weeny bit of socialism in your program?"[7] Senator Bennett Clark (Dem., Mo.) added an amendment that would exempt any private firm that had an existing, more liberal pension program from having to participate in the Social Security program. And Huey Long twice attempted to filibuster the entire bill. But once again, the final vote showed that when Congress was presented with the choice of no program or the one FDR offered, it was no contest. The Senate passed the Social Security Act by a vote of 77 to 6. Roosevelt refused to sign the bill unless the Clark Amendment was removed, and it was not until this was accomplished in Conference Committee, on August 14, 1935, that he signed the Social Security Act of 1935 into law.

As expected, the law was almost immediately challenged in court. In 1937, in two cases, *Steward Machine Co. v. Davis* and *Helvering v. Davis*, the Supreme Court, departing from earlier New Deal rulings, upheld the constitutionality of the act. Speaking for the Court, Justice Benjamin Cardoso argued that the problem of the aged may be included under the Constitution's mandate to promote the general welfare and is "plainly national in area and dimensions" and thus need not be left to the states. The American social welfare state was born.

## 5. The Social Security Act of 1935

[*The Social Security Act is broken into separate Titles for each of its different programs. Title I creates the program for old-age assistance, Title II the federal old-age benefits program ("social security"), Title III the unemployment compensation program, Title IV the Aid for Dependent Children Program, Title V the program for Maternal and Child Welfare, Title VI public health programs, and Title XI the program for Aid to the Blind. Title VII creates the Social Security Administration to administer the system, while Titles VIII and IX authorize the taxation necessary to fund the programs.*]

*PREAMBLE*

An act to provide for the general welfare by establishing a system of Federal old-age benefits, and by enabling the several States to make more adequate provision for aged persons, blind persons, dependent and crippled children, maternal and child welfare, public health, and the administration of their unemployment compensation laws; to establish a Social Security Board; to raise revenue; and for other purposes.

*Be it enacted by the Senate and House of Representatives of the United States of America in Congress assembled,*

**TITLE I—GRANTS TO STATES FOR OLD-AGE ASSISTANCE**

Appropriation

SECTION 1. For the purpose of enabling each State to furnish financial assistance, as far as practicable under the conditions in such State, to aged needy individuals, there is hereby authorized to be appropriated for the fiscal year ended June 30, 1936, the sum of $49,750,000, and there is hereby authorized to be appropriated for each fiscal year thereafter a sum sufficient to carry out the purposes of this title. . . .

## Payment to States

SEC. 3. (a) From the sums appropriated therefor, the Secretary of the Treasury shall pay to each State which has an approved plan for old-age assistance, for each quarter, beginning with the quarter commencing July 1, 1935,

(1) an amount, which shall be used exclusively as old-age assistance, equal to one-half of the total of the sums expended during such quarter as old-age assistance under the State plan with respect to each individual who at the time of such expenditure is sixty-five years of age or older and is not an inmate of a public institution, not counting so much of such expenditure with respect to any individual for any month as exceeds $30 *[i.e., the federal government will pay for one-half of the first $30 dollars of an old-age assistance pension, the state must pay for the rest]*, and

(2) 5 per centum of such amount, which shall be used for paying the costs of administering the State plan or for old-age assistance, or both, and for no other purpose. . . .

### TITLE II—FEDERAL OLD-AGE BENEFITS

## Old-age Reserve Account

Section 201. (a) There is hereby created an account in the Treasury of the United States to be known as the Old-Age Reserve Account. . . .

(b) It shall be the duty of the Secretary of the Treasury to invest such portion of the amounts credited to the Account as is not, in his judgment, required to meet current withdrawals. Such investment may be made only in interest-bearing obligations of the United States or in obligations guaranteed as to both principal and interest by the United States *[i.e., the Old-Age Reserve Account may contain only U.S. Treasury bills and bonds]*.

## Old-Age Benefit Payments

SEC. 202. (a) Every qualified individual . . . shall be entitled to receive, with respect to the period beginning on the date he attains the age of sixty-five, or on January 1, 1942, whichever is the later, and ending on the date of his death, an old-age benefit . . . *[the size of the benefit to range from a minimum of $10 a month to a maximum of $85 a month, based upon a benefit calculation formula]*.

## Payments Upon Death

SEC. 203. (a) If any individual dies before attaining the age of sixty-five, there shall be paid to his estate an amount equal to 3½ per centum of the total wages determined by the Board to have been paid to him. . . .

## Definitions

SEC. 210. When used in this title—(a) The term "wages" means all remuneration for employment . . . except that such term shall not include that part of the remuneration which, after remuneration equal to $3,000 has been paid . . . is paid by such employer with respect to employment during [a] calendar year. (b) The term "employment" means any service, of whatever nature, performed within the United States by an employee for his employer, except—

(1) Agricultural labor; (2) Domestic service in a private home; (3) Casual labor not in the course of the employer's trade or business; (4) Service performed as an officer or member of the crew of a vessel documented under the laws of the United States or of any foreign country; (5) Service performed in the employ of the United States Government or of an instrumentality of the United States; (6) Service performed in the employ of a State, a political subdivision thereof, or an instrumentality of one or more States or political subdivisions; (7) Service performed in the employ of a corporation, community chest, fund, or foundation, organized and operated exclusively for religious, charitable, scientific, literary, or educational purposes, or for the prevention of cruelty to children or animals, no part of the net earnings of which inures to the benefit of any private shareholder or individual.

## TITLE III—GRANTS TO STATES FOR UNEMPLOYMENT COMPENSATION ADMINISTRATION

## Appropriation

SECTION 301. For the purpose of assisting the States in the administration of their unemployment compensation laws, there is hereby authorized to be appropriated, for the fiscal year ending June 30, 1936, the sum of $4,000,000, and for each fiscal year thereafter the sum of $49,000,000, to be used as hereinafter provided.

## Payments to States

SEC. 302. (a) The Board shall from time to time certify to the Secretary of the Treasury for payment to each State which has an unemployment compensation law approved by the Board under Title IX, such amounts as the Board determines to be necessary for the proper administration of such law during the fiscal year in which such payment is to be made. The Boards determination shall be based on

    (1) the population of the State;

    (2) an estimate of the number of persons covered by the State law and of the cost of proper administration of such law; and

    (3) such other factors as the Board finds relevant. . . .

### TITLE IV—GRANTS TO STATES FOR AID TO DEPENDENT CHILDREN

#### Appropriation

SECTION 401. For the purpose of enabling each State to furnish financial assistance, as far as practicable under the conditions in such State, to needy dependent children, there is hereby authorized to be appropriated for the fiscal year ending June 30, 1936, the sum of $24,750,000, and there is hereby authorized to be appropriated for each fiscal year thereafter a sum sufficient to carry out the purposes of this title. The sums made available under this section shall be used for making payments to States which have submitted, and had approved by the Board, State plans for aid to dependent children. . . .

#### Payment to States

SEC. 403. (a) From the sums appropriated therefor, the Secretary of the Treasury shall pay to each State which has an approved plan for aid to dependent children, for each quarter, beginning with the quarter commencing July 1, 1935, an amount, which shall be used exclusively for carrying out the State plan, equal to one-third of the total of the sums expended during such quarter under such plan, not counting so much of such expenditure with respect to any dependent child for any month as exceeds $18, or if there is more than one dependent child in the same home, as exceeds $18 for any month with respect to one such dependent child and $12 for such month with respect to each of the other dependent children.

#### Definitions

SEC. 406. When used in this title—

(a) The term dependent child means a child under the age of sixteen who has been deprived of parental support or care by reason of the death, continued absence from the home, or physical or mental incapacity of a parent, and who is living with his father, mother, grandfather, grandmother, brother, sister, stepfather, stepmother, stepbrother, stepsister, uncle, or aunt, in a place of residence maintained by one or more of such relatives as his or their own home;

(b) The term aid to dependent children means money payments with respect to a dependent child or dependent children.

## TITLE V—GRANTS TO STATES FOR MATERNAL AND CHILD WELFARE

### Part 1—Maternal and Child Health Services
### Appropriation

SECTION 501. For the purpose of enabling each State to extend and improve, as far as practicable under the conditions in such State, services for promoting the health of mothers and children, especially in rural areas and in areas suffering from severe economic distress, there is hereby authorized to be appropriated for each fiscal year, beginning with the fiscal year ending June 30, 1936, the sum of $3,800,000. The sums made available under this section shall be used for making payments to States which have submitted, and had approved by the Chief of the Children's Bureau, State plans for such services.

### Payment to States

SEC. 504. (a) . . . the Secretary of the Treasury shall pay to each State which has an approved plan for maternal and child-health services . . . an amount, which shall be used exclusively for carrying out the State plan, equal to one-half of the total sum expended during such quarter for carrying out such plan. *[The state must pay for the other half of the expenses of the plan.]*

### Part 2—Services for Crippled Children
### Appropriation

SEC. 511. For the purpose of enabling each State to extend and improve (especially in rural areas and in areas suffering from severe economic distress), as far as practicable under the conditions in such State, services for locating crippled children and for providing medical, surgical, corrective, and other services and care, and facilities for diagnosis, hospitalization, and aftercare, for children who are crippled or who are suffering from conditions which lead to crippling, there is hereby authorized to be appropriated for each fiscal year beginning with the fiscal year ending June 30, 1936, the sum of $2,850,000. The sums made available under this section shall be used for making payments to States which have submitted, and had approved by the Chief of the Childrens' Bureau, State plans for such services.

Part 3—Child Welfare Services

SEC. 521. (a) For the purpose of enabling the United States, through the Children's Bureau, to cooperate with State public-welfare agencies establishing, extending, and strengthening, especially in predominantly rural areas, public-welfare services (hereinafter in this section referred to as child-welfare services) for the protection and care of homeless, dependent, and neglected children, and children in danger of becoming delinquent, there is hereby authorized to be appropriated for each fiscal year, beginning with the year ending June 30, 1936, the sum of $1,500,000. Such amount shall be allotted by the Secretary of Labor for use by cooperating State public-welfare agencies on the basis of plans developed jointly by the State agency and the Children's Bureau. . . .

Part 4—Vocational Rehabilitation

SEC. 531. (a) In order to enable the United States to cooperate with the States and Hawaii in extending and strengthening their programs of vocational rehabilitation of the physically disabled . . . *[is appropriated]* the sum of $841,000 for each such fiscal year in addition to the amount of the existing authorization, and for each fiscal year thereafter the sum of $1,938,000.

**TITLE VI—PUBLIC HEALTH WORK**

Appropriation

SECTION 601. For the purpose of assisting States, counties, health districts, and other political subdivisions of the States in establishing and maintaining adequate public-health services, including the training of personnel for State and local health work, there is hereby authorized to be appropriated for each fiscal year, beginning with the fiscal year ending June 30,1936, the sum of $8,000,000 to be used as hereinafter provided.

State and Local Public Health Services

SEC. 602. (a) The Surgeon General of the Public Health Service, with the approval of the Secretary of the Treasury, shall . . . allot to the States the total of . . . the amount appropriated for such year pursuant to section 601 . . . on the basis of (1) the population; (2) the special health problems; and (3) the financial needs; of the respective States. . . .

**TITLE VII—SOCIAL SECURITY BOARD**

Establishment

SECTION 701. There is hereby established a Social Security Board. . . . to be composed of three members to be appointed by the President, by and with the advice and consent of the Senate. During his term of membership on the Board, no member shall engage in any other business, vocation, or employment. Not more than two of the members of the Board shall be members of the same political party. . . .

## Duties of the Social Security Board

SEC. 702. The Board shall perform the duties imposed upon it by this Act and shall also have the duty of studying and making recommendations as to the most effective methods of providing economic security through social insurance, and as to legislation and matters of administrative policy concerning old-age pensions, unemployment compensation, accident compensation, and related subjects.

### TITLE VIII—TAXES WITH RESPECT TO EMPLOYMENT

*[Title VIII is the tax to support the old age-benefits program.]*

## Income Tax on Employees

SECTION 801. In addition to other taxes, there shall be levied, collected, and paid upon the income of every individual a tax equal to the following percentages of the wages . . . received by him after December 31, 1936 . . . :

(1) With respect to employment during the calendar years 1937, 1938, and 1939, the rate shall be 1 per centum.

(2) With respect to employment during the calendar years 1940, 1941, and 1942, the rate shall be 1 ½ per centum.

(3) With respect to employment during the calendar years 1943, 1944, and 1945, the rate shall be 2 per centum.

(4) With respect to employment during the calendar years 1946, 1947, and 1948, the rate shall be 2 ½ per centum.

(5) With respect to employment after December 31, 1948, the rate shall be 3 per centum.

## Deduction of Tax from Wages

SEC. 802. (a) The tax imposed by section 801 shall be collected by the employer of the taxpayer by deducting the amount of the tax from the wages as and when paid. . . .

## Excise Tax on Employers

SEC. 804. In addition to other taxes, every employer shall pay an excise tax, with respect to having individuals in his employ, equal to the following percentages of the wages . . . paid by him after December 31, 1936, with respect to employment. . . .

(1) With respect to employment during the calendar years 1937, 1938, and 1939, the rate shall be 1 per centum.

(2) With respect to employment during the calendar years 1940, 1941, and 1942, the rate shall be 1 ½ per centum.

(3) With respect to employment during the calendar years 1943, 1944, and 1945, the rate shall be 2 per centum.

(4) With respect to employment during the calendar years 1946, 1947, and 1948, the rate shall be 2 ½ per centum.

(5) With respect to employment after December 31, 1948, the rate shall be 3 per centum.

### TITLE IX—TAX ON EMPLOYERS OF EIGHT OR MORE

*[Title IX is the tax to support the unemployment compensation program.]*

### Imposition of Tax

SECTION 901. On and after January 1, 1936, every employer . . . shall pay for each calendar year an excise tax, with respect to having individuals in his employ, equal to the following percentages of the total wages . . . payable by him . . . with respect to employment . . . during such calendar year:

(1) With respect to employment during the calendar year 1936 the rate shall be 1 per centum;

(2) With respect to employment during the calendar year 1937 the rate shall be 2 per centum;

(3) With respect to employment after December 31, 1937, the rate shall be 3 per centum.

### Credit Against Tax

SEC. 902. The taxpayer may credit against the tax imposed by section 901 the amount of contributions, with respect to employment during the taxable year, paid . . . into an unemployment fund under a State law. The total credit allowed to a taxpayer under this section for all contributions paid into unemployment funds with respect to employment during such taxable year shall not exceed 90 per centum of the tax against which it is credited. . . .

### Unemployment Trust Fund

SEC. 904. (a) There is hereby established in the Treasury of the United States a trust fund to be known as the Unemployment Trust Fund . . . The

Secretary of the Treasury is authorized and directed to receive and hold in the Fund all moneys deposited therein by a State agency from a State unemployment fund. . . .

**TITLE X—GRANTS TO STATES FOR AID TO THE BLIND**

Appropriation

SECTION 1001. For the purpose of enabling each State to furnish financial assistance, as far as practicable under the conditions in such State, to needy individuals who are blind, there is hereby authorized to be appropriated for the fiscal year ending June 30, 1936, the sum of $3,000,000, and there is hereby authorized to be appropriated for each fiscal year thereafter a sum sufficient to carry out the purposes of this title. The sums made available under this section shall be used for making payments to States which have submitted, and had approved by the Social Security Board, State plans for aid to the blind.

**TITLE XI—GENERAL PROVISIONS**

Reservation of Power

SEC. 1104. The right to alter, amend, or repeal any provision of this Act is hereby reserved to the Congress.

Short Title

SEC. 1105. This Act may be cited as the Social Security Act.
August 14, 1935.

**NOTES**

1. Some states as well the federal government did offer unemployment benefits to government workers. Four other states passed unemployment legislation within several weeks of the passage of the Social Security Act.

2. Jacob S. Hacker and Paul Pierson, "Business Power and Social Policy: Employers and the Formation of the American Welfare State," paper presented at the 2000 annual meeting of the American Political Science Convention, p. 20.

3. Public Papers and Address of Franklin D. Roosevelt, 1934, p. 452.

4. Arthur M., Schlesinger, Jr., *The Age of Roosevelt: The Coming of the New Deal* (New York: Houghton Mifflin, 1988), pp. 308–309.

5. Mark H. Leff, "Taxing the Forgotten Man: The Politics of Social Security Finance in the New Deal," *Journal of American History* 70, No. 3 (1983): 368.

6. *Economic Security Act.* Hearings on HR 4120 before the House Ways and Means Committee, 74 Congress 1st Session (1935), p. 949.

7. Arthur Altmeyer, *The Formative Years of Social Security* (Madison: University of Wisconsin Press, 1966), p. 38.

# 6

## The Social Security Act Amendments of 1939

By the end of the 1930s, Social Security had survived its toughest political tests. In 1936, Alf Landon, the GOP nominee for president, made opposition to the program a campaign theme in his effort to unseat President Roosevelt. Landon's crushing defeat demonstrated Social Security's popularity. A year later, the Supreme Court found the program to be constitutional.

Though it was now clear that the Social Security Act would survive, debate over the program did not end. Liberals continued to believe that Title II, the old-age insurance plan, was too stingy, while conservatives still worried about the fiscal impact of the entire enterprise. In 1939 these worries strangely combined to produce a major change in Social Security. Today, when one thinks of "Social Security," one is actually thinking of the American old-age insurance program as recreated in 1939. In the 1935 act, the old-age insurance program was a reserve or annuity-style plan, a plan in which an individual received back, upon retirement, his or her own contributions plus interest. The 1939 Amendments began shifting the program to a "pay-as-you-go" plan, in which a retired individual's benefits were paid, not from his or her own taxes, but from the annual contributions of those currently in the workforce. The Amendments also added a survivors benefit to social security. In the 1935 program, a worker's benefits ended with his or her death. In 1939, this was changed to continue benefits, at a reduced level, to the worker's spouse or dependent children.

The 1935 act had given the Social Security Board the authority to offer recommendations for the improvement of the Social Security programs, but the real initiative for the 1939 Amendments came from Republican Michigan Senator Arthur Vandenberg. The 1935 act had created a reserve account to hold the contributions paid into Social Security until they were returned as benefits. Like many Republicans, Vandenberg was deeply skeptical of how this account would be used. At best, it would be a huge temptation for those wishing to expand the federal government; at worst, it was part of a Roosevelt scheme to get the financing for more New Deal programs. Since Social Security taxes began in 1937, and benefits were not scheduled until 1942, the reserve account was already sizable. Vandenberg and others estimated it would grow to $47 billion by 1980. In the late 1930s this was an almost unbelievable amount of money, enough to buy every farm in the United States with 14 billion dollars to spare![1] How could anyone reasonably believe that politicians could keep their hands off it? This was the gist of an article Senator Vandenberg published in an April 1937 *Saturday Evening Post*.[2] Vandenberg proposed making the programs benefits more liberal, starting the benefits in 1940 rather than 1942, and postponing the tax increase scheduled for 1940, all in an effort to prevent the creation of this political menace. Of course, the lack of a reserve account would mean that beneficiaries would have to be paid mostly out of that year's taxes on workers, because their own contributions had not been "stored" anywhere and could not be returned to them. Vandenberg believed, however, that this would be just as safe as a reserve plan, and would be less expensive to operate.

Later that year, Senator Vandenberg approached Arthur Altmeyer, the first chair of the Social Security Board, and asked if he would agree to establish a commission to reexamine Titles II and VII (the old-age insurance plan and its financing). Altmeyer thought it politically impossible to refuse. In November 1937, a committee was appointed that included prominent economists, Vandenberg allies, business executives, union leaders, and representatives from public interests, to consider the reform of Social Security. Although Altmeyer was not enthusiastic about making changes, he believed that some reforms had to be made to head off the more extreme proposals of Vandenberg and others.

Expecting every idea under the sun to be raised, Altmeyer suggested a fallback position to Roosevelt: Get rid of the reserve account and increase benefits, but hold firm on the scheduled tax increases. Anything beyond this would be financially ruinous, he claimed. Roosevelt agreed.

Sure enough, members of the Advisory Commission proposed a variety of ambitious reforms. Liberals who had lost the 1935 debate on financing again demanded the end of the contribution system, to be replaced by benefits paid from the general revenues. This would allow for more generous benefits, and for redistributing income to poorer retirees. The still influential Senator Robert Wagner was known to support this position. Others called for combining old-age assistance (the Title I poverty program) and old-age insurance. They were scandalized that many senior citizens could draw higher pensions from the former than from the latter. Business representatives objected to the whole idea of the reserve account. It was, they believed, financially unsound. The government was using the Social Security tax to buy U.S. bonds to place in the reserve account on behalf of contributing workers. But some day the bonds would come due and the U.S. government would have to raise the revenue to pay them off. Where would that money come from? The economists on the commission had a different problem with the account. They believed that the taxes sitting in the account constituted income that U.S. workers could not spend. This forced reduction in spending served as a drag on the U.S. economy, and could be a barrier to getting out of the Depression.

The one thing upon which almost everyone seemed to agree was eliminating the reserve account. But if this was done, how could the financial soundness of the program be guaranteed? One method, heartily endorsed by the board and liberal supporters, was to expand the number of workers paying into the program. Thus the committee recommended including agricultural workers, those working in education and the nonprofit sector, and others, in Social Security. Moreover, workers over age 65 would be allowed to continue to earn up to $14.99 a month, while paying the tax. (Above that amount, they would see their monthly benefits reduced.) Another method was to change the financing of the program. The committee argued that federal revenues "derived from sources other than pay-roll taxes" could be used to support the program.[3] This was a polite way of recommending the use of general revenues to pay benefits to retirees. This recommendation appeared to fly in the face of both FDR's and Treasury Secretary Henry Morgenthau's adamant opposition to the use of anything other than payroll taxes in 1935. However, Morgenthau was convinced to change his views. He now argued that since virtually all Americans would be receiving Social Security, making it unlike the far narrower program contemplated three years earlier, it was both morally and fiscally appropriate to dedicate general revenues to the program. He was also impressed, as were other administration officials, by the economists' claims about the economic drag caused by the existing system.

To quiet further fears about the government's use of Social Security contributions, the committee suggested the creation of a trust fund to be managed by designated, independent trustees, into which all Social Security taxes would automatically be credited, and from which all benefits would be paid. In other words, contributions would not, even for an instant, pass through the operating budget of the United States.

Once this movement towards a "pay-as-you-go" system was accepted, the possibilities were opened for increasing old-age insurance benefits. The committee called for benefits to begin in 1940 rather than in 1942, and under a new formula that would give the first retirees more generous payments than contemplated under the 1935 act. Under the original plan, benefits were to be based on an eligible worker's *lifetime earnings*. The only earnings that counted were those upon which the Social Security tax was paid. The first retirees, who obviously spent most of their working lives before the existence of the program, would have paid tax on a relatively small amount of their earnings, and they would, accordingly, not receive much in the way of benefits. To change this, Social Security actuaries suggested paying benefits instead on covered *average monthly earnings*. This would almost immediately bring retirees' benefits up to an acceptable level. Note, however, that this change eroded the link between taxes paid and benefits received. The desire to ensure that the level of benefits was sufficient also introduced into the program the criterion of need, or welfare, as a basis for determining benefits. This radical goal was purposely left unspoken by advocates. The new 1939 benefits formula was that each eligible retired worker would receive in benefits 40 percent of the first $50 he or she had earned in an average month plus 10 percent of the next $200. These amounts would be increased by 1 percent for every year an employee had paid taxes into Social Security.

The committee proposed a second dramatic expansion of benefits. Under the 1935 law, Social Security benefits were linked to the individual who had paid the taxes. When he or she died, the benefits expired. The advisory committee suggested including the worker's family in the benefits. Specifically, a married couple, only one of whom had worked, would receive the benefit earned by the working spouse plus a supplemental allowance of 50 percent of that benefit for the nonworking spouse. A nonworking widow would receive three-quarters of the benefit. Dependent children would receive one half of their deceased parent's benefit until they reached the age of 16 (or 18, if in school). In cases where there were no other dependents, the deceased's aged parents might be eligible for benefits. This new category of benefits was called "survivor's benefits." As a result, the program would be retitled Old-Age and Survivors Insurance.

Noting that every other country that had a retirement system also insured its workers against permanent disability, members of the Social Security Administration tried to add disability benefits to the program. However, the more fiscally conservative members of the committee balked at the unknown expense of this addition, and no timetable for the inclusion of this class of benefits was offered.

Securing Roosevelt's assent to its proposals, the committee finished its business and reported its recommendations to Congress in December 1938. Congressional hearings then essentially replayed the debate of 1935. A version of the Townsend Plan was revived and offered on the House floor as an alternative to Social Security. It was defeated easily (by a vote of 302 to 97), but had the serendipitous effect, according to the *New York Times*, of making the 1939 proposals look very minor, thus easing their passage.[4] Conservatives and southerners forced some changes during House Ways and Means Committee Hearings. They refused to contemplate expansion of the program to cover agricultural workers. Maritime workers were the only new group allowed into the program. And they ignored the recommendation for creating a disability program. Otherwise, the Ways and Means Committee endorsed the advisory committee's proposals and sent them to the floor of the House. The Ways and Means was a very powerful committee, and the House of Representatives largely deferred to the decisions it made. As a result, there was little floor debate. The labor movement tried to reverse the decision to keep agricultural workers out of Social Security, but an AFL-promoted amendment to include these workers was voted down. Another amendment to restrict Social Security benefits solely to American citizens was also easily defeated. The final vote for adding the 1939 Amendments to the Social Security Act was 364 to 2.

While the House vote attested to the overwhelming popularity that Social Security had already gained, passage in the Senate was more difficult. Senator Robert LaFollette (Rep., WI) continued to favor a program that would offer each American a flat pension financed out of general revenues. He saw no need for all the conditions entailed in the Social Security Act and the proposed amendments to it. In committee hearings, he raked Social Security Chair Altmeyer over the coals, pointing out the many difficulties of the Social Security system and demanding written answers to over one hundred detailed questions. Behind LaFollette was a group of like-minded experts, and this last-ditch effort to redirect America's social insurance policy so worried Altmeyer that he sought and gained Roosevelt's support in fighting it. Problems opened on a second front when Sen. Downey (Dem., CA), picking up a liberal theme, proposed that the new Old Age and Survivors Insurance be combined with the Title I Old-Age Assistance to create one old-age program. Downey's motion to recommit the bill for further study was rejected by a vote of 18 to 47, the closest vote on the 1939 amendments. The fact that 12 of the 16 Republicans voted to recommit indicates that the GOP continued to oppose the whole idea. Republicans simply did not have the votes to do anything about it.

As in 1935, both houses of Congress first voted for the bill by huge margins, and then fell into a rankerous quarrel when it came time to meet in conference committee. This time the issue was the Connally amendment, added in the Senate, that would change the funding formula for the Title I Old-Age Assistance program. Senator Connally (Dem., TX) wanted a new formula that would increase the federal government matching grants to the states for this program. This would benefit poorer states, making it easier for them to support their programs, but it would also raise the federal matching grants above the 50 percent incorporated into the 1935 act. The House and Senate snagged on this issue. Altmeyer wanted to compromise between the two, but FDR refused. The principle that each state had to pay at least half of a federal-state government program, was, in Roosevelt's eyes, nonnegotiable. (Thus supporters *were* able to increase the federal match for the Aid to Dependent Children program from one third to one half via the 1939 amendments.) Eventually, President Roosevelt got his way. The Senate agreed to drop the amendment, and the revisions to the Social Security Act became law.

These revisions fundamentally recast Social Security. As the first overhaul of a very large program, the 1939 amendments resulted in a number of changes. The favorable Supreme Court decision enabled the rewriting of the bill to develop explicitly the social insurance aspects that the 1935 drafters had feared might not pass constitutional muster. For example, the old Title VIII tax was replaced by the new Federal Insurance Contributions Act (FICA). But the most significant change was the entirely rewritten Title II. The addition of survivor's benefits, the supplemental pension for spouses, the ability to use nonpayroll taxes to finance the program, and the computation of benefits based on average monthly earnings, all served to change Social Security from what had been essentially an annuity program to one where benefits were not restricted to one's individual contributions. The 1939 amendments thus made possible the huge expansion in Social Security that was to come.

## 6. Social Security Act Amendments of 1939

[Many amendments were made in 1939. Most were minor. The major changes were the rewriting of Title II, and the development of Title VI to finance the program as recast.]

**TITLE II—AMENDMENT TO TITLE II OF THE SOCIAL SECURITY ACT**

Sec. 201. Effective January 1, 1940, title II of such Act is amended to read as follows:

**TITLE II—FEDERAL OLD-AGE AND SURVIVORS INSURANCE BENEFITS**

Sec. 201(a) There is hereby created on the books of the Treasury of the United States a trust fund to be known as the "Federal Old-Age and Survivors Insurance Trust Fund" . . . The Trust Fund shall consist of the securities held by the Secretary of the Treasury for the Old Age Reserve Account and the amount standing to the credit of the Old Age Reserve Account on the books of the Treasury on January 1, 1940 . . . and, in addition, such amounts as may be appropriated to the Trust Fund. . . . There is hereby appropriated to the Trust Fund . . . amounts equivalent to 100 per centum of the taxes (including interest, penalties, and additions to the taxes) received under the Federal Insurance Contributions Act and covered into the Treasury.

(b) There is hereby created a body to be known as the Board of Trustees of the Federal Old-Age and Survivors Insurance Trust Fund . . . which Board of Trustees shall be composed of the Secretary of the Treasury, the Secretary of Labor, and the Chairman of the Social Security Board . . . The Secretary of the Treasury shall be the Managing Trustee . . .

(c) It shall be the duty of the Managing Trustee to invest such portion of the Trust Fund as is not, in his judgment, required to meet current withdrawals. Such investments may be made only in interest-bearing obligations of the United States or in obligations guaranteed as to both principal and interest by the United States. *[This paragraph states that the trust fund may only invest in U.S. Treasury bills and bonds.]*

### Old-Age and Survivors Insurance Benefit Payments

Wife's Insurance Benefits

(b) (1) Every wife . . . of an individual entitled to primary insurance benefits, if such wife (A) has attained the age of sixty-five, (B) has filed application for wife's insurance benefits, (C) was living with such individual at the time such application was filed, and (D) is not entitled to receive primary insurance benefits, or is entitled to receive primary insurance benefits each of which is less than one-half of a primary insurance benefit of her husband, shall be entitled to receive a wife's insurance benefit for each month. . . .

(2) Such wife's insurance benefit for each month shall be equal to one-half of a primary insurance benefit of her husband, except that, if she is entitled to receive a primary insurance benefit for any month, such wife's insurance benefit for such month shall be reduced by an amount equal to a primary insurance benefit of such wife.

Child's Insurance Benefits

(c) (1) Every child . . . of an individual entitled to primary insurance benefits, or of an individual who died a fully or currently insured individual . . . after December 31, 1939, if such child (A) has filed application for child's insurance benefits, (B) at the time such application was filed was unmarried and had not attained the age of 18, and (C) was dependent upon such individual at the time such application was filed, or, if such individual has died, was dependent upon such individual at the time of such individual's death, shall be entitled to receive a child's insurance benefit for each month. . . .

(2) Such child's insurance benefit for each month shall be equal to one-half of a primary insurance benefit of the individual with respect to

whose wages the child is entitled to receive such benefit, except that, when there is more than one such individual such benefit shall be equal to one-half of whichever primary insurance benefit is the greatest.

Widow's Insurance Benefits

(d) (1) Every widow . . . of an individual who died a fully insured individual after December 31, 1939, if such widow (A) has not remarried, (B) has attained the age of sixty-five, (C) has filed application for widow's insurance benefits, (D) was living with such individual at the time of his death, and (E) is not entitled to receive primary insurance benefits, or is entitled to receive primary insurance benefits each of which is less than three-fourths of a primary insurance benefit of her husband, shall be entitled to receive a widow's insurance benefit for each month. . . .

(2) Such widow's insurance benefit for each month shall be equal to three-fourths of a primary insurance benefit of her deceased husband, except that, if she is entitled to receive a primary insurance benefit for any month, such widow's insurance benefit for such month shall be reduced by an amount equal to a primary insurance benefit of such widow.

Parent's Insurance Benefit

(f) (1)Every parent . . . of an individual who died a fully insured individual after December 31, 1939, leaving no widow and no unmarried surviving child under the age of eighteen, if such parent (A) has attained the age of sixty-five, (B) was wholly dependent upon and supported by such individual at the time of such individual's death and filed proof of such dependency and support within two years of such date of death, (C) has not married since the individual's death, (D) is not entitled to receive any other insurance benefits under this section, or entitled to receive one or more benefits for a month, but the total for such month is less than one-half of a primary insurance benefit of such deceased individual, and (E) has filed application for parent's insurance benefits, shall be entitled to receive a parent's insurance benefit for each month. . . .

(2) Such parent's insurance benefit for each month shall be equal to one-half of a primary insurance benefit of such deceased individual, except that, if such parent is entitled to receive an insurance benefit or benefits for any month (other than a benefit under this subsection), such parent's insurance benefit for such month shall be reduced by an amount equal to the total of such other benefit or benefits for such month. Sec. 209(e) *[This section defined the terms "primary insurance benefit" and "average monthly wage" as used in the 1939 Amendments. Each definition is actually a new formula for calculating monthly pension benefits. Together, they substantially raised the average social security pension from the formulas in the 1935 Act.]*

*[Following the favorable Supreme Court decision, legislators felt now able to incorporate the Social Security payroll taxes, as amended in 1939, into the U.S. Internal Revenue Code. Title VI was rewritten to accomplish this via the creation of the FICA (Federal Insurance Contributions Act) tax. This Title has since been repealed, and these taxes have been directly placed in the Internal Revenue Code.]*

### TITLE VI—AMENDMENT TO THE INTERNAL REVENUE CODE

Sec. 601. Section 1400 of the Internal Revenue Code is amended to read as follows:

Section 1400. Rate of Tax.

In addition to other taxes, there shall be levied, collected, and paid upon the income of every individual a tax equal to the following percentages of the wages. . . .

With respect to wages received during the calendar years 1939, 1940, 1941, and 1942, the rate shall be 1 per centum.

(1) With respect to wages received during the calendar years 1943, 1944, and 1945, the rate shall be 2 per centum.

(2) With respect to wages received during the calendar years 1946, 1947, and 1948, the rate shall be 2½ per centum.

(3) With respect to wages received after December 31, 1948, the rate shall be 3 per centum.

. . . . .

Sec. 607. Subchapter A of chapter 9 of the Internal Revenue Code is amended by adding at the end therof the following new section: "Section 1432. This subchapter may be cited as the Federal Insurance Contributions Act."

Sec. 608. Section 1600 of the Internal Revenue Code is amended to read as follows:

Section 1600. Rate of Tax.

Every employer . . . shall pay for the calendar year 1939 and for each calendar year thereafter an excise tax, with respect to having individuals in his employ, equal to 3 per centum of the total wages . . .

August 11, 1939

### NOTES

1. Edward Berkowitz and Kim McQuaid, *Creating the Welfare State: The Political Economy of Twentieth Century Reform* (New York: Praeger, 1988) p. 132.

2. Arthur H. Vandenberg, "The 47,000,000,000 Blight," *The Saturday Evening Post* (April 24, 1937), pp. 5–7.

3. Final Report of the Advisory Council on Social Security, Senate Doc. 4, 76th Congress, 1st Session, December 10, 1938. Quoted in Robert B. Stevens, ed., *Stat-*

*utory History of the United States: Income Security* (New York: Chelsea House Publishers, 1970), p. 218.

4. Quoted in Carmen Solomon, "Major Decisions in the House and Senate Chambers on Social Security," *CRS Report for Congress, Congressional Research Service*, December 29, 1986, p. 16.

# 7

# The Servicemen's Readjustment Act of 1944 (The G.I. Bill)

Better known as the "G.I. Bill," the Servicemen's Readjustment Act was the first important social legislation of the post-World War II era. Two of the most prominent features of contemporary American life, the vastly increased importance of higher education and the suburbanization of the United States, may, in good measure, be attributed to this bill. However, its impact on America's social insurance system has been much debated. Some believe the G.I. Bill not only furthered the nation's social protections but served as a bulwark that protected the still fragile Social Security system in the politically hostile environment of the 1940s. But others view the bill as a step back, a return to an earlier view of social insurance, more like that of the Civil War pension system, and away from the idea of a universal, comprehensive social insurance system for all Americans.

The G.I. Bill passed Congress without a dissenting vote. But that unanimity masquerades one of the stranger legislative histories of any major act. The bill was introduced by two unlikely bedfellows, the reactionary, avowedly racist Democratic Mississippi congressman John Rankin and Senator Bennett Clark (Dem., MO). Clark's most famous political moment came when he fell asleep at the 1944 Democratic Convention after nominating his fellow Missourian, Harry Truman, for vice president. Supporters then had to work overtime to convince the Senate's leading social-welfare advocates, Robert Wagner (Dem., NY) and Robert LaFollette (Rep., WI) and they had to overcome the indifference, if not hostility, of President Roosevelt himself to attain passage.

The bill obviously emerged from the experience of World War II. Once victory appeared certain, discussions began of how to integrate the 16 million soldiers and sailors back into civilian life once the war was over. In 1942, Roosevelt asked the National Resource Planning Board (NRPB) to consider this question. Everyone remembered the tremendous problems after World War I that had culminated in a veteran's march on Washington (the so-called "Bonus March") in 1929. There was also a widespread fear that the Great Depression would reappear after the war, and that vets would return to a country with no jobs to give them.

The Social Security Act of 1935 made the provision of pensions, America's response to its nineteenth-century wars, redundant. The NRPB studied both Canadian and state policies toward World War I veterans, but none offered much of a model. American veterans had been given only preferential hiring in the civil service and vocational rehabilitation services for the disabled. What was else could be done? To many, including the major veteran's organizations, the answer was cash bonuses for service. This approach harkens back to the idea of using social programs to reward meritorious service. The American Legion demanded a $500 bonus for each person who had served in uniform. The proposal was extremely popular, a Gallup poll showing 88 percent of Americans behind it.[1] However, it had one rather important enemy, Franklin D. Roosevelt. Roosevelt had previously vetoed bonuses for World War I veterans and was equally opposed to them for the new veterans. Roosevelt believed the bonus system divided the country into two classes of Americans, veterans, who deserved special treatment, and everyone else. He thought this a bad idea. Social policies should be universal and available to all, lest the politically marginalized receive nothing. He, and other New Dealers, favored a second approach to helping veterans integrate back into society via the provision of temporary rehabilitation and education programs. In fact, he had proposed creating a "Federal Rehabilitation Service" along these lines. It would offer assistance to all Americans, not just veterans.

FDR actually had a far more ambitious idea in store. He was developing his "Economic Bill of Rights," a stirring set of social guarantees to every American that he would present to Congress in 1944. Veteran's benefits were an unwanted distraction.

However, it was no longer the New Deal era. Following the elections of 1942, the "conservative coalition," a combination of Republicans and southern Democrats, firmly controlled the Congress. Roosevelt's relations with Congress had deteriorated badly. By 1944, Congress, led by the Democrats' own Senate majority leader, Alben Barkley (KY), overrode FDR's veto to impose its own budget upon him, an unthinkable event 10 years earlier. In this environment, Roosevelt's grandiose idea was a dead letter.

Roosevelt thus adopted a defensive strategy. He would oppose the bonus. In doing so, he faced not only the Legion, but the press baron William Randolph Hearst, who had taken up the issue in his newspapers. Hearst assigned two reporters to cover the bonus debate, and attacked bonus opponents daily in editorials and political cartoons. Told by advisors that he was going to have to offer something or "the opposition may steal the thunder," the president retreated to the idea of "mustering-out pay."[2] The distinction was rather slight. Mustering-out pay would be a small cash payment to allow veterans time to reintegrate into the civilian economy. It would be the exact same (lower) amount of cash for every veteran, whereas bonuses might be scaled by where and how long one had served. The former at least preserved the idea of equal treatment so important to Roosevelt. This legislative battle dominated Congress in 1943. The American Legion developed a very effective public relations campaign around case histories of forgotten and abused old soldiers. Yet, Andrew Jackson May (Dem., KY) the chair of the House Military Affairs Committee, who was fearful of the bonuses' cost, was able to ensure that the final bill was closer to FDR's position than that of the bonus adherents. Veterans were given the small allowance of $100 if they had served less than 60 days, $200 if over 60 days, and $300 if overseas.

The bonus debate, however, was just the preliminary skirmish. By late 1943 a larger battle had begun, one that ended in a four-cornered competition for who could offer veterans the most. For the first time since the 1920s, the GOP had hopes of wresting control of Congress in the upcoming 1944 elections. Veteran's benefits were too good an election issue to pass up. Even otherwise fiscally conservative Republicans jumped at the opportunity to appear pro-veteran. Not surprisingly, Democrats, not wanting to be on the wrong side of such a popular issue, upped the ante. Both parties were pressured by veteran's organizations. The American Legion, the Veterans of Foreign Wars, and other organizations were themselves in a competition to attract new veterans, and each used support for expanded veteran's programs as their bait. Sitting atop all of this was Hearst, still using the issue to boost readership of his newspapers.

At their 1943 national encampment, the Veterans of Foreign Wars passed a resolution calling for the government to pay for the education of veterans whose studies had been interrupted or delayed by war service. Bennett Clark, a senator in electoral trouble, sponsored the resolution as the first-ever veteran's education bill. This was but the first of 640 veteran's bills to be introduced in Congress that session. Meanwhile, at about the same time, Roosevelt announced his support for a modest set of educational benefits for veterans. Specifically, the government would pay for one calendar year of education for honorably discharged veterans, with a smaller number of "exceptional ability or skill" to be selected by the government for an additional three years of training. (The latter to be selected through IQ tests.)

Cost was a major reason for the administration's narrow program. But the administration itself was in disarray, with no one certain which agency should run the program, or how. Some agencies, such as the Federal Security Agency, told Congress they opposed the administration's proposal altogether. As a result, the initiative passed to the veteran's groups and their congressional allies. And these groups had much more expansive ideas. They also made it clear that benefits should be exclusively for veterans. Thus, they engineered the defeat of Roosevelt's Federal Rehabilitation Service, replacing it with a veterans-only rehabilitation bill.

In November 1943, the American Legion undertook to develop a "master plan" of veteran's benefits. Past Legion President Henry Colmery sat down and wrote out a proposed bill in a matter of days. In it, he included benefits for health, unemployment, education, and housing, as well as a bonus. Other veteran's groups were skeptical. They thought a piecemeal approach to legislation would work better in Congress. But in January 1944, the American Legion introduced its "Bill of Rights for G.I. Joe and Jane." The name was a stroke of genius, and Hearst had a field day excoriating those who would oppose such an honorable measure. Clark was the obvious choice to sponsor the bill in the Senate, and, for the House, the Legion chose John Rankin of Mississippi. Rankin was the chair of the House World War Veteran's Legislation Committee and had the great advantage of not being Andrew Jackson May, who had just stalled the bonus bill, or John Lesinski, the equally lukewarm chair of the Invalid Pension Committee. Veteran's organizations combined to pressure the House leadership into giving Rankin's committee jurisdiction of the entire bill.

The Legion bill had six titles. The first expedited the health claims of disabled veterans. The second dealt with mustering-out pay, and was later dropped when the mustering-out pay measure described above was passed. The third was an education plan that mirrored Roosevelt's plan above. It stipulated that veterans would receive a subsistence allowance of $50 (if single) or $75 (if married) per month while in school. The amount was set low to discourage veterans with little interest in education from entering the program. The fourth was a loan program for purchasing a home, farm, or business. This was an entirely new idea, and drew from one of the less controversial New Deal programs, the National Housing Act of 1934. That act had created the Federal Housing Administration (FHA) to help would-be buyers purchase a home. A Veteran's Housing Administration would be given the resources to insure long-term mortgages, with maximum annual interest rates, on behalf of veterans. Fifth, the Legion called for centralizing all veteran's programs under the Veteran's Administration.[3] Finally, there was an unemployment plan. Veterans could obtain up to $25 a week, for one year, if they could not find work.

The G.I. Bill quickly obtained many congressional sponsors, Republican and Democrat. However, a committee turf battle in the House, where the other chairs did not want to cede their authority to Rankin, held up consideration until that May. This gave time for open warfare to break out among the various veteran's organizations. On February 16, 1943, the VFW, the Disabled American Veterans, the Military Order of the Purple Heart, and the Regular Veteran's Association published identical open letters opposing the G.I. Bill. Ostensibly, they disliked various portions of the bill, but they may have been as much motivated by a desire not to yield veteran's leadership to the American Legion. These groups then proposed an alternative, a bonus ranging up to $5,000. The U.S. Army and Navy both indicated their support for this renewed bonus idea. Though sponsors were found for "The Veteran's Adjustment Pay Act of 1944," Congress had just compromised on the mustering-out bill and was disinclined to reopen the issue. In any event, the American Legion was collecting one million signatures in support of its plan. Ultimately, the Legion was able to swing the VFW back on board, although the other organizations remained hostile.

Educators, too, divided over the bill. The American Council on Education came out in support. But some elite institutions, fearing a watering down of higher education, opposed the bill. The presidents of Harvard University and the University of Chicago, for example, did not like the educational portions of the bill. However, it is fair to say that education groups had nowhere near the political clout of the veteran's groups that were debating the legislation.

In the Senate, where turf was not a problem, the bill sailed to passage. Senators made a few changes, liberalizing education benefits, and agreeing to Senator Wagner's desires for liberalizing the application of the unemployment standards. But the House was another story. Rankin, the chief sponsor, suddenly shifted to opposing the unemployment plan, indicating he might detain the bill in his committee. What had happened? Essentially, he had changed his mind because of his combined prejudices against higher education, African-Americans, and labor unions. He believed higher education to be largely worthless, producing an "overeducated and undertrained" population that would as likely as not be communist-influenced, too. He felt the unemployment program would end up subsidizing African-American veterans, who "would remain unemployed for at least a year" if they could.[4] Finally, he was adamant that no veteran should have to pay a labor union for his job, in other words, he refused to have anything to do with a bill that might help a union-closed shop.

Rankin's committee finally did report a bill, but one that represented the ideas of its chair. The question then became whether supporters of the original bill could stop Rankin's version on the floor of the House. After a bitter session, Rankin prevailed. The House voted unanimously for his substitute version of the G.I. Bill. This sent the bill to a conference committee of seven senators and seven representatives to resolve the House and Senate differences. According to conference committee rules, a majority of the members of each house must vote for the bill as revised in the committee, in order for it to be sent back to the houses for final passage. As it turned out, three of the House members would accept the Senate version. A fourth supportive member was at home because of illness. Hours before the final conference decision, the American Legion found that member (John Gibson of Georgia) and flew him to Washington in time to cast the deciding vote. The Senate version had prevailed. On June 22, 1944 President Roosevelt signed the Servicemen's Readjustment Act of 1944 into law.

Though Congress would revisit and revise the requirements of the G.I. Bill in succeeding years, generally liberalizing them, the 1944 bill established a huge program of benefits for America's veterans. The program ultimately cost the federal government $14.5 billion. The educational and housing portions of the bill had the greatest impact. A surprisingly large number of veterans took advantage of these programs. Over the next 10 years, more than 2.2 million veterans would attend college using the G.I. Bill, while another 5.6 million attained other forms of training. This surge of new students created the world's largest system of higher education. Perhaps more important, it created the most educated citizenry in human history. Today's "knowledge society" is the product. At an individual level, thanks to a college education, many veterans were able to earn incomes that would otherwise have been beyond their reach. The taxes on this additional income from veterans alone more than repaid the government's average $1,857 investment in them.

The effect of the housing portions of the G.I. Bill is less widely known but equally as important. Before the FHA and VHA, a buyer typically had to pay 30 percent down to buy a home or business. Moreover, mortgages varied greatly in length and terms. Riskier buyers might find that no one would lend to them for fear of default. The G.I. Bill changed all this. Now the Veteran's Housing Administration insured loans to all approved veterans, at mortgage terms lengthened as far as 30 years. The guaranteed insurance reduced both interest rates and the need for a large down payment, as sellers felt more certain they would be repaid. The lengthened terms reduced the average monthly payment, enabling many more people on modest incomes to afford a house. The effects of this portion of the bill (known today as "VHA mortgages") were immediate. In just the year 1947 alone, more than 542,000 veterans purchased a home using VHA insurance. This accounted for 42.8 percent of all home loans made that year. Even into the early 1950s, more than one quarter of all housing loans were VHA loans. America's "crabgrass frontier" of owner-occupied, single-family homes, spread across suburbia, is yet another legacy of the Servicemen's Readjustment Act.[5]

Based on the changes it brought to American life, few bills can compare. Yet the G.I. Bill also redirected America's approach to social insurance. "A product of conservative revival," it returned America's social insurance policy to the doctrine of rewarding meritorious or deserving citizens and away from the more universal conception of social insurance that Franklin Roosevelt had tried to develop in the 1930s.[6]

# 7. The Servicemen's Readjustment Act of 1944 (The G.I. Bill)

An Act to Provide Federal Government aid for the readjustment in civilian life of returning World War II veterans.

*[The GI Bill contains six Titles. Title I provides for veteran hospitalization and claims, Title II creates education programs for veterans, Title III provides home and business loans, Title IV offers job counseling and employment placement services, Title V specifies benefits for unemployed veterans, and Title VI pertains to the administration of the bill.]*

*Be it enacted by the Senate and House of Representatives of the United States of American in Congress assembled,* That this Act may be cited as the "Servicemen's Readjustment Act of 1944."

**TITLE I—HOSPITALIZATION, CLAIMS, AND PROCEDURES**

Section 101. The Administrator of Veterans' Affairs and the Federal Board of Hospitalization are hereby authorized and directed to expedite and complete the construction of additional hospital facilities for war veterans. . . .

**TITLE II**

Chapter IV—Education of Veterans

1. Any person who served in the active military or naval service on or after September 16, 1940, and prior to the termination of the present war, and who shall have been discharged or released therefrom under conditions other than dishonorable, and whose education or training was impeded, delayed, interrupted, or interfered with by reason of his entrance into the service, or who desires a refresher or retraining course, . . . shall be eligible for and entitled to receive education or training under this part: Provided, that such course shall be initiated not later than two years after either the date of his discharge or the termination of the present war, whichever is the later: Provided further, that no such education or training shall be afforded beyond seven years after the termination of the

present war: And provided further, that any such person who was not over 25 years of age at the time he entered service shall be deemed to have had his education or training impeded, delayed, interrupted, or interfered with.

2. Any such eligible person shall be entitled to education or training, or a refresher or retraining course, at an approved educational or training institution, for a period of one year . . . Upon satisfactory completion of such course of education or training . . . such person shall be entitled to an additional period or periods of education or training, not to exceed the time such person was in the active service on or after September 16, 1940, and before the termination of the war . . . but in no event shall the total period of education or training exceed four years:

3. Such person shall be eligible for and entitled to such course of education or training as he may elect, . . . and at any approved educational or training institution at which he chooses to enroll . . . which will accept or retain him. . . .

5. The Administrator shall pay the educational or training institution, for each person enrolled in full time or part time course of education or training, the customary cost of tuition, and such laboratory, library, health, infirmary, and other similar fees as are customarily charged, and may pay for books, supplies, equipment, and other necessary expenses, exclusive of board, lodging, other living expenses, and travel, as are generally required for the successful pursuit and completion of the course by other students in the institution: *Provided,* That in no event shall such payments, with respect to any person, exceed $500 for an ordinary school year. . . .

6. While enrolled in and pursuing a course under this part, such person, upon application to the Administrator, shall be paid a subsistence allowance of $50 per month, if without a dependent or dependents, or $75 per month, if he has a dependent or dependents. . . .

11. As used in this part, the term 'educational or training institutions' shall include all public and private elementary, secondary, and other schools furnishing education for adults, business schools and colleges, scientific and technical institutions, colleges, vocational schools, universities, and other educational institutions, and shall also include business or other establishments providing apprentice or other training on the job. . . .

## TITLE III—LOANS FOR THE PURCHASE OR CONSTRUCTION OF HOMES, FARMS, AND BUSINESS PROPERTY

### Chapter V—General Provisions for Loans

Sec. 500. (a) Any person who shall have served in the active military or naval service of the United States at any time on or after September 16,

1940, and prior to the termination of the present war and who shall have been discharged or released therefrom under conditions other than dishonorable after active service of ninety days or more, or by reason of an injury or disability incurred in service in line of duty, shall be eligible for the benefits of this title. Any such veteran may apply within two years after separation from the military or naval forces, or two years after termination of the war, whichever is the later date, but in no event more than five years after the termination of the war, to the Administrator of Veterans' Affairs for the guaranty by the Administrator of not to exceed 50 per centum of a loan or loans for any of the purposes specified in sections 501, 502, and 503: Provided, That the aggregate amount guaranteed shall not exceed $2,000. . . .

## Purchase or Construction of Homes

Sec. 501. (a) Any application made by a veteran under this title for the guaranty of a loan to be used in purchasing residential property or in constructing a dwelling on unimproved property owned by him to be occupied as his home may be approved by the Administrator of Veterans' Affairs. . . .

## Purchase of Farms and Farm Equipment

(1) Sec. 502. Any application made under this title for the guaranty of a loan to be used in purchasing any land, buildings, livestock, equipment, machinery, or implements, or in repairing, altering, or improving any buildings or equipment, to be used in farming operations conducted by the applicant, may be approved by the Administrator of Veterans' Affairs. . . .

## Purchase of Business Property

Sec. 502. Any application made under this title for the guaranty of a loan to be used in purchasing any business, land, buildings, supplies, equipment, machinery, or tools, to be used by the applicant in pursuing a gainful occupation (other than farming), may be approved by the Administrator of Veterans' Affairs. . . .

**TITLE IV**

## Chapter VI—Employment of Veterans

Sec. 600. (a) In the enactment of the provisions of this title Congress declares as its intent and purpose that there shall be an effective job counseling and employment placement service for veterans, and that, to this end, policies shall be promulgated and administered, so as to provide for them the maximum of job opportunity in the field of gainful employment. . . .

**TITLE V**

Chapter VII—Readjustment Allowances for Former Members of the Armed Forces Who Are Unemployed

Sec. 700. (a) Any person who shall have served in the active military or naval service of the United States at any time after September 16, 1940, and prior to the termination of the present war, and who shall have been discharged or released from active service under conditions other than dishonorable, after active service of ninety days or more, and by reason of an injury or disability incurred in service in line of duty, shall be entitled . . . to receive a readjustment allowance *[a cash payment to assist the veteran in reentering the civilian workforce]* . . . for each week of unemployment, not to exceed a total of fifty-two weeks. . . .

June 22, 1944

**NOTES**

1. Davis R.B. Ross, *Preparing for Ulysses: Politics and Veterans During World War II* (New York: Columbia, 1969), p. 85.

2. Michael J. Bennett, *When Dreams Come True: The G.I. Bill and the Making of Modern America* (Washington: Brassey's, 1996), p. 88.

3. There was one exception. The Selective Service System would retain responsibility over veterans' reemployment rights.

4. Both quotes are from John Rankin, quoted in Ross, p. 108.

5. See Kenneth T. Jackson, *Crabgrass Frontier: The Suburbanization of the United States* (New York: Oxford University Press, 1985).

6. Geoffrey Perret, *Days of Sadness, Years of Triumph: The American People 1939–1945* (New York: Coward, McCann and Geoghegan, 1973), p. 121.

# 8

## The Social Security Act Amendments of 1950

Franklin Roosevelt never gave up his dream of a comprehensive social insurance system for all Americans. In his penultimate state of the union address, he called for an "economic bill of rights" that would add medical care and disability insurance to an expanded Old Age and Survivors Insurance Program (OASI) that would cover everyone in the United States. However, he was unable to make any progress toward these goals before his death. Part of the reason was World War II. But resistance to new or expanded social programs remained strong. In fact, Congress repeatedly refused even to implement the Social Security tax increases that had been scheduled in the 1939 Amendments. As a result, the existing program was starved of revenue, and the monthly benefits to retirees were not increased.

The odd result was that, for most senior citizens, the old-age assistance poverty program remained more important than OASI ("Social Security"). By 1949, only one in five retired workers received a social security pension. This was only half the number that received an old-age assistance stipend. Moreover, the average old-age assistance payment was $42 a month, while the average social security check was but $25 a month.[1] Frustrated reformers eventually seized on this discrepancy. They called for a new start for the Social Security program, one that would reward work over welfare, and one that would truly include all Americans.

Their efforts ended in another set of amendments to the 1935 Social Security Act. While the amendments made a number of changes to the act, four stand out. Social Security was made a virtually universal pension system. Most occupations previously excluded from coverage were brought into the program. The 1950 Amendments also raised the average monthly benefit by 77.5 percent, the largest single increase in the history of the program. In effect, this redefined Social Security as a "livable" pension rather than a bare minimum with which to avoid poverty. The survivor's benefit was extended to new classes of Americans, including dependent husbands, dependent widowers, and children of insured women. Finally, the amendments added a modest program of public assistance for disabled Americans to the Social Security Act.

Through the 1940s, neither Social Security taxes nor benefits had changed. The most prominent opponent of implementing the scheduled FICA tax increases was still Republican Senator Arthur Vandenberg of Michigan. But he had a great deal of support in Congress, enough to prevent the increases even over FDR's opposition. The seeming stagnation of the program led Arthur Altmeyer, soon to be the chair of the reorganized Social Security Administration, to approach Senator Robert Wagner (Dem., NY) with the idea of making the expansion of Social Security to cover all workers a plank in the 1944 Democratic platform. But the conclusion of World War II, the death of Roosevelt, and the succession of Harry Truman to the presidency turned attention from the issue.

Once the war was over and he was established in office, Truman returned to the idea of reforming Social Security. Like FDR, his primary interests were to add medical and disability coverage, but he also wanted to expand the coverage of the existing program. He called for Social Security reform in both his 1947 and 1948 budget and state of the union messages. He underlined his support by again including this issue in his May 24, 1948 special message to Congress. However, unlike Roosevelt, Truman faced a Republican-controlled Congress. Even after dropping medical insurance, the most controversial of his proposed changes, he was unable to interest Congress in his proposed reforms. Though a score of bills were introduced to expand the coverage of Social Security, none came even close to passage.

Congress, in fact, was heading in the opposite direction. In 1948 it narrowed the definition of an employee under the Social Security Act, overriding a Truman veto, to cut 500,000 workers from the OASI program.

If opponents of an expanded Social Security Act saw this as a victory, however, they were soon to be disappointed. Truman made this vote a major theme in his 1948 presidential campaign. It contributed to his upset defeat of Dewey, and to electing Democrat majorities to both houses of Congress. Truman returned to the White House in a much stronger position from which to press his reforms through Congress.

Not only did Democrats control Congress, but the unexpected economic prosperity of the postwar years meant that employment was high and retirement contributions to Social Security were larger than anticipated. The trust fund was healthy, with 13 billion dollars in 1950. Not only did it appear that benefits could be significantly raised just by implementation the 1939 tax schedule, but the steadily rising wage rates made existing benefit levels look ever more paltry. In addition, the previous year an advisory committee created by the Senate Finance Committee had submitted its recommendations to Congress, endorsing sweeping changes to the OASI program.

Truman renewed his call for an expanded social security in his 1949 state of the union address. On February 21, he transmitted the drafts of two separate bills, one for public assistance and child welfare, another for Social Security and disability, to Chairman Doughton (Dem., NC) of the House Ways and Means Committee. A medical plan was placed in yet a third bill. The creation of separate bills was urged by Altmeyer and others, who thought this would provoke less controversy than one omnibus bill, and increase the odds of getting something through Congress. The strategy proved to be correct. The health care bill was viciously attacked by the American Medical Association and business groups, and died in Congress. But with these opponents focused elsewhere, the Social Security reforms passed by comfortable margins.

The public assistance and child welfare bill simply increased federal appropriations for these programs and made some changes in eligibility and in the methods of payment. (But segregationists were able to stop Truman's desire to add an obligation that states give similar treatment to persons in similar circumstances in order for state public assistance plans to receive federal matching grants.) Hence these reforms encountered no real resistance in Congress.

The president's requests for changes in the OASI program were more ambitious. Drawing on the Advisory Commission report recommendations, and his own advisors, Truman called for ending almost all the exclusions to eligibility written into the 1935 Act. Specifically, Social Security should be extended to cover the self-employed, farm workers, domestic workers, employees in the non-profit sector, and government workers. And qualifying for coverage would be made somewhat easier for everyone. Next, Social Security retirees should receive an immediate, large increase in benefits. Then, every year thereafter, the benefit amount should rise by 1 percent for every year of an individual's coverage in the program.[2] Retirees would also be allowed to earn up to $50 a month without losing any retirement benefits. Existing law allowed them to receive only up to $14.99 before their pension was reduced. Finally, in addition to this expansion of the OASI program, Truman wanted a new benefits program for workers who had become disabled, whether temporarily or permanently, and could not work.

The Ways and Means Committee held extensive hearings over the summer before reporting the bill to the full House on August 22, 1949. Support divided along party lines. Republicans argued that the OASI program should be conceived as but a "basic floor" of protection and not as a full pension plan.[3] Thus, they opposed expanding either coverage or benefits. They also opposed the disability benefits program because it would unfairly compete with private insurers. Together with conservative southern Democrats, they were able to limit the proposed disability program to only permanent and totally disabled workers, toughen eligibility requirements for inclusion in the OASI program, and roll back Truman's proposed 1 percent annual increase in OASI benefits to one half of one percent. The committee also continued to insist that farm workers be excluded from the program. With these compromises, the committee voted 23 to 2 to report the revised bill. A turf battle between the Ways and Means and the House Rules Committees threatened to tie up the bill, but eventually it was forwarded to the House floor under a closed rule, meaning that amending or changing the bill on the floor was prohibited. Under this restrictive measure, all the House could do was to vote yes or no. The key vote was one to send the bill back to the committee. This failed 113 to 232. The House then voted 333 to 14 to pass the Amendments to the Social Security Act. That almost 100 members attempted to bury the bill by returning it to the committee, but would not go on record as voting against it, indicates how politically popular Social Security had become. No one wanted to be seen opposing it.

The House vote was so late that the Senate was unable to consider the bill until it reconvened in 1950. Once again, the two parties took quite different positions. The Republican majority leader, Robert Taft of Ohio, continued to propound Sen. Vandenberg's position, arguing for rolling OASI and old-age assistance into one program, with no eligibility requirements and equal pensions for all retirees. This would be financed through a flat percentage of the income tax. The GOP argued this was fairer, simpler to administer, and a more honest accounting of public funds. But he did not have the votes. Instead, the Senate Finance Committee reported a slightly liberalized version of the House bill to the floor. The committee made three important changes to the House bill. It tinkered again with coverage, adding farm workers back but making nonprofit participation in the OASI optional. It eliminated even the one half of a percent annual increase for years of coverage in the program. And it removed the disability program. On the floor, a vote to restore the disability program failed. After a series of other minor amendments, the bill passed 81 to 2.

In conference, the House and Senate split their differences. Farm workers were kept in the program, but nonprofit participation was made voluntary.[4] Government workers were also excluded from OASI. As of September 1950, the average benefit for social security recipients was increased 77.5 percent using a new benefit formula mid-way between that passed in each house. The eligibility and computation formulas for future benefits were liberalized, but no annual benefit increases were included. The conferees also raised the FICA tax, in increments, to ensure the increased benefits could be paid while keeping the program fiscally sound. Beginning in 1954, the tax was scheduled to rise from 4 percent (shared equally by employer and employee) until it reached 7.5 percent after 1969. The self-employed would have to contribute three-quarters of this amount.

The conference committee restored a disability program, but limited it to individuals who were totally and permanently disabled. It fashioned a program similar to the other Social Security public assistance programs, providing matching grants for state-run programs. This narrow program was more in tune with Republican (and Senate) desires for a "charity" program than Truman's interest in general disability insurance, but it did serve as the precedent for future federal action in this area.

President Truman signed the 1950 Amendments to the Social Security Act on August 28, 1950. The law extended social security coverage to an additional 10 million working Americans, and raised the average monthly benefit from $26 to $46. Social Security had been transformed into a nearly universal old-age pension system upon which Americans could expect to live, albeit modestly, during their retirement.

## 8. The Social Security Act Amendments of 1950

[Nearly one hundred pages in length, the 1950 Amendments were as extensive as those of 1939. The Amendments were organized into four titles: Title I—Amendments to Title II of the Social Security Act; Title II—Amendments to Internal Revenue Code; Title III—Amendments to Public Assistance and Maternal and Child Welfare Provisions of the Social Security Act; and Title IV—Miscellaneous Provisions. The most important changes are those below.]

*Be it enacted by the Senate and House of Representatives of the United States of America in Congress assembled,* That this Act . . . may be cited as the "Social Security Act Amendments of 1950."

**TITLE I—AMENDMENTS TO TITLE II OF THE SOCIAL SECURITY ACT**

Old-Age and Survivors Insurance Benefit Payments
Definition of Employment

Section 210—For the purposes of this title—

(a) The term 'employment' means . . . any service, of whatever nature, performed after 1950 either (A) by an employee for the person employing him, irrespective of the citizenship or residence of either, (i) within the United States, or (ii) on or in connection with an American vessel or American aircraft . . . or (B) outside the United States by a citizen of the United States as an employee for an American employer (as defined in subsection (e)); except that, in the case of service performed after 1950, such term shall not include . . .

*[Excluded from this definition were agricultural labor, if part-time, paid less than $50 a quarter, connected with the production or harvesting of certain designated agricultural commodities, or in connection with the ginning of cotton, domestic service by a student, employees of another family member, service on non-American vessels or aircraft, federal workers that are covered in a U.S. retirement system, state or local government workers, those employed by a religious, charitable, educational, or other tax-exempt organization, enrolled students employed by their school, work for a foreign government or international organization, student nurses, fisherman, and newspaper deliverers. Later amendments have since rescinded almost all of these exclusions.]*

Quarter and Quarter of Coverage

*[Section 213 explicitly includes self-employed income under the OASI.]*

Section 213. (a) For the purposes of this title—

(2) (B) The term 'quarter of coverage' means, in the case of a quarter occurring after 1950, a quarter in which the individual has been paid $50 or more in wages or for which he has been credited . . . with $100 or more of self-employment income. . . .

## Computation of Primary Insurance Amount

*[This section sets out a new, liberalized benefits formula.]*

Primary Insurance Benefit

(a) (1) The primary insurance amount of an individual who attained age twenty-two after 1950 and with respect to whom not less than six of the quarters elapsing after 1950 are quarters of coverage shall be 50 per centum of the first $100 of his average monthly wage plus 15 per centum of the next $200 of such wage; except that if his average monthly wage is less than $50 . . . *[two special conversion tables are used for wages of less than $50 to boost the benefits of these individuals above the level they would otherwise be eligible for]*.

## Coverage of State and Local Employees

'Voluntary Agreements for Coverage of State and Local Employees'

Section 218. (a) (1) The Administrator shall, at the request of any State, enter into an agreement with such State for the purpose of extending the insurance system established by this Title to services performed by individuals as employees of such State or any political subdivision thereof. Each such agreement shall contain such provisions, not inconsistent with the provisions of this section, as the State may request.

**TITLE II—AMENDMENTS TO THE INTERNAL REVENUE CODE**

## Self-Employment Income

Section 208 (a) Chapter I of the Internal Revenue code is amended by adding at the end thereof the following new subchapter:

"SUBCHAPTER E—TAX ON SELF-EMPLOYMENT INCOME

Sec. 480. Rate of Tax.

In addition to other taxes, there shall be levied, collected, and paid for each taxable year beginning after December 31, 1950, upon the self-employment income of every individual, a tax as follows . . . *[the tax is set at ¾ the combined employee and employer payroll tax]*.

**TITLE III—AMENDMENTS TO PUBLIC ASSISTANCE AND MATERNAL AND CHILD WELFARE PROVISIONS OF THE SOCIAL SECURITY ACT**

Section 351. The Social Security Act is further amended by adding after Title XIII thereof the following new title:

**"TITLE XIV—GRANTS TO STATES FOR AID TO THE PERMANENTLY AND TOTALLY DISABLED"**

## Appropriation

*[Section 1401 creates partial federal funding for states that chose to operate a disability program.]*

Section 1401. For the purpose of enabling each State to furnish financial assistance, as far as practicable under the conditions in such State, to needy individuals eighteen years of age or older who are permanently and totally disabled, there is hereby authorized to be appropriated for the fiscal year ending June 30, 1951, the sum of $50,000,000, and there is hereby authorized to be appropriated for each fiscal year thereafter a sum sufficient to carry out the purposes of this title. The sums made available under this section shall be used for making payments to States which have submitted, and had approved by the Administrator, State plans for aid to the permanently and totally disabled.

## Payment to States

*[Section 1403 stipulates that the federal government will pay three-fourth of the costs of the state disability program for the first $20 spent per individual per month, and one half of any costs above that amount.]*

Section 1403. (a) From the sums appropriated therefor, the Secretary of the Treasury shall pay to each State . . . the sum of the following proportions of the total amounts expended during such quarter as aid to the permanently and totally disabled under the State plan, not counting so much of such expenditure with respect to any individual for any month as exceeds $50—

(A) three-fourths of such expenditures, not counting so much of any expenditure with respect to any month as exceeds the product of $20 multiplied by the total number of such individuals who received aid to the permanently and totally disabled for such month, plus

(B) one-half of the amount by which such expenditures exceed the maximum which may be counted under clause (A); . . .

August 28, 1950

## NOTES

1. Edward Berkowitz and Kim McQuaid, *Creating the Welfare State: The Political Economy of Twentieth Century Reform,* (New York: Praeger, 1988), p. 176.

2. The Advisory Committee had actually opposed the 1 percent benefit increase, arguing that the focus should be on larger immediate benefits.

3. Carmen D. Solomon, "Major Decisions in the House and Senate Chambers on Social Security," *CRS Report for Congress. Congressional Research Service,* December 29, 1986, p. 27.

4. Numerous eligibility requirements continued to exclude a number of farm workers, however. Farm workers were not entirely included until more amendments to the law were made in 1954.

# 9

# Federal Disability Insurance: The Social Security Act Amendments of 1956

Few prospects are more frightening than becoming unable to work because of a disability. Although some employers offer insurance for such an eventuality, and private disability insurance is available, even today only about one in four working Americans are covered under such insurance.[1] Unless one is wealthy, suffering a disability without insurance could mean an ensuing lifetime of unemployment and poverty. The original Social Security Act included no provisions for disability, except for the Title X grant-in-aid program for the blind. In 1956, this was rectified. The Old-Age and Survivors Insurance program (OASI) was refashioned to include disabled workers. Not only was the first major new federal program added to Social Security since its passage in 1935, but it has become the primary financial protection against job loss due to disability for most working Americans. Social Security disability insurance today covers 95 percent of American workers. The 1956 amendments thus filled a serious gap in America's system of social insurance.

The lack of a disability plan in the original Social Security Act was not because the dire situation of disabled workers was unrecognized. In fact, by the mid-1920s virtually every state did have a worker's compensation program for those who had suffered injuries on the job. Vocational rehabilitation programs were also being passed. The problem, rather, was financial and political. The Depression had been catastrophic for the existing private disability insurance industry. Claims, and industry losses, were huge. This seemed to offer the lesson that, under the wrong conditions, a disability insurance system could be extremely expensive. The potential cost made a disability program appear politically dangerous to these reformers attempting to get Social Security through Congress. And government disability insurance had powerful enemies. Not only the insurance industry but also the American Medical Association was opposed to the idea. The AMA believed that the day the government, not the doctor, decided who was disabled, and what treatment was appropriate, was the day that "socialized medicine" had arrived in the United States. Doctors would have lost control over their patients and their earning power.

These realities had prevented serious consideration of a disability program in the first decade of Social Security's existence. Yet, many members of Congress were nettled by a seeming unfairness in the operation of the OASI toward disabled workers. If a worker became disabled, he or she would be unable to accumulate quarters of Social Security coverage close to the date of retirement, *and*, his or her average monthly income might be calculated using quarters when the worker was disabled. This seemed to punish disabled workers for the injury they had suffered. President Truman had requested action on this issue, but, as we have seen, a divided Congress would only consent to pass a grant-in-aid program to assist state plans for permanently and totally disabled workers in its 1950 amendments to the Social Security Act. Obtaining a true federal disability program would be a politically difficult undertaking.

Thus, proponents began with a different idea, the "disability freeze." In 1952, liberal Democrats in the House of Representatives proposed amending the OASI program so that the quarters during which a worker was disabled would not be included in calculating his or her eligibility for coverage or his or her average monthly income. This seemingly innocuous idea generated a firestorm of protest from the AMA, which demanded to know whether the doctor or the government would determine the existence of a disability. After some parliamentary maneuvers the bill passed the House, but the "freeze" was dropped in the Senate version. The conference committee then fashioned a rather cynical compromise. It put a disability freeze in the OASI program, but the freeze was to terminate on June 30, 1953, one day before the first date (July 1) that a worker was allowed to apply for it!

Needless to say, this did not satisfy supporters of a disability plan. They returned to the issue when the Social Security Act next came up for amendment, in 1954. Yet, that year interest in the disability plan fell before an even bigger issue. President Eisenhower was the first Republican to hold the presidency since the birth of the Social Security system. In 1954 he would deliver his first proposals for changing the program. Would he attempt to dismantle it? Would he pursue the ideas of Taft, Vandenburg, and earlier Republicans, and attempt radically to reshape the program? To proponents' great relief, Eisenhower announced himself a supporter of the existing program. He focused successfully on further expanding eligibility under OASI. And he, and the new Housing, Education, and Welfare (HEW) secretary, Oveta Culp Hobby, endorsed the disability freeze. Eisenhower's position on the freeze was surprising. Apparently, members of the Social Security bureaucracy and the undersecretary of HEW, Nelson Rockefeller, had persuaded their superiors of this course. They found an opening in the administration's evident desire to boost vocational rehabilitation services and explained that the freeze would give disabled workers hope for the future and encourage them to enter rehabilitation programs. Even Eisenhower's support, though, did not guarantee passage. The AMA, supported by the Chamber of Commerce, again fought the idea that the federal government should be making medical decisions. This opposition led to a compromise: Determinations of disability would be made only at the state level, by state vocational rehabilitation agencies. As the House Ways and Means Committee noted, "[t]hese agencies have well-established relationships with the medical profession. . . ."[2] With this proviso, the disability freeze easily passed the Congress. For guidance, Congress provided states with the definition of a "disability" that remains current law.[3]

What supporters were still unable to obtain was a full-blown disability insurance plan—monthly stipends to individuals who could not work. Senator Herbert Lehman (Dem., NY) signaled that liberals would continue this fight by offering and then withdrawing an amendment to create a federal insurance program for permanent and temporary disability at the end of the Senate debate on the 1954 amendments.

The 1954 elections returned Democrat majorities to both houses, a favorable development for disability insurance supporters. But it also became clear that the Eisenhower administration was going to oppose any further government expansion on this issue. In other words, for the first time in the history of Social Security, reformers were going to have to fight the White House. In the House, Democrats could use their control of parliamentary procedure to defeat Ike, but in the Senate things were not going to be as easy.

In January 1955 President Eisenhower opened the battle by calling on Congress for further Social Security reform, but pointedly excluding any mention of disability benefits. Six months later, Jere Cooper (Dem., TN), chair of the House Ways and Means Committee, announced that his committee would be holding executive (i.e., secret) sessions to consider the over one hundred Social Security reform bills that had been introduced that year. Republicans vainly protested for public hearings. In the secret sessions, the committee constructed a disability insurance plan. The plan would offer a payment of monthly benefits to all totally and permanently disabled workers over age 50, to be computed in the same manner as OASI benefits. Disabled children under the age of 18 would also receive monthly benefits if their parent or guardian covered under OASI died or retired. The plan would be financed by an additional one quarter of one percent tax on workers and their employers (or three-eighths of one percent for the self-employed). The committee reported a bill to revise Social Security that included the disability plan and it was sent to the floor under a suspension of the rules. This meant that a two-thirds vote was needed for passage, but also that no amendments would be allowed from the floor, and debate would be limited to 40 minutes. Though there were many complaints about using this procedure, the bill passed 372 to 31. On a single yes or no vote, who wanted to vote against the entire Social Security program? Meanwhile, Secretary Hobby continued to protest that more study was needed.

The Senate does not have similar procedures by which to control debate, and, when its Finance Committee began hearings in early 1956, the lobbying was intense. President Eisenhower warned against financially unsound changes to the OASI program in his state of the union address. The AMA, the Chamber of Commerce, and the National Association of Manufacturers began their campaign against a disability insurance program. The AMA, in particular, remained hostile. But unlike in earlier years, pro-Social Security interest groups were emerging as well. The most important was the AFL-CIO, which was finally united in its desire to expand Social Security, and lobbied vigorously for the disability program. The now large "Social Security bureaucracy" of administrators, social workers, and policy advisors also entered the fray. Because of their positions in the government, though, their activities often took place behind the scenes.

After hearing from the many interest groups who had not been able to testify in the House, the Finance Committee concluded its hearings in late March 1956. The final witness was Marion Folsom, who had succeeded Culp as the HEW secretary. Folsom outlined the administration's opposition to the program. He argued that defining "disability" was extremely difficult, that the grant-in-aid program to the states passed in 1950 was sufficient for the problem, and that more study was needed. He emphasized a key difference between the existing OASI and a new insurance plan. The costs of the former were predictable, one could estimate them into the future, but no one could estimate future levels of disability, and, hence, the true cost of the program was unknowable. The Eisenhower administration, supported by business interests, preferred to focus on vocational rehabilitation as the solution to the problem of worker disability.

The committee found this argument compelling, and reported a bill to the floor that removed the disability program. From the House bill, it kept only the children's disability benefits, slightly liberalizing the terms. It was believed that most of these cases would be of congenital or early childhood conditions, and thus would not have the definitional problems or potentially huge cost associated with the adult program. The Finance Committee report then added an additional argument against the adult program: The existence of monthly benefits might create the perverse incentive of inducing people who could work to claim or maintain disabled status.

The Senate floor debate included other controversial issues, such as lowering the age of OASI eligibility to 62 for women and changing the funding formula for public assistance, but none was so closely contested as disability insurance. To appease worries about its unpredictable cost, Senator Kerr (Dem., OK) suggested creating a separate trust fund for the disability program. The portion of the Social Security tax intended for the disability program would be directly deposited into a disability trust fund that would operate exactly like the old-age insurance trust fund. This would ensure that the OASI trust fund would never be "raided" for monies with which to pay disability benefits.

Senator Walter George (Dem., GA) offered an amendment that would restore the disability insurance program as passed by the House of Representatives, but with the disability trust fund. This was quickly recognized as not only a critical Social Security vote, but as a key test of the Democrats' ability to impose their will on the White House. Democratic Senate Majority Leader Lyndon Johnson (TX) went to extraordinary lengths to unite his party behind the amendment, while the administration and its allies in the business and medical communities fought just as fiercely against it. In the event, the Democrats split 41 to 7 in favor of the George amendment, ensuring its approval by just one vote (47 to 45). The rest was anticlimactic. On August 1, 1956 President Eisenhower, though indicating his lack of enthusiasm about the disability program, signed the 1956 amendments to the Social Security Act into law.

As passed, the OASI was reorganized as the Old Age, Survivors, and Disability Insurance program (OASDI). Under it, disability benefits would be paid monthly to every American between the ages of 50 and 65 who was insured under the OASI program at the time of the disability and who met the federal test of disability. There was a six-month waiting period, and no provisions for temporary or partial benefits. Critics have noted that it was, in its essence, an early retirement program rather than a cradle-to-grave disability program. As noted above, a small program for disabled children was also included in the 1956 amendments. As it turns out, the disability portion of OASDI has grown dramatically over the years. In 1960, further amendments removed the age requirement, making disability benefits available to any Social Security-eligible worker. By 2000, over six million Americans received over $100 billion a year through its auspices. It has become the primary form of financial protection against disability for most American workers.

## 9a. Social Security Amendments of 1956

An Act to amend title II of the Social Security Act to provide
disability insurance benefits for certain disabled individuals
who have attained age fifty, to reduce to age sixty-two the age
on the basis of which benefits are payable to certain women,
to provide for child's insurance benefits for children who are
disabled before attaining the age eighteen, to extend coverage,
and for other purposes.

[The 1956 Amendments, though not as lengthy as those of 1950 or
1939, are still extensive. Below are the portions of the bill relevant to
its major innovation, the Old Age, Survivors, and Disability Insurance
program. The definition of "disability" was created in the Social Security Amendments of 1954. Because of its importance, it is placed
after the text of the 1956 Amendments below.]

*Be it enacted by the Senate and House of Representatives of the United States of America in Congress, assembled,* That this Act may be cited as the "Social Security Amendments of 1956."

## TITLE I—AMENDMENTS TO TITLE II OF THE SOCIAL SECURITY ACT

*Child's Insurance Benefits for Children Who Are Disabled Before Attaining Age Eighteen* Section 101. (a) Section 202 9(d) (1) of the Social Security Act is amended to read as follows:

(1) Every child . . . of an individual entitled to old-age insurance benefits, or of an individual who died a fully or currently insured individual after 1939, if such child—

(A) has filed application for child's insurance benefits,

(B) at the time such application was filed was unmarried and either (i) had not attained the age of eighteen, or (ii) was under a disability . . . which began before he attained the age of eighteen, and

(C) was dependent upon such individual at the time such application was filed, or, if such individual has died, at the time of such individual's death, shall be entitled to a child's insurance benefit for each month. . . .

*Disability Insurance Benefits For Certain Disabled Individuals Who Have Attained Age Fifty*

Section 103 (a) Title II of the Social Security Act is amended by inserting after section 222 the following new sections:

### Disability Insurance Benefits Payments

Disability Insurance Benefits

Section 223. (a) (1) Every individual who—

(A) is insured for disability benefits . . .

(B) has attained the age of fifty and not attained the age of sixty-five

(C) has filed an application for disability insurance benefits, and

(D) is under a disability . . . at the time such application is filed, shall be entitled to a disability insurance benefit for each month beginning with the first month after his waiting period . . . in which he becomes so entitled to such insurance benefits and ending with the month preceding the first month in which any of the following occurs: his disability ceases, he dies, or he attains the age of sixty-five.

(2) Such individual's disability insurance benefit for any month shall be equal to his primary insurance amount for such month . . . as though he became entitled to old-age insurance benefits in the first month of his waiting period. . . .

(e) Section 201 of *[the Social Security Act]* is amended to read as follows:

### Federal Old-Age and Survivors Insurance Trust Fund and Federal Disability Insurance Trust Fund

Section 201. (b) There is hereby created on the books of the Treasury of the United States a trust fund to be known as the 'Federal Disability Insurance Trust Fund.' The Federal Disability Insurance Trust Fund shall consist of such amounts as may be appropriated to, or deposited in, such fund as provided in this section. There is hereby appropriated to the Federal Disability Insurance Trust Fund for the fiscal year ending June 30, 1957, and for each fiscal year thereafter, out of any moneys in the Treasury not otherwise appropriated, amounts equivalent to 100 per centum of—

(1) ½ of 1 per centum of the wages . . . paid after December 31, 1956, and reported to the Secretary of the Treasury or his delegate pursuant to title F of the Internal Revenue Code of 1954 . . . ; and

(2) ⅜ of 1 per centum of the amount of self-employment income. . . .

(h) Benefit payments required to be made under section 223 *[the Disability Insurance Program]* shall be made only from the Federal Disability Insurance Trust Fund. All other benefit payments required to be made under this title shall be made only from the Federal Old-Age and Survivors Insurance Trust Fund . . .

(i) The heading of title II of the Social Security Act is amended to read as follows:

'TITLE II—FEDERAL OLD-AGE, SURVIVORS, AND DISABILITY INSURANCE BENEFITS'

August 1, 1956

The Definition of Disability
[Defining "disability" is key to a program of disability insurance. The 1956 Amendments did not define this term. It merely incorporated the definition given in the 1954 Amendments to the Social Security Act. This continues to be the current definition of a disability under the Social Security Act.]

# 9b. Social Security Amendments of 1954

**TITLE I—AMENDMENTS TO TITLE II OF THE SOCIAL SECURITY ACT . . .**

Disability; Period of Disability

(i) (1) The term 'disability' means (A) inability to engage in any substantial gainful activity by reason of any medically determinable physical or mental impairment which can be expected to result in death or to be of long-continued and indefinite duration, or (B) blindness; and the term 'blindness' means central visual acuity of 5/200 or less in the better eye with the use of a correcting lens . . . Nothing in this title shall be construed as authorizing the Secretary or any other officer or employee of the United States to interfere in any way with the practice of medicine or with relationships between practitioners of medicine and their patients, or to exercise any supervision or control over the administration or operation of any hospital.

(2) The term 'period of disability' means a continuous period of not less than six full calendar months (beginning and ending as hereinafter provided in this subsection) during which an individual was under a disability . . . No such period shall begin as to any individual unless such individual, while under a disability, files an application for a disability determination with respect to such period; and no such period shall begin as to any individual after such individual attains retirement age. . . .

September 1, 1954

## NOTES

1. Michael J. Graetz and Jerry L. Mashaw, *True Security: Rethinking American Social Insurance* (New Haven: Yale University Press, 1999), p. 88.

2. Quoted in United States House of Representative, Committee on Ways and Means, Staff Report, "Committee Staff Report on the Disability Insurance Program," 93rd Congress, Second Session, July 1974, p. 111.

3. The definition is included with the text of the amendments that follows this section.

# 10

# Aid to Families with Dependent Children and the Emergence of Modern Welfare: The Public Welfare Amendments of 1962

In 1992, Bill Clinton made the pledge to "end welfare as we know it" a central theme in his successful presidential campaign. By that time "welfare" had become one of the most reviled words in American politics. But what was "welfare as we know it," and where did it come from? The passage of the Public Welfare Amendments of 1962 was the key moment in creating the modern American welfare system. The act embodied changes in rhetoric and direction that would underpin the growth and development of federal public assistance policy until the Clinton presidency 30 years later.

The framers of Social Security believed that the act of 1935, along with its later extensions, would largely solve the problem of poverty in America. The set of guarantees given to Americans, including a livable pension, disability protection, and benefits for spouses and surviving children, should allow nearly everyone, in Roosevelt's words, to live in "freedom from want." The Social Security Act, however, had included programs for those Americans who, it was believed, would still need extra help, such as the blind. The two biggest programs were the Old-Age Assistance (OAA) program and the Aid to Dependent Children (ADC) program. These programs were to be set up and managed by the states. The federal government would help by providing matching grants for financing. They are also "means-tested programs." That is, eligibility to receive benefits under them is restricted to Americans with low incomes. This is unlike the Old Age, Survivor, and Disability Insurance (OASDI) program, which is federally run, and is an "entitlement." Every American may qualify to receive benefits under it.

Advocates for Social Security genuinely thought that as more Americans were brought under the OASDI program, the OAA and ADC programs would wither away. That is why neither program attracted a great deal of controversy at the time of the passage of the Social Security Act. Unfortunately, that is not what happened. ADC, in particular, continued to expand. By 1960, over two million children, and 795,000 families, were enrolled in the program.[1] As a result, federal government grants for public assistance had risen to $2.1 billion, five times what they had been at the end of World War II.[2] The program did not seem to be working. In 1961 a Democrat Representative from Indiana, Winfield Denton, sadly noted, "We were hopeful . . . that Social Security would take the place of most of the welfare. It doesn't seem to be doing that, does it?"[3]

As the program grew, the characteristics of the typical beneficiary greatly changed. In 1935, 8 of 10 ADC recipients were widowed mothers. By 1960, widows accounted for only 1 in 10 cases. The vast majority had become women who were divorced or who had never married. Over half of the cases were of illegitimate births. This politicized the program. Many distinguished between the "deserving" poor, who were worthy of government support, and individuals who were allegedly relying on federal monies to support objectionable lifestyles. The prominent Republican Senator Barry Goldwater (AZ) spoke for many when he said, "I do not believe that the mere fact of having little money entitles everybody, regardless of circumstance, to be permanently maintained by the taxpayers at an average or comfortable standard of living."[4]

Throughout the 1950s, Congress tinkered with ADC to make the program more effective and efficient. In 1950, to help poor families, it authorized payments to the caretaker (usually the mother) as well as to the eligible child. Beginning in 1952, the federal share of public assistance programs was increased almost every other year. In 1956, cost sharing for rehabilitative services to help the poor was authorized (though not appropriated), and states were allowed to try demonstration projects for reducing welfare dependency. In 1960, a medical assistance plan for the poor was created. But nothing seemed to slow the growth in welfare cases, and welfare costs.

By the early 1960s, a sense of the need for reform was in the air. Two catalysts helped turn that feeling into action. One was a series of ADC controversies that put the program in the public spotlight. The other was the election of John F. Kennedy as president.

Kennedy came into office on a platform of change. This was an era in which Social Security was still widely seen as a Democrat issue, and it was only natural for Kennedy to desire this program to be included in his "New Frontier." Yet, Roosevelt's Social Security plan was largely completed, so Kennedy had to turn elsewhere. He appointed Wilbur Cohen, a leader in the fight for the disability insurance program, to head a task force on social welfare. This led to the Ad Hoc Committee on Social Welfare, and a thorough examination of America's public assistance programs.

Even before the committee reported its findings, Kennedy asked Congress to include children who were poor because of an unemployed parent under ADC. The original requirement had been that only a child with a deceased, disabled, or absent parent could be eligible under ADC. Social workers believed that the existing requirement was breaking families apart, as unemployed spouses "abandoned" their families so as to make them ADC eligible. Wilbur Mills (Dem., AR), the chair of the Ways and Means Committee, was able to push the bill through the House, once again using a closed bill to prevent debate on the floor. But he insisted on making this change temporary. It would be an experiment to last 15 months. The Senate curbed Kennedy's request by reducing this to 14 months, and by making the inclusion voluntary. States were given the choice of adopting or rejecting this change. But once passed, the principle of supporting entire families was established.

Meanwhile, a series of controversies were garnering ADC a good deal of unwanted attention. The first was in Louisiana. There, in 1960, the state ADC program adopted a "suitable home" requirement. Among other things, this denied aid to mothers who had given birth out of wedlock. Some 23,000 children, most of them African-American, were removed from the program.[5] This resulted in a worldwide outcry. An embarrassed Social Security commissioner quickly imposed a new regulation forbidding states to deny assistance using a suitable home test without first having made other provisions to care for the child.

This regulation was to take effect July 1, 1961, but by then public attention had turned to a second ADC crisis. One month earlier, the city manager of Newburgh, New York, imposed an additional 13 eligibility requirements for ADC recipients in his jurisdiction. These included conditions such as proof that the recipient had had a job when moving to Newburgh, a curtailment of aid to those having additional illegitimate children, and a limit of three months' aid to able-bodied individuals. The result was another storm of criticism (and, often, support).

These events gave additional force to the ad hoc committee's recommendations, which were reported in September. The committee called for a major revision of the ADC program, suggesting 14 specific changes. Arguing that the then current focus on merely providing financial support for the poor was misguided, it called for a new emphasis on imparting the skills necessary for the poor to help themselves. "The ultimate aim is to help families become self-supporting and independent by strengthening all their own resources."[6] This would entail a substantial reform of the program. First, it would need to be oriented as much around families as children. Families should be assisted to become self-supporting, with a minimum disruption to family life. Second, it should focus on "rehabilitation," the provision of skills necessary to care for oneself and to enter the workforce. Third, ADC needed to be closely integrated with other poverty programs to coordinate antipoverty efforts. Fourth, an increase in training and support for social work was necessary to lower case loads and assist social workers in their rehabilitation efforts. By implication, more federal support would be needed. Finally, tying the reforms to popular concerns, the committee recommended developing programs to combat illegitimacy and create public work jobs for the poor.

On February 1, 1962, Kennedy sent a special message to Congress, asking for legislation to enact the recommendations of the ad hoc committee. Kennedy made clear his desire to reorient public assistance. Proposing "far-reaching changes," he claimed that "public welfare . . . must be more than a salvage operation. . . . Its emphasis must be directed increasingly toward prevention and rehabilitation . . . we must place more stress on services instead of relief."[7] He argued his plan would save families, reduce juvenile delinquency, lower illegitimacy, and attack dependency.

The GOP greeted Kennedy's ideas skeptically. Many Republicans thought the changes, especially the proposed increase in social workers, would only pad the welfare rolls. But, except for the social worker-dominated American Public Welfare Association, there was virtually no lobbying activity around the bill. In fact, most members of Congress were ambivalent about its contents, and certain there was little political advantage to be gained. In the House, for example, only 7 of the 25 members of the Ways and Means Committee took an active part in the bill's hearings.[8] Only one House member, New York City's William Fitts Ryan, spoke in its favor on the floor. This gave Wilbur Mills, the Ways and Means Committee chair, complete latitude to guide the bill through the House. He made but several slight changes to Kennedy's proposals. The most important were to raise the federal matching share for public assistance programs and to strike Kennedy's wish that residency requirements be banned from state welfare programs. Republicans opposed the increase in the federal matching share, but under the closed rule then generally given to Ways and Means Committee legislation, there was little they could do. Once the GOP motion to recommit the bill failed by a vote of 155 to 233, the Public Welfare Amendments easily passed the House.

The story was similar in the Senate. The bill was debated on the floor for 11 days, but that debate was almost entirely over an unsuccessful amendment to add health care for the aged to the OASDI program. An amendment from Paul Douglas (Dem., IL) that enabled OAA recipients to earn up to $25 a month without having their benefits reduced was the only programmatic change made. (The Conference Committee eventually settled on a figure of $30.) The bill passed the Senate on a voice vote, and was signed into law by President Kennedy on July 25, 1962.

The Public Welfare Amendments of 1962 made a large number of changes to U.S. public assistance programs. More important than any of these changes, however, was the rhetorical reorientation of America's welfare policy. This shift in purpose is best exemplified in the renaming of the Aid to Dependent Children program to the "Aid to Families with Dependent Children" (AFDC) program. The goal of welfare was now seen as that of "rehabilitating" families, keeping them together while helping parents or other caretakers to learn the skills necessary for them to enter the workforce and leave the welfare rolls. To this end, the amendments made permanent the 1961 law permitting payments to a family whose primary wage earner was unemployed (called AFDC-UP), and authorized AFDC benefits for both parents as well as their children. They allowed states to require unemployed adults to enter community work programs in order to receive AFDC benefits. The Amendments raised the federal matching formula for the rehabilitation portions of state public assistance plans to 75 percent, and increased federal grants-in-aid to other elements of the state plans along more complicated formulas. And more federal funds for training and hiring social workers were authorized (however, money for this portion of the Amendments was never appropriated).

The Public Welfare Amendments of 1962 stand at the beginning of the massive increase in the American welfare system that occurred over the following three decades. Nearly one million cases were added to the AFDC in the years immediately following the amendments, and the caseload rose to 14 million by the mid-1990s. This is seven times the number in 1962. The cost of welfare also soared. By 1994, over 14 billion dollars were spent annually on public assistance programs. A more subtle indication of the change that occurred is the fact that the percentage of eligible Americans who sought to be enrolled in public assistance programs rose from one third in the early 1960s to over 90 percent in the early 1970s. In some locales the result was dramatic. By 1970 one in seven residents of New York City, for example, was on public assistance.[9] The Public Welfare Amendments of 1962, then, substantially changed the contours of American public assistance. But it did not succeed in ending the need for it. Instead, it produced a complex system of expanded public assistance: welfare "as we know it."

## 10. Public Welfare Amendments of 1962

An Act to extend and improve the public assistance and child welfare services programs of the Social Security Act, and for other purposes

*Be it enacted by the Senate and House of Representatives in Congress assembled,* That this Act . . . may be cited as the "Public Welfare Amendments of 1962."

**TITLE I—PUBLIC WELFARE AMENDMENTS**

Part A—Improvement in Services to Prevent or Reduce Dependency

. . . Federal Financial Participation in Costs of Services
Sec. 101. (a) (1) the Social Security Act is amended by . . . inserting . . . the following:

(4) in the case of any State, *[federal matching funds will be]* an amount equal to the sum of the following proportions of the total amounts expended . . . —

(A) 75 per centum of so much of such expenditures as for . . .

(i) services which are prescribed . . . to applicants for or recipients of assistance under the plan to help them attain or retain capability for self-care, or

(ii) other services, specified by the Secretary *[of Health, Education, and Welfare]* as likely to prevent or reduce dependency . . .

(iii) any of the services . . . which the Secretary may specify as appropriate for individuals who . . . have been or are likely to become applicants or recipients of assistance under the plan, if such services are requested by such individuals. . . .

(iv) the training of personnel employed or preparing for employment by the State agency or by the local agency administering the plan in the political subdivision; plus

(B) one-half of so much of such expenditures (not included under subparagraph (A)) as are for services provided . . . to applicants for or recipients under the plan, and to individuals requesting such services. . . .

### Expansion and Improvement of Child Welfare Services

Increase in Authorization of Appropriations

*[This section provided a schedule of increased appropriations, from 25 million dollars for the fiscal year ending June 30, 1961 to 50 million dollars for the year ending June 30, 1967.]*

Coordination with Dependent Children Program and Extension of Child Welfare Services

*[This section requires that State programs under Titles IV (Aid to Dependent Children) and V (Grants to States for Maternal and Child Welfare) be coordinated with each other, and with other poverty programs, if they are to receive federal funding. These programs must also be targeted at communities with the greatest need for them.]*

Day Care

Section 527. (a) In order to assist the States to provide adequately for the care and protection of children whose parents are, for part of the day, working or seeking work, or otherwise absent from the home or unable for other reasons to provide parental supervision, the portion of the appropriations . . . not allotted under section 522 shall be allotted by the Secretary among the States solely for use . . . for day care services . . . which are licensed by the State, or are approved . . . by the State agency. . . .

Welfare Services for Child under Dependent Children Program

Section 103. . . . the Social Security Act is amended . . . *[to]* provide for the development and application of a program for such welfare and related services for each child who receives aid to families with dependent children as may be necessary in the light of the particular home conditions and other needs of such child, and provide for coordination of such programs, and any other services provided for children under the State plan, with the child-welfare services plan developed as provided in part 3 of title V, with a view toward providing welfare and related services which will best promote the welfare of such child and his family. *[This is a mandate that each state offer a set of welfare services specifically tailored to the needs of each individual child who received them, and that the services provided the child be coordinated with each other.]*

Technical Amendments to Reflect Emphasis on Rehabilitation and
Other Services

Section 104. (a) (1) The heading of title IV of the Social Security Act is amended to read as follows:

**"TITLE IV—GRANTS TO STATES FOR AID AND SERVICES TO NEEDY FAMILIES WITH CHILDREN"**

Community Work and Training Programs

Section 105. (a) Title IV of the Social Security Act is amended by adding at the end thereof the following new section:

Community Work and Training Programs

. . . For the purpose of assisting the States in encouraging through community work and training programs of a constructive nature, the conservation of work skills and the development of new skills for individuals who have attained the age of 18 and are receiving aid to families with dependent children, . . . expenditures . . . for any month with respect to a dependent child . . . shall not be excluded from aid to families with dependent children because such expenditures are made in the form of payments for work performed in such month by any one or more of the relatives with whom such child is living if such work is performed for the State agency or any other public agency under a program . . . *[This mandates that the public assistance benefits provided to a child's relative in the form of a cash payment for work performed under a public welfare program not be used to exclude a child from AFDC benefits.]*

Aid For Both Parents of Dependent Children

Section 109.... the Social Security Act... is amended by inserting "(and the spouse of such relative if living with him and if such relative is the child's parent and the child is a dependent child by reason of the physical or mental incapacity of a parent or is a dependent child under section 407)" after "relative with whom any dependent child is living."...

*[This section makes the spouse of a dependent child's physically or mentally incapacitated parent also eligible for public assistance, if that spouse lives with the dependent child.]*

**PART C—IMPROVEMENT OF PUBLIC WELFARE THROUGH EXTENSION OF TEMPORARY PROVISIONS AND INCREASE IN FEDERAL SHARE OF PUBLIC ASSISTANCE PAYMENTS**

Extension of Aid with Respect to Dependent Children of Unemployed Parents or in Foster Family Homes

Section 131. *[This section essentially made permanent two changes to Title IV that were enacted in 1961 on a temporary basis. The first, entitled "Dependent Children of Unemployed Parents," extended the definition of a dependent child to "include a needy child under the age of eighteen who has been deprived of parental support or care by reason of the unemployment ... of a parent." The second, entitled "Federal Payments for Foster Home Care of Dependent Children," extended the definition of a dependent child to one who had been placed in a foster home. The Public Welfare Amendments of 1962 authorized them for the succeeding five years.]*

July 25, 1962

**NOTES**

1. Department of Health and Human Services, Office of the Assistant Sec. for Planning and Evaluation, Human Services Policy, *AFDC: The Baseline,* June 1998.

2. Congressional Quarterly, *Congress and the Nation 1946–1964* (Washington: CQ Press), p. 1274.

3. At a 1961 House Appropriations Hearing, quoted in Gilbert Y. Steiner, *Social Insecurity: The Politics of Welfare* (Chicago: Rand McNally, 1966), p. 26.

4. Steiner, p. 7.

5. Lisa Levenstein, "From Innocent Children to Unwanted Migrants and Unwed Moms: Two Chapters in the Public Discourse on Welfare in the United States, 1960–1961," *Journal of Women's History* 11, no. 4 (Winter 2000): 10–33.

6. United States Government. Department of Health, Education, and Welfare. *Report of the Committee on Public Welfare* (September 1961), p. 13.

7. United States Government, *Public Papers of the Presidents, John F. Kennedy*, p. 98.

8. Steiner, p. 45.

9. These figures are from R. Kent Weaver, *Ending Welfare As We Know It* (Washington: Brookings Institution Press, 2000), p. 55; B. Guy Peters, *American Public Policy: Promise and Performance, 5th edition* (New York: Chatham House Publishers, 1999), p. 299.

# 11

## The War on Poverty: The Economic Opportunity Act of 1964

Lyndon Johnson's War on Poverty is the most famous episode in American welfare policy. Its failure critically undermined the country's support for future large-scale welfare programs. The War on Poverty was waged via the Economic Opportunity Act (EOA) of 1964, which created a number of new programs designed to attack destitution in America. The Act also created the Office of Economic Opportunity (OEO) to supervise these and other antipoverty initiatives. The director of the OEO was to be America's "poverty czar," charged with overseeing the elimination of poverty in the United States. The OEO, the czar, and indeed many of the programs contained in the Act have all since disappeared. But the legacy of the War on Poverty has structured the American debate on social welfare until the present day.

The 1960s was a decade of ferment. The civil rights movement, the student movement, and the antiwar movement were but the major examples of a society engaged in a profound examination of itself. But it was also a decade a vaulting ambition. President Kennedy opened the 60s by announcing the United States would place a man on the moon within 10 years. The attack on poverty, initially given a 10-year timetable as well, combined America's self-reflection with its sense of almost limitless power.

The Public Welfare Amendments of 1962 were among the first products of this critical self-examination. Worries over rising juvenile delinquency, and the rediscovery of the existence of widespread poverty in America, had driven their enactment. But, while the 1962 amendments had signaled a decisive shift in America's approach to welfare, they did not contain any major programmatic initiatives. Indeed, competing perspectives were voiced within the administration over exactly what to do. Wilbur Cohen, a major figure in every social welfare debate since Social Security, and then an assistant secretary of Health, Education, and Welfare, believed that fighting racial discrimination and further expanding the AFDC program were the best answers. Willard Wirtz, the Labor secretary, wanted a large program of public employment to end poverty. David Hackett, the chair of the President's Committee on Juvenile Delinquency, not surprisingly focused on America's youth. Programs should be developed to inculcate the skills necessary to get and keep good jobs.

However, it was Walter Heller, the chair of Kennedy's Council of Economic Advisors (CEA), who began the full-blown debate within the administration over poverty. Examining the statistics, Heller realized that economic growth no longer seemed to be reducing the numbers of Americans living in poverty. The belief that the combination of a growing economy and old-age insurance would work to eradicate poverty that had animated American social policy since the Social Security Act of 1935 was false. Some Americans apparently did not have the skills or opportunity to enter the workforce and keep jobs, even when economic times were good. On October 29, 1963 the CEA released a memo, "Program for a Concerted Assault on Poverty," which summarized this finding. The next day Heller called for new ideas on attacking poverty from across the administration.[1]

Heller's initiative was sadly interrupted by the assassination of President Kennedy. However, Lyndon Johnson, when informed of the poverty discussions, was enthusiastic. He told Heller to make a poverty initiative the new administration's highest priority. Johnson wanted something enacted before the 1964 election, though there was as yet no plan.

Hackett was the first to offer a detailed proposal. In a 39-page memo, he offered a pilot program to reduce poverty. It called for the creation of numerous task forces to identify the specific difficulties facing various demographic groups, such as poor farmers, Native Americans, Mexican-Americans, and so forth, and then to develop demonstration projects for each. These projects would employ different approaches to fighting poverty, in effect, creating a giant experiment to discover what policies would be the most effective. Efforts directed at young people would be stressed. It is no accident that Hackett's plan smacks of a social science study. Officials were increasingly drawing on the work of social scientists in designing social programs. A result of the massive expansion of these disciplines after World War II, this "professionalization of reform" would become a major influence on all subsequent welfare debates.

Hackett's draft went to the CEA and then to presidential speech writer Theodore Sorenson. Heller recommended limiting the initiative to 10 demonstration projects, to ensure efforts were not spread too thin. Hackett's emphasis on youth was kept. Heller and Sorenson added the idea of a cabinet-level "Council on Poverty" to oversee this and other poverty programs.

At the end of 1963, Heller journeyed to the LBJ ranch to present this program to the president. Johnson found it uninspiring. He wanted a much more spectacular initiative, one that America would notice. He saw no reason to limit the demonstration projects, why shouldn't every community have one? He told Heller to go back to Washington and think bigger.

By January 6, 1964, President Johnson had yet to see this bigger program, but he nevertheless announced in his state of the union address that the "administration today, here and now, declares unconditional war on poverty."[2] His advisors did not think this analogy wise, but Johnson was never one to worry about rhetorical excess. Later in the month, he asked Sargent Shriver, the head of the Peace Corps, to write the legislation for his War on Poverty. Shriver set up a task force, and, in a series of secret meetings, developed a bill over the next six weeks.

Not only had so ambitious a social policy never before been attempted, Shriver had two more practical problems. First, Johnson wanted the most expansive of programs, but on a shoestring budget. Many point to the huge increase in federal revenues during the 1960s in explaining the large social policies of that era. Government revenues grew from $94 billion in 1961 to $150 billion in 1967.[3] But, in fact, Johnson was loathe to spend any of it, at least before the election of 1964. He placed a one-billion-dollar ceiling on the program, and insisted that half of that amount must come from existing programs. When Willard Wirtz approached him with his idea of adding a public employment program that would cost $1.25 billion (to be financed by a nickel a pack cigarette tax), Johnson dismissed the idea out of hand. He insisted there be no new taxes for his War on Poverty.

This financial stricture led task force members to focus primarily on the issue of "opportunity," and to develop a set of modest programs to assist the poor in pulling themselves up by their own bootstraps. Though this accords better with the views of most Americans, it is also true that the money was not there to develop or reform income maintenance programs. The problem of poverty thus became defined more as lack of opportunity than lack of income. Hence the name, the "Economic Opportunity Act."

Shriver's second problem was a war within the War over whether to emphasize youth programs or community action programs. The rationale for the former was that poverty was best cured by giving individuals the skills necessary to lead a productive life while they were still young. The basis for the latter was the argument of many sociologists and social workers that the poor could not be expected to break out of the cycle of poverty until they could take control of their own lives. Programs should be structured to promote the active input and involvement of the poor themselves. This led to the notion of providing grants directly to local poverty organizations (to be called community action boards or agencies), sidestepping conservative or paternalistic state and local governments. In fact, a number of academics favoring this approach would later move to arguing that public confrontations and demonstrations by these organizations were necessary to energize the community and break the passivity of the poor.

Task force members drew heavily upon a plan already implemented in New York City called "Mobilization for Youth" (MFY). This plan had been developed by academics and social workers under the auspices of the Ford Foundation. Begun in 1961, it tried to combine youth activities with community action principles. The EOA looks remarkably similar to the MFY, though as Daniel Patrick Moynihan notes, this was more a sign of the times than any conscious attempt directly to copy the MFY. However, task force members had great difficulty designing the community action program. No one knew what "community action" actually meant. Shriver remained skeptical enough of the whole idea to demote Community Action Programs to Title II of the bill, behind the more convincing youth programs. By March 1964, a plan was ready. It consisted of a combination of new programs, new grants for community action activities and pilot projects, and some additional business incentives, all placed within a new Office of Economic Opportunity (see

**Table 11.1**

**Key New Programs and Policies of the Economic Opportunity Act**

| Program | Eligible Groups | Purpose of Program |
|---|---|---|
| Job Corps | youth aged 16–21 | education, vocational training, work experience (40% to be in Youth Conservation Corps*) |
| Work Training | youth aged 16–21 | federal assistance for state and local youth work training programs |
| Work Study | low-income students | part-time work, on campus, to pay for education |
| Adult Education* | persons over 18 | obtain skills in reading and writing English |
| Rural Loans | low-income rural families | finance agricultural or rural enterprises |
| Migrant workers | migrant workers | housing, sanitation, education, daycare |
| Business Loans | small business | aid to employ the long-term unemployed |
| Volunteers in Service to America (VISTA) | volunteers | training of volunteers who wish to help fight poverty |
| Community Action Program | Community Action Agencies | grants to assist locally designed anti-poverty programs |

*provisions added in Congress.

Table 11.1). The OEO director would become the principal advisor to the president on matters of poverty and welfare policy. The most expensive provision was the over $300 million in grants to be issued to community action agencies. These grants would be administered by local nonprofit groups with the "maximum feasible participation of local residents."

In retrospect, it is odd how limited were the programs charged with such a difficult goal. Combined, the EOA programs amounted to but one percent of the federal budget. Even so, on March 16, 1964 Johnson presented the bill to Congress as "a milestone" in the fight against poverty. A parade of interest groups, including the United Auto Workers, the National Council of Churches, the Urban League, and a number of big-city mayors, announced their support. The only active opposition appeared to be on the political left, where reformers believed the EOA was far too limited to effect any transformation in American life.

Yet shortly before Johnson forwarded his legislation, Republicans announced their own program to conquer poverty. The GOP believed LBJ's initiative to be nothing but an election tactic, one they wished to defeat. The GOP offered a seven-point program. Much of it was vague, but it included improving schools, hiring more social workers, and finding new solutions to the problems of low-income families. They envisioned their program as implemented by the states in a manner similar to the Social Security public assistance programs. The Republican plan meant the War on Poverty would be a partisan issue after all.

In congressional hearings, Republicans stated their usual objections to federal welfare programs. There were already more than 40 federal antipoverty programs in place, and they questioned the need for another. They believed the states were more constitutionally entitled and better positioned to undertake these sorts of programs. Noting that the states spent 44 times the funds on their own poverty programs as were contained in all the EOA programs combined, Rep. Peter Frelinghuysen (NJ), a Republican leader on this issue, questioned how big an impact the EOA could possibly have. Republicans were supported by the Chamber of Commerce and the National Association of Manufacturers.

The EOA went to the House Education and Labor Committee, where Democrats added an adult literacy program that President Kennedy had desired. The Republicans' biggest ally turned out to be the Democrat chair of the Rules Committee, the very conservative Howard W. Smith (VA). Smith did not like the bill. He claimed it was because of its vagueness, but more probably it was because it seemed to promise racial integration and perhaps even co-education in the federal programs that would be set up. For two months, he would not allow the EOA to go to the floor.

President Johnson had anticipated this difficulty. Knowing that a coalition of Republicans and segregationist Democrats could unite to defeat the bill, Johnson had chosen his floor manager carefully. It would not be the African-American chair of the Education and Labor Committee, the flamboyant Adam Clayton Powell, who by rights should have shepherded the bill through the House, but instead the conservative Georgia Democrat, Phil M. Landrum. Landrum was able to sympathize with Smith's worries, and coax the chair to a vote in the Rules Committee, which Landrum then carried by the barest 8 to 7 vote.

While Smith was holding up the bill in the House, it was considered in the Senate. There few substantive changes were made. Instead, the debate turned to "states rights." Conservatives of both parties argued that the OEO, and its ability to offer grants directly to local organizations, undermined state governments. An amendment to give governors a veto over projects in their states passed before being reconsidered and defeated by one vote. (Barry Goldwater, AZ, an opponent of the EOA and the Republicans' candidate for president, for some reason did not cast the deciding vote that would have saved the amendment.) The EOA's most determined opponent, Texas Republican John Tower, then nearly constructed an alliance of Republicans and southern Democrats essentially over the issue of racially integrating the Job Corps camps. To save the bill, Shriver was forced to concede to governors the right to veto Job Corps camps and antipoverty contracts with private agencies. This concession saved the bill, which then passed the Senate 61 to 34.

On the floor of the House, the Republicans also reached for the votes of southern Democrats. To prevent this (and to avoid a protracted conference committee), Landrum offered the Senate bill as a substitute for the original House bill. Expecting a close vote, a number of side deals were struck, everything from a guarantee that an administrator disliked by the North Carolina delegation would not be appointed to the OEO to a promise that 40 percent of the Job Corps positions would be in rural conservation camps. Even so, a maneuver by Howard Smith appeared to defeat the bill. His motion to strike the enacting clause passed 170 to 135 on a teller vote.[4] Democrat floor leaders were forced to quickly call for a roll call vote, using the extra time to round up the votes necessary to reverse Smith's motion. Their success made anticlimactic the 226 to 185 vote to pass the Economic Opportunity Act. Liberals, however, had to swallow one last bitter pill. Mississippi Democratic Representative John Bell Williams successfully added a loyalty oath (an oath swearing that one has not been a member of an organization seeking to overthrow the United States government) for Job Corps enrollees before Lyndon Johnson signed the EOA into law on August 20, 1964.

Only with great difficulty could the EOA, and the War on Poverty, be argued to be a success. The numbers of poor Americans did fall by some 8 million in the five years after its passage. And federal expenditures on welfare programs did double. But this was a period of tremendous economic prosperity, and it is difficult to credit the decline in poverty primarily to the EOA. Welfare caseloads, perhaps a better indicator of the truly needy, did not drop. Within a year of its enactment, the EOA had become so controversial that Johnson considered dismantling the OEO. He decided not to, but he did lose his interest in its programs.

The flagship EOA programs, the Job Corps and the Community Action Program, both encountered tremendous political hostility. Beset with bureaucratic problems, and a series of crimes and riots in the first camps, the early Job Corps was not much more than a good idea. It could not even accommodate all wishing to enter it. Today 110 Job Corps camps remain (now called campuses), and, over the past 25 years, some 1.7 million Americans have been trained in the program. But whatever its current merits, its initial problems permanently cost it political popularity and congressional support, sharply limiting both its size and its ambition.

Community Action programs encountered the same fate. Initially, over one thousand local boards were created. But their activities led to political opposition on every front. Mayors and governors recognized the political threat of community organizations over which they had no control, and became determined opponents of the program. Welfare activists and self-styled radicals took control of some local programs and engaged in widely condemned activities. Progressives accused the OEO of ignoring the "maximum feasible participation" mandate by excluding the poor from running their programs. By 1965, internal OEO memos showed a desperate worry over the program's "rapidly deteriorating public image." In 1981 the program was ended altogether. A successor program continues to offer antipoverty grants, but via block grants through state governments.

The OEO itself was terminated in 1974. EOA programs survive, but in revised forms and in different agencies. The OEO was ultimately the victim of dashed expectations. Given an impossible mandate and meager resources, it could not succeed. In the words of James Patterson, "perhaps no government program in modern American history promised so much more than it delivered."[5] The scale of its promises dwarfed its achievements, and that failure has colored the American welfare debate for nearly 40 years.

# 11. The Economic Opportunity Act of 1964

An Act to mobilize the human and financial resources of the Nation to combat poverty in the United States.

*Be it enacted by the Senate and the House of Representatives of the United States of America in Congress Assembled,* That this Act may be cited as the 'Economic Opportunity Act of 1964.'

**FINDINGS AND DECLARATION OF PURPOSE**

Sec. 2 Although the economic well-being and prosperity of the United Sates have progressed to a level surpassing any achieved in world history, and although these benefits are widely shared throughout the Nation, poverty continues to be the lot of a substantial number of our people. The United States can achieve its full economic and social potential as a nation only if every individual has the opportunity to contribute to the full extent of his capabilities and to participate in the workings of our society. It is, therefore, the policy of the United Sates to eliminate the paradox of poverty in the midst of plenty in this Nation by opening to everyone the opportunity for education and training, the opportunity to work, and the opportunity to live in decency and dignity. It is the purpose of this Act to strengthen, supplement, and coordinate efforts in furtherance of that policy.

**TITLE I—YOUTH PROGRAMS**

Part A—Job Corps

STATEMENT OF PURPOSE

Sec. 101. The purpose of this part is to prepare for the responsibilities of citizenship and to increase the employability of young men and young women aged sixteen through twenty-one by providing them in rural and urban residential centers with education, vocational training, useful work experiences, including work directed toward the conservation of natural resources, and other appropriate activities.

ESTABLISHMENT OF JOB CORPS

Sec. 102. In order to carry out the purposes of this part, there is hereby established within the Office of Economic Opportunity . . . a Job Corps. . . .

Sec. 109. Within the Job Corps there is authorized a Youth Conservation Corps in which at any time no less than 40 per centum of the enrollees under this part shall be assigned to camps where their work activity is directed primarily toward conserving, developing, managing, and protecting the public natural resources of the Nation, and developing, managing, and protecting public recreation areas. . . .

### Part B—Work-Training Programs

STATEMENT OF PURPOSE

Sec. 111. The purpose of this part is to provide useful work experience opportunities for unemployed young men and young women, through participation in State and community work-training programs, so that their employability may be increased or their education resumed or continued and so that public agencies and private nonprofit organizations (other than political parties) will be enabled to carry out programs which will permit or contribute to an undertaking or service in the public interest that would not otherwise be provided, or will contribute to the conservation and development of natural resources and recreation areas. . . .

Sec. 113. (a) The Director is authorized to enter into agreements providing for the payment by him of part or all of the cost of a State or local program submitted hereunder, if he determines . . . that—

(1) enrollees in the program will be employed either (A) on publicly owned and operated facilities or projects, or (B) on local projects sponsored by private nonprofit organizations . . . other than projects . . . to be used for sectarian instruction or as a place for religious worship;

(2) the program will increase the employability of the enrollees. . . .

(3) the program will permit or contribute to an undertaking or service in the public interest that would not otherwise be provided, or will contribute to the conservation, development or management of the natural resources. . . .

(4) the program will not result in the displacement of employed workers or impair existing contracts for services;

(5) the rates of pay and other conditions of employment will be appropriate and reasonable. . . .

Sec. 114. (a) Participation in programs under this part shall be limited to young men and women . . . who have attained the age of sixteen but have not attained the age twenty-two. . . .

## Part C—Work-Study Programs

STATEMENT OF PURPOSE

Sec. 121. The purpose of this part is to stimulate and promote the part-time employment of students in institutions of higher education who are from low-income families and are in need of the earnings. . . .

GRANTS FOR WORK-STUDY PROGRAMS

Sec. 123. The Director is authorized to enter into agreements with institutions of higher education . . . under which the Director will make grants to such institutions to assist in the operations of work-study programs as hereinafter provided.

Sec. 124. An agreement entered into pursuant to Section 123 shall—

(c) provide that employment . . . shall be furnished only to a student who (1) is from a low-income family, (2) is in need of the earnings from such employment in order to pursue a program of study at such institution, (3) is capable . . . of maintaining good standing in such course of study while employed under the program . . . and (4) has been accepted for enrollment as a full-time student at the institution. . . .

(d) provide that no student shall be employed . . . more than fifteen hours in any week. . . .

## Part D—Authorization of Appropriations

Sec. 131 . . . there is hereby authorized to be appropriated the sum of $412,500,000 for the fiscal year ending June 30, 1965; and for the fiscal year ending June 30, 1966, and the fiscal year ending June 30, 1967, such sums may be appropriated as the Congress may hereafter authorize by law.

## TITLE II—URBAN AND RURAL COMMUNITY ACTION PROGRAMS

### Part A—General Community Action Programs

STATEMENT OF PURPOSE

Sec. 201. The purpose of this part is to provide stimulation and incentive for urban and rural communities to mobilize their resources to combat poverty through community action programs.

### Community Action Programs

Sec. 202. (a) The term 'community action program' means a program—

(1) which mobilizes and utilizes resources, public or private, of any . . . geographical area . . . in an attack on poverty;

(2) which provides services, assistance, and other activities of suffi-

cient scope and size to give promise of progress toward elimination of poverty or a cause or causes of poverty. . . .

(3) which is developed, conducted, and administered with the maximum feasible participation of residents of the areas and members of the groups served; and

(4) which is conducted, administered, or coordinated by a public or private nonprofit agency, or a combination thereof. . . .

FINANCIAL ASSISTANCE FOR DEVELOPMENT OF COMMUNITY ACTION PROGRAMS

Sec. 204. The Director is authorized to make grants to, or in contract with, appropriate public or private nonprofit agencies, or combinations thereof, to pay part or all of the costs of development of community action programs.

## Part B—Adult Basic Education Programs

DECLARATION OF PURPOSE

Sec. 212. It is the purpose of this part to initiate programs of instruction for individuals who have attained age eighteen and whose inability to read and write the English language constitutes a substantial impairment of their ability to get or retain employment commensurate with their real ability, so as to help eliminate such inability and raise the level of education of such individuals with a view to making them less likely to become dependent on others, improving their ability to benefit from occupational training and otherwise increasing their opportunities for more productive and profitable employment, and making them better able to meet their adult responsibilities.

Sec. 216. (a) . . . the Director shall make grants to States which have State plans approved by him. . . .

## Part C—Voluntary Assistance Program for Needy Children

STATEMENT OF PURPOSE

Sec. 219. The purpose of this part is to allow individual Americans to participate in a personal way in the war on poverty, by voluntarily assisting in the support of one or more needy children, in a program coordinated with city or county social welfare agencies.

[TITLE IV—EMPLOYMENT AND INVESTMENT INCENTIVES. This title relates to small-business concerns.]

## TITLE V—WORK EXPERIENCE PROGRAMS

STATEMENT OF PURPOSE

Sec. 501. It is the purpose of this title to expand the opportunities for constructive work experience and other needed training available to persons who are unable to support or care for themselves or their families. . . .

Sec. 502. In order to stimulate the adoption of programs designed to help unemployed fathers and other needy persons to secure and retain employment or to attain or retain capability for self-support or personal independence, the Director is authorized to transfer funds . . . to enable him to make payments for experimental, pilot, or demonstration projects. . . .

Authorization of Appropriations

Sec. 503. . . . there is hereby authorized to be appropriated the sum of $150,000,000 for the fiscal year ending June 30, 1965; and for the fiscal year ending June 30, 1966, and the fiscal year ending June 30, 1967, such sums may be appropriated as the Congress may hereafter authorize by law.

## TITLE VI—ADMINISTRATION AND COORDINATION

### Part A—Administration

OFFICE OF ECONOMIC OPPORTUNITY

Sec. 601. (a) There is hereby established in the Executive Office of the President the Office of Economic Opportunity. . . .

AUTHORITY OF DIRECTOR

Sec. 602 . . . the Director is authorized . . . to. . . .

(n) . . . perform such functions and take such steps as he may deem to be necessary or appropriate to carry out the provisions of this Act. . . .

August 20, 1964

## NOTES

1. Daniel Patrick Moynihan, *Maximum Feasible Misunderstanding: Community Action and the War on Poverty* (New York: The Free Press, 1969), p. 79.

2. United States Government. Public Papers of the Presidents, Lyndon Baines Johnson, 1963–64, volume 1, p. 112.

3. Irwin Unger, *The Best of Intentions: The Triumphs and Failures of the Great Society Under Kennedy, Johnson and Nixon* (New York: Doubleday, 1996), p. 75.

4. In a teller vote, a member on each side of the question is chosen to be the vote counter, or "teller." The other representatives walk up the center aisle towards the rear of the House, first the "yeas" and then the "nays." The tellers count each group as they walk past and report back to the chair. This method of voting was ended in 1971.

5. James T. Patterson, *America's Struggle Against Poverty: 1900–1980* (Cambridge: Harvard University Press, 1981), p. 152.

# 12

# The Food Stamp Act of 1964

The food stamp program is perhaps the best known, and is the most distinctive, of America's social welfare policies. Virtually everyone has seen food stamps being used at their local supermarket. But why did the United States undertake such an unusual antipoverty program? Either the provision of the food itself, or simply the cash with which to buy it, seems so much simpler. The answer begins with the fact that food stamps are an extension neither of the Social Security system nor of the changes in social welfare policy that had occurred in the years just before its passage. They are the product of entirely different politics.

Though the food stamp program may not be a typical public assistance program, it has become one of America's most important. By fiscal year 2000, approximately 17.2 million Americans, and 7.3 million households, received food stamps. The average beneficiary received $73 a month, and the average household obtained $173 per month. Congress appropriates over $21 billion a year for the food stamp program, making it one of the largest domestic programs. Given its size, it is not surprising that the program has been controversial since it was first conceived.

Few people, whether supporters or critics, realize just how long ago that was. The United States was distributing "orange stamps" and "blue stamps" before World War II. This first food stamp program was a Great Depression effort simultaneously to help farmers and provide relief to the poor. Agricultural surplus was one of the many problems of that era. American farmers could not find markets for everything they grew. In 1933 the Roosevelt administration began purchasing part of the surplus and distributing it to local relief agencies. They, in turn, gave it to the poor. In the late 1930s officials in the U.S. Department of Agriculture arrived at what they believed to be a better way of doing this. If they provided families on relief with coupons, the families could go directly to a nearby market and obtain the food themselves. Orange-colored coupons, called orange Stamps, were sold to the poor at face value to be used to purchase the foods needed to obtain a nutritious diet. Blue Stamps were included with the purchase as a free "bonus." These could be used to obtain any food designated as being in surplus. A popular belief that the stamps were often fraudulently obtained or used led to criticism of the program, and it lapsed after the war.

Several senators then pressed to reestablish the program. As in the 1930s, they focused on food stamps as a way to reduce crop surpluses and help the American farmer. It is this origin as a solution to an agricultural surplus problem that makes the food stamp program unlike any other public assistance program. Indeed, the program had been, and would be, lodged in the Department of Agriculture, not in any of the public welfare agencies.

There was initially little support for reviving the program, and food stamps would almost certainly have disappeared forever if it were not for a solitary congresswoman. In 1952 St. Louis elected Leonor Sullivan (Dem.) to the U.S. House of Representatives. Congresswoman Sullivan made food stamps her issue. She fought, ever more tenaciously, for a dozen years to secure its passage. If ever there is a case of one member of Congress making a difference, it is the Food Stamp Act of 1964. Sullivan saw the potential of turning food stamps into an antipoverty program. As she later explained, "I became deeply concerned by the accounts of undernourishment among needy school children and others in St. Louis at about the same time the main concern on agricultural matters here in Washington seemed to be the unmanageable surpluses of food. The more I thought about this contradiction, the more indignant I became."[1]

Sullivan proceeded to introduce food stamp legislation in every session of Congress. For many years she had little success. Republicans were almost unanimously against the program. Opposed to its cost, they noted that, whether by history or statute, the states, not the federal government, were responsible for public assistance programs in the United States. And they complained that agricultural surpluses and poverty were two distinct issues. If this was actually a welfare program, Congresswoman Sullivan and other supporters should say so. Food stamps should be explicitly introduced as public assistance legislation and judged on that basis. Through the 1950s food stamp opponents were supported by the Eisenhower administration and its extremely conservative agriculture secretary, Ezra Taft Benton. When directed by Congress to investigate the worth of food stamp programs, Benton's department found them wanting. Food stamps would assist in reducing the agricultural surplus only if many families were allowed into the program, but the cost of doing this would be enormous. It also thought food stamps were less effective than the existing in-kind distribution programs.

A subtler reason for Sullivan's difficulties lay with the institutional structure of the House of Representatives. Since food stamps involved agriculture, food stamp legislation went to the House Agriculture Committee. Republican committee members could reliably be expected to fight these bills. But so could many of that committee's Democrats. These were rural southern Democrats, disproportionately represented on the committee because they had great interest in the farm bills over which it had jurisdiction. These Democrats did not share the opinions of Leonor Sullivan and her urban counterparts. First, they were fiscally conservative. Second, they saw nothing in these bills to benefit *their* constituents. Their districts grew tobacco and cotton, two crops for which food stamps were completely irrelevant. Third, and the most complex motive, was the nature of farm labor in the South of the 1950s. Sharecropping and day labor were common. These workers, often African-American, were extremely poor and would almost certainly be eligible for food stamps were they to be available. Many plantation and other large-scale farmers worried that this would make them less willing to work under the hard conditions that they had historically been offered. The result was that the southern Democrats repeatedly joined the Republicans to kill the food stamp bills in committee.

But Representative Sullivan was not deterred. Realizing that her obstacle was the Agriculture Committee, she set out to make life difficult for her own party's leaders until they would agree to pressure the committee on her behalf. She attempted to upset the normal order of business in the House by, for example, objecting to unanimous consent agreements on the House agenda that the leadership had carefully negotiated. (A single objection on the floor is sufficient to nullify such an agreement.) By 1959, after numerous travails, she finally had the support of the House leadership, and was able to get a food stamp bill onto the floor and passed. Hubert Humphrey (Dem., MN) led a similar bill through the Senate. But, even from the perspective of a food stamp supporter, the cost was high. To obtain the bill, it had been necessary to limit it to two years at a cost not to exceed $250 million annually, and to make it optional for each state. Even more important, the Department of Agriculture was given the choice of whether to implement the program. Secretary Benton, not surprisingly, chose not to do so.

Sullivan went back to the drawing board. But events began to favor her. John Kennedy, a food stamp cosponsor when in the Senate, became president in 1961. And a national reawakening to the problem of hunger was under way. The latter was signified by the remarkable success of Michael Harrington's exploration of poverty in America, *The Other America*, when it was published in 1962.[2] More prosaically, it was evidenced by the development of a new "hunger lobby" of civil rights and poverty activists who came to Washington demanding legislation.

Kennedy's very first executive order was to initiate a food stamp pilot program, to be authorized under the 1959 statute. Seven states were selected, including West Virginia, where many claim JFK had been first exposed to the extent of the nation's poverty. Alert to the need for bipartisanship, Sullivan made sure that at least one of the pilot programs was in a GOP district. (The apparent partisanship behind the siting of the pilot programs would still become a major issue in the upcoming congressional debate.)

Kennedy's decision meant that a workable food stamp program had to be devised. Fortunately, officials who had administered the prewar program were still in the Department of Agriculture. They had a number of practical problems. What should be the value of the stamps to be distributed? Should they be sold or given away? Where would they be used? How would fraud be controlled? They first decided that if the object of the program was nutritional adequacy, a baseline nutritious diet must be established. The Department of Agriculture had already developed measures, and cost estimates, of such a diet. It had formulated a "USDA economy food plan," the most inexpensive but healthy diet that a family could purchase over the course of week. In 1961, this diet was estimated to cost $5 per person a week.[3]

This would appear to be an appropriate level at which to set a family's food stamp allotment. However two problems were quickly realized. For the very poor, this allotment might be more than they were used to spending on food. Thus, they might be tempted to continue spending at their old level, and sell or trade the additional stamps. On the other hand, as incomes rose, so did spending on food. Many of these households were probably already spending more than the "economy plan." This created a trickier problem. If only the "economy plan" value of food stamps was allocated, the program would not do much to raise consumption and increase the nutrition for these families. But if higher allocations were given, there would again be the temptation to sell or trade the stamps. The solution was to create a sliding scale. The absolute poorest (i.e., those with no income at all) would receive somewhat less than recommended under the "economy food plan," then, as incomes rose, the allotment of food stamps would rise in tandem.

This raised a second question. Should the stamps be granted or sold to poor households? Acutely aware that accusations of a black market in food stamps had sunk the prewar program, planners decided that the stamps should be purchased. This would create an incentive for the purchaser to use the stamps for his or her own household. The purchase price was set as the amount that a family usually spent on food. This again led to a sliding scale. The higher the income, the higher the purchase requirement.

To further prevent fraud, as few foods as possible were excluded from the program. If many products were banned, there would be the temptation to illegally swap or sell stamps to obtain forbidden foods. Tobacco, alcohol, coffee, tea, cocoa, and bananas were made the only food products one could not buy using the stamps.[4] Stores would have to register and be approved to the handle the stamps, another antifraud protection.

Thus far the program had addressed the proper incentives to purchasers, and protections against fraud. But what about the original aims, boosting nutrition and reducing specific food surpluses? One could argue, as did critics, that both had been sacrificed to obtain the program. However, planners did add a final component to the program, "bonus stamps." Bonus stamps, indistinguishable from regular food stamps, were given to poor families at the time they purchased their stamps. This enabled them to increase their food consumption above what they could otherwise afford. Bonus stamps, too, were distributed on a sliding scale; the poorer the family, the more bonus stamps they received.

The result was a rather complicated set of distribution regulations. To see how the sliding scale of food stamp purchases operated, consider the 1961 food stamp plan in Kentucky.[5] A very poor family, one with an income between $25 and $34 a month, should they decide to enter the program, was obligated to purchase $18 of food stamps monthly. To this would be added bonus stamps valued at $42, so that the family's total monthly value in food stamps was $60. A second family, still poor, but earning between $125 and $134 a month, would have to purchase $64 in food stamps, and would be given an additional $24 worth of bonus stamps, to equal the equivalent of $88 a month.

As the pilot programs proceeded, the Kennedy administration liked what it saw. As a result, it initiated a second round of pilots, and prepared to obtain legislation for the permanent authorization of the program in 1963. Admitting that the program had little effect on farm surpluses, it focused on positive research results about its effects on the nutritional levels of the poor. It expected Congress to pass a $360 million food stamp program that year. Instead, the agriculture committee simply sat on the bill.

Two months after President Kennedy's assassination, Lyndon Johnson returned to it. The committee responded to his demand for action by formally tabling the bill. In other words, it voted to engage in no further consideration of the food stamp program. Sullivan was enraged, and responded by objecting on the floor to every unanimous consent procedure involving farm subsidies. Behind the scenes, the House leadership undertook more punitive action. It swung the votes necessary in the Rules Committee to prevent the tobacco research bill, a major subsidy for tobacco growers, from also reaching the floor. This was too much for tobacco district Representatives. Sullivan introduced a new bill, three members reversed their Agriculture Committee votes, and the bill was voted out, 18 to 16. But the bill was by no means headed for passage. The House leadership was not certain they had the votes on the floor. In a classic episode of logrolling, the Congressional practice of trading of votes for one bill in exchange for votes on another, they linked the Food Stamp Act to a wheat-cotton subsidy bill that the Department of Agriculture feared was heading for defeat. Urban Democrats were instructed to vote for the subsidy bill, and rural and southern Democrats were asked to vote for food stamps in exchange.

On the floor, Republicans, with the support of the Chamber of Commerce and some farm groups, continued to fight the bill, reiterating their belief in the apparent phoniness of the bill. Though masquerading as a farm bill, it did nothing for farmers. They thought it merely another ambitious, expensive, and questionable federal welfare program. But they could not shake the deal the Democratic caucus had struck, and the bill passed 229 to 189, on an almost straight party-line vote. After this epic struggle, the Senate was content simply to revise the list of excluded products (adding products such as soft drinks) and pass the bill by a voice vote. President Johnson signed it into law on August 31, 1964.

Though the Food Stamp Act had passed, the necessary legislative maneuverings had deeply compromised it. Not only was the size of the program reduced, it was made optional. That is, states could introduce or reject the program as they saw fit. The federal government would pay half of the costs, should they decide to begin a program. In 1965, only 29 states chose to implement such a program. The program was also bedeviled by low participation rates. Many eligible families did not enter the program. Whether this was due to onerous regulations, the stigma of being seen using the stamps, or some other reason was never clear. The fragility of its passage encouraged continued criticism of the program.

For these reasons, the Food Stamp Act of 1964 turned out to be merely the first step toward the present food stamp program. Attempts to change or improve its operations periodically followed. In 1970, a federal regulation made the purchasing requirements considerably more generous. In 1973, food stamps were made mandatory in all states. Four years later the Food Stamp Act of 1977 entirely rewrote the program. The purchase requirement was dropped altogether. These changes considerably liberalized the program, making it the sizable program of today.

More recently, the program has been on the defensive. Significant cuts were made in the 1980s. The 1996 Personal Responsibility and Work Opportunity Reconciliation Act further reduced benefits, restricted eligibility, limited the number of months an individual without a dependent child may receive food stamps, and increased fraud penalties. That Act also allowed states to experiment with methods other than food stamps to deliver food subsidies to the poor. As of 2001, California, Alabama, and Washington have done so.

As these many revisions suggest, the food stamp program continues to be controversial. Is it the "most important change in the public welfare policy in the United States since the passage of the

Social Security Act of 1935" or is it yet another program with a "tangled history of government regulations, fraud, computer deficiencies and court decisions . . . snarled in bureaucracy?"[6] Or is it both? No matter what one's conclusion, any program that is used weekly by more than one out of 15 Americans must be considered to be among the most significant to be enacted by Congress.

## 12. The Food Stamp Act of 1964

An Act to strengthen the agricultural economy; to help achieve a fuller and more effective use of food abundances; and to provide for improved levels of nutrition among low-income households through a cooperative Federal-State program of food assistance to be operated through normal channels of trade; and for other purposes.

*Be it enacted by the Senate and House of Representatives of the United States of America in Congress assembled,* That this act may be cited as "The Food Stamp Act of 1964."

### DECLARATION OF POLICY

Sec. 2. It is hereby declared to be the policy of Congress, in order to promote the general welfare, that the Nation's abundance of food should be utilized cooperatively by the States, the Federal government, and local governmental units to the maximum extent practicable to safeguard the health and well-being of the Nation's population and raise levels of nutrition among low-income households. The Congress hereby finds that increased utilization of foods in establishing and maintaining adequate national levels of nutrition will tend to cause the distribution in a beneficial manner of our agricultural abundances and will strengthen our agricultural economy, as well as result in more orderly marketing and distribution of food. To effectuate *[put into practice]* the policy of Congress and the purposes of this Act, a food stamp program, which will permit those households with low incomes to receive a greater share of the Nation's food abundance, is herein authorized. . . .

### ESTABLISHMENT OF THE FOOD STAMP PROGRAM

Sec. 4. The Secretary *[of Agriculture]* is authorized to formulate and administer a food stamp program under which, at the request of an appropriate State agency, eligible households within the State shall be provided with an opportunity more nearly to obtain a nutritionally adequate diet through the issuance to them of a coupon allotment which shall have a greater monetary value than their normal expenditures for food. The coupons so received by such households shall be used only to purchase food from retail food stores which have been approved for participation in the food stamp program. Coupons issued and used as provided in this Act shall be redeemable at face value by the Secretary through the facilities of the Treasury of the United States. . . .

### ELIGIBLE HOUSEHOLDS

Sec. 5. (a) Participation in the food stamp program shall be limited to those households whose income is determined to be a substantial limiting factor in the attainment of a nutritionally adequate diet. . . .

### ISSUANCE AND USE OF COUPONS

Sec. 6. (a) Coupons shall be printed in such denominations as may be determined to be necessary, and shall only be issued to households which have been duly certified as eligible to participate in the food stamp program. . . .

(c) Coupons issued to eligible households shall be simple in design and shall include such words or illustrations as are required to explain their purpose and define their denomination. . . .

### VALUE OF THE COUPON ALLOTMENT AND CHARGES TO BE MADE

Sec. 7. (a) The face value of the coupon allotment which State agencies shall be authorized to issue to households which are certified eligible to participate in the food stamp program shall be in such an amount as will provide such households with an opportunity more nearly to obtain a low-cost nutritionally adequate diet. . . .

(b) Households shall be charged such portion of the face value of the coupon allotment issued to them as is determined to be equivalent to their normal expenditures for food. [This provision was eliminated in the Food Stamp Act of 1977.]

### VIOLATIONS AND ENFORCEMENT

Sec. 14.(b) Whoever knowingly uses, transfers, acquires, or possesses in any manner not authorized in this Act shall, if such coupons are of the value of $100 or more, be guilty of a felony. . . .

(c) Whoever presents, or causes to be presented, coupons for payment or redemption of the value of $100 or more, knowing the same to have been received, transferred, or used in any manner in violation of the

provisions of this Act or the regulations issued pursuant to this Act, shall be guilty of a felony. . . . *[Offenses involving less than $100 are misdemeanors.]*
   August 31, 1964

**NOTES**

   1. Randall Ripley, "Legislative Bargaining and the Food Stamp Act, 1964," in Frederick N. Cleveland, ed., *Congress and Urban Problems* (Washington: The Brookings Institution Press, 1969), p. 282.
   2. Michael Harrington, *The Other America* (New York: Macmillan Press, 1962).
   3. Jeffrey M. Berry, *Feeding Hungry People: Rulemaking in the Food Stamp Program* (New Brunswick: Rutgers University Press, 1984), p. 26. This paragraph relies on Berry's account.
   4. Kenneth Finegold, "Agriculture and the Politics of U.S. Social Provision: Social Insurance and Food Stamps," in Margaret Weir, Ann Shola Orloff, and Theda Skocpol, eds., *The Politics of Social Policy in the United States* (Princeton: Princeton University Press, 1988), p. 222. The Senate later added to this list.
   5. Berry, p. 27. Recall that the program was optional and each state had its own requirements.
   6. Both quotes were made in 1977, the high-water mark of the program. The first is by Richard Nathan, former deputy undersecretary of HEW, in Maurice MacDonald, "Food Stamps: An Analytical History," *Social Service Review* 51, no. 4 (December 1977): 642. The latter is by Phillip M. Gregg, "The Food Stamp Program: Is It a State or Federal Problem?" *Illinois Issues*, August 17, 1977, p. 16.

# 13

# Medicare and Medicaid: The Social Security Amendments of 1965

Medicare stands second only to Social Security among social legislation passed in the twentieth century. Providing comprehensive medical coverage to individuals over 65, the program has not only assisted millions of senior citizens in obtaining health care, vastly improving their quality of life, it has also transformed the practice of American medicine. Medicare is the fastest growing, and perhaps the most complicated, of America's social insurance programs. Its complexity and price tag ensure that the program will continue to be hotly debated in coming years. Medicaid, a companion program that covers the health needs of the indigent, has similarly expanded in cost and coverage. It is today one of the major expenses of state governments, and lays behind many a budget battle. Yet it, too, has provided significant benefits to millions of Americans. In retrospect, that the United States would provide such programs may seem obvious. But, in fact, they were—and are—extremely controversial, and were enacted only after a bitter and protracted struggle of nearly 30 years.

That struggle began during the administration of Franklin D. Roosevelt. Roosevelt, as we have seen, had initially intended to include a health care plan in his Social Security program. He decided to drop the idea because its cost, complexity, and potential political opposition threatened to sink the entire bill. That did not stop his political allies, led by the New York Senator Robert Wagner, from introducing a first comprehensive health care bill in 1940. This bill died, as did the more ambitious Wagner-Murray-Dingell bill of 1943. Roosevelt then included medical coverage in his "Economic

Bill of Rights." Congress ignored his request. Harry Truman, emboldened by his upset victory in 1948, next sent to Congress a series of bills that would have given every American health insurance for all medical, dental, hospital, and nursing care expenses. This compulsory, universal health care plan was to be financed by a 3 percent payroll tax, divided, as with Social Security, between employers and employees. It was the most comprehensive, and most ambitious, health care legislation ever introduced. Public opinion polls favored action. But these bills, too, failed. They did not even reach the floor of either house.

The Democratic party was on record as favoring such a program, it controlled Congress virtually throughout this period, and yet no health care program could be passed. What was the problem? One stumbling block was the financing. No one knew how much a health care program would cost. Actuaries (professionals who compute insurance risks) could estimate the cost of Social Security—how many eligible workers there were, when they would retire, how long, on average, they would live, and so forth. From this one could arrive at a reasonable projection of the cost of the program, and so how to finance it. But experts could only guess at the cost of a health program. Who would use it, and how often? Would people go to the doctor or the hospital more often if they knew the government would pay for it? Would the kinds of health services offered change? This guessing game meant that the true financial burden of a health care program on the government would not be known until after it was passed. This worried many members of Congress, including conservative Democrats.

Second, a powerful combination of interest groups was arrayed against the idea. The Chamber of Commerce, the National Grange, the American Farm Bureau Federation, the insurance industry, the American Pharmaceutical Association, the American Legion, the National Catholic Welfare Conference, and the American Medical Association were among those that lobbied against the Truman plan. The American Medical Association (AMA) was the most deeply hostile. It was implacable in its opposition to *any* government-run health plan. And the AMA was not just another interest group. It represented well over one hundred thousand American physicians. Physicians had a unique authority in this debate. Who else knew more about medicine? They were key to the effectiveness of any plan Congress might pass. Administering a program in the face of the opposition of the people who would actually deliver the services would be difficult, to say the least. Doctors were also wealthy and respected individuals in their community. The AMA had the money with which to lobby and the public deference with which to be heard.

The AMA fought national health care for one simple reason. Doctors believed a government program would eventually "socialize" medicine. It was thought that Washington would dictate the treatments they could offer and the fees they could charge. That the first health care proposals would have dramatically restricted the practice of medicine is beyond doubt. The Wagner-Murray-Dingell bill, for example, would have created an approved list of physicians from which patients could select, and would have authorized the surgeon general to set mandated fees for medical services and to limit the number of patients in a physician's practice. The fear of these restrictions drove the AMA to fight government health care plans at almost any cost.

The AMA won its battle against Truman's national health insurance. An AMA advertising blitz was widely credited with defeating several prohealth plan members of Congress in the 1950 election. After this, Democrats beat a hasty retreat. Their 1952 election platform did not endorse national health insurance, and Adlai Stevenson avoided the issue in his campaign for president. Four years later, the party chose to ignore the issue health care altogether. Combined with the victory of Dwight Eisenhower, this seemed to seal the fate of a government health care plan in the United States.

The Eisenhower approach to health care was an abrupt departure from that of Roosevelt and Truman. In the 1940s, Ohio's Robert Taft, "Mr. Republican," had outlined a GOP position on health care similar to its view of Social Security. That is, if America needed any program at all, it should be targeted at the needy, funded through general revenues, and operated by the states. Building on that approach, Oveta Culp Hobby, the first secretary of Health, Education, and Welfare (HEW), suggested a program of using the government to help every American obtain private health care insurance. Democratic opposition and insurance industry skepticism doomed this proposal, and it was easily defeated in the House of Representatives.

Meanwhile, adherents of national health insurance were licking their wounds and reassessing their strategy. Even before Truman left office, his advisors were suggesting that the program be trimmed back and targeted at senior citizens. This was purely tactical. In the words of one official, "it is difficult for me to see how anyone with a heart can oppose this [type of program]."[1] The notion of a retirement age was by now widely shared. Who would want a retiree to have to continue to go out and earn the money to buy a health insurance policy? More cynically, to the extent the aged relied on their children for financial support, those children ought to welcome a program that would relieve them of the burden of paying for their parents' health care. This suggested tying the program to the Social Security System. This thinking was endorsed enthusiastically by officials in the Social Security Administration, who had been pushing for the addition of health care since Social Security's inauguration.

After the election of 1952, this view went underground, but it did not disappear. While liberals in Congress annually sponsored, and annually lost, this narrowed idea for health care, behind the scenes an informal alliance was growing among the Social Security Administration, "exiled" Democrat politicos, and the AFL-CIO. The latter may have been the most important of the three. In the 1950s, the 14-million-member labor union was at the height of its political power. The labor battles of the 1930s and 1940s were over. Now a permanent, highly institutionalized part of the American political scene, the AFL-CIO even had a Social Security committee devoted to organizing labor's support to protect and expand the program. The disability program then being debated in Congress was its top priority. But health care came next. Thus in 1957, the year after the Old-Age, Survivors, and Disability Insurance program was enacted, the head of that committee, Nelson Cruikshank, a Social Security Administration official, Robert Ball, and two former officials, I.S. Falk (then with the United Mine Workers), and the ubiquitous Wilbur Cohen (then at the University of Michigan) gathered to write a new health care plan to be attached to Social Security.

The plan was to be for individuals over 65 who were eligible for OASDI benefits. It would offer hospitalization (60 days a year), nursing home care (120 days after leaving a hospital), payment of surgeon's fees, hospital diagnostic services, and hospital drugs. It would be financed through an additional payroll tax. Note what was not in the plan. Any care in a doctor's office or at home ("outpatient" care) was excluded, as were physician's fees for services provided in a hospital. In part this was to reduce the cost of the program, but mostly it was an attempt to mitigate the hostility of the AMA.

The authors then went shopping for a congressional sponsor. The bill would have to originate in the House Ways and Means Committee, so that was where the sponsor must be found. The chair, Jere Cooper (Dem., TN), so helpful in the disability fight, said no. Wilbur Mills (Dem., AR), second in seniority, and, in the eyes of many, the power behind the throne, also said no. Down the list they went, until the rather obscure Rhode Island Democrat Aime Forand agreed to introduce what then became known as the Forand bill. The Democratic Study Group, the caucus of liberal Democrats in Congress, pressed to make the bill a priority. But the reluctance evidenced by the most influential Democrats on the Ways and Means Committee signaled the fate of the Forand bill. It did not make it out of the committee.

However, with labor and liberals behind it, the bill would not go away. In 1960, the committee again engaged in its annual consideration and tabling (i.e., killing) of the bill. Seven Democrats joined all the Republicans in sinking it. But it was getting harder. It was an election year, and Democrats such as Hubert Humphrey and John F. Kennedy began using the bill for their campaigns. Pat McNamara, a Democratic Michigan senator up for reelection, used his subcommittee on aging as a platform for hearings on the issue. A parade of senior citizens testified that paying for health care was their biggest worry. With 18 cosponsors, McNamara introduced legislation in the Senate. With all this attention given the issue, Republicans did not want to be seen as stonewalling. The Eisenhower administration and Vice President Nixon, also on the campaign trail, needed a response.

Many Republicans, however, sided with the Senate Minority Leader Everett Dirksen (IL) in opposing any compromise. He believed even the smallest program would become a hole "through which the government would come."[2] Nevertheless, the HEW secretary, Arthur Flemming, eventually arrived at an alternative to the Forand bill, a state-run program similar to the existing public assistance programs. Unlike Forand, the Eisenhower program was truly comprehensive. Virtually every medical procedure, whether outpatient or inpatient, was covered. But it would be limited to senior citizens earning less than $2,500 a year ($3,800 for couples). The wealthier could and should buy private insurance. Those who were eligible would be asked to pay $24 a year, and a deductible of $250 ($400 for couples). In exchange they would be reimbursed for 80 percent of nearly every medical expense. Flemming called this program "Medicare." Ironically, the proposal died but the name lived on.

Wilbur Mills, now the chair of the Ways and Means Committee, looked to be in a fix. An opponent of national health insurance, he was caught between the demands of fellow Democrats and this new pressure from the White House. But, calling the committee into executive session, Mills deftly navigated between the two. He knew his own party's opposition to the Eisenhower approach. Yet he preferred it to the Forand bill. So he simply redrafted "medicare" as the "Mills bill," reducing its benefits in the process. Correctly seen by Forand as "a watered-down version" of the White House plan, it would create a program called "Medical Assistance to the Aged." It would be a new public assistance program to be operated under Social Security. A state could choose to offer such a program, and, if it did, the federal government would share in its cost under a formula weighted to help poorer states. It would be relatively comprehensive, but limited to indigent senior citizens, who must exhaust all their health insurance and all their other financial resources before they became eligible. Using his powers as chair, he placed the Mills bill on the floor under a closed rule. It could not be altered or amended. Knowing full well that Democrats were itching to vote for a health care plan, he essentially dared them to vote against the only plan available, his. On June 23, 1960 it passed.

Disappointed liberals turned to the Senate, hoping that Lyndon Johnson, in his last days as majority leader, would undo the Mills bill. Johnson tried his best to get a Forand-type bill adopted, but he ran up against Mills' fellow Oklahoman, the powerful Robert Kerr (Dem.). Seated on the Finance Committee, Kerr oversaw the health care hearings. Clinton Anderson (Dem., NM) offered a more moderate version of Forand, only to see Kerr engineer its defeat and substitute a slightly liberalized version of the Mills bill, now called the Kerr-Mills bill. After defeating Anderson (this time joined by John F. Kennedy) once again on the floor, the Kerr-Mills bill passed 91 to 2, and the Medical Assistance to the Aged program came into existence. It was the fervent hope of Mills, Kerr, and the outgoing Eisenhower administration that this would be the end of the health care debate.

But they did not get their wish. John Kennedy, now president, renewed the call for a federal health care plan within several weeks of his inauguration. But neither Mills, nor the Senate finance chair,

Harry Byrd (Dem., VA), was interested in his ideas. They would not sponsor Kennedy's bill, and the more junior Cecil King (Dem., CA) had to team with Clinton Anderson to introduce it. The King-Anderson bill suffered the same annual fate once meted the Forand bill. Frustrated Democrats finally attempted an end run on the Senate floor. In 1962 they reached out to liberal Republicans, and their informal leader, Jacob Javits of New York. King-Anderson was rewritten to bring them on board. It was changed to include all seniors, not just Social Security-eligible, and to allow covered persons the option of either a federal insurance plan or assistance in obtaining a private insurance plan. Financing was to be through the payroll tax for those in Social Security, and from the general revenues for those who were not. Now called the Anderson-Javits bill, Senators attempted to amend it to a public welfare bill.

Outside of Congress, the politicking was furious. A key moment came when the United Auto Workers organized a nationwide rally for the bill on May 20, 1962. President Kennedy addressed supporters from Madison Square Garden. The television networks broadcast his speech around the nation. The next night the AMA countered, its president appearing on national TV to oppose to the plan. Letters to Congress indicated that the AMA had won this battle for public opinion, and congressional advocates realized it would be an extremely close vote.

Fighting for the last vote, the Senate's Democrat whips could not understand why Jennings Randolph of West Virginia, a reliable supporter of social legislation, would not announce his intentions. On August 17, they found out. He stood to cast the deciding vote to defeat Anderson-Javits.[3] Only later did the story emerge. The state of West Virginia had illegally overspent on one of its public assistance programs, and needed special federal legislation. The sponsor of the public welfare bill, none other than Robert Kerr, had been more than happy to make a deal. Health care had lost once again.

The elections of 1962 brightened the spirits of Medicare backers. Democrats netted three seats in the Senate, enough to reverse the vote. The death of Robert Kerr removed another obstacle. This meant the struggle would move to the House. Unfortunately for supporters, this meant they would have to overcome the opposition of the man many believe to be the most skillful legislator ever to sit in the U.S. House of Representatives, Wilbur D. Mills.

While Republicans continued to oppose the bill because they

feared its cost, disliked the idea of a huge new federal program in an area once reserved for the states, and had long included physicians among their most loyal supporters, Mills, and like-minded southern Democrats, had more complex motivations. They came from rural districts, where labor was weak, and doctors were often the most respected members of the small towns that dotted them. People were conservative, and not likely to support big government programs. Mills, for example, resisted party leaders in part because of his own political experience. He had had to defeat an even more conservative, incumbent Democrat to hold his Arkansas seat after the state lost two seats in the 1960 redistricting. But Mills had no difficulties with federalizing health care, nor had he any particular loyalty to doctors. Rather, he was fervently loyal to another federal program, Social Security. It was this that led him to oppose Medicare. Mills believed that the complexity of health care meant that a program that was both financially and politically successful was extremely unlikely. Since it was tied to the Social Security system, Medicare's failure could bring down the entire program. Anything that might destroy Social Security, the greatest legacy of the New Deal, was too great a gamble. It was ultimately for this reason that Democrat leaders had no success, over nearly 10 years, in getting Wilbur Mills to end his opposition.

Mills used his dominance of the Ways and Means Committee to stymie first Kennedy, and then Johnson. He did this even as the antihealth care interest group coalition was melting away. Hospitals, nurses, and other providers were recognizing the potential financial bonanza for them should Medicare pass, and therefore shifted to support it. Only the insurance industry and the AMA remained. The AMA, however, redoubled its efforts. In 1963 it launched "Operation Hometown," a multimillion dollar anti-Medicare campaign. It even assessed special dues on doctors to pay for the expense.

Every tactic was tried in an effort to head off the program. The most remarkable was in 1964, when it appeared John C. Watts (Dem., KY) might become the thirteenth and deciding vote for Medicare on the Ways and Means Committee. Shortly thereafter, the AMA publicly called the recently released surgeon general's report linking smoking and cancer "inconclusive," claiming more study was needed. Mr. Watts, representing a tobacco district, quietly resumed his opposition.[4] By the end of 1964, Mills had defeated Medicare once more, and that October, a *New York Times* editorial questioned whether it had finally fallen into the permanent "limbo of perennial issues."[5]

The *Times'* pessimism was premature. In November 1964, Lyndon Johnson was reelected president in one of the largest landslides in U.S. history. Forty-four new Democrats were swept into the House of Representatives on his coattails. For opponents of Medicare, the world turned upside down. No one recognized this quicker than Representative Mills. After the election, Mills announced that if Medicare was financed through a separate payroll tax with a trust fund separate from that of Social Security, he could support it. Johnson agreed. When the 89th Congress convened in January 1965, a revised King-Anderson bill was the first to be introduced. It now called for the provision of 60 days of hospitalization and 60 days of nursing home care, along with hospital diagnostic services for Americans over the age of 65.

The AMA recognized it was on the ropes and responded with a counterproposal: "Eldercare." This would expand the Kerr-Mills program and enable the government to buy private insurance for the needy aged. It was never seriously considered. The beleaguered GOP realized it was certain to lose. Believing it was imperative not to appear too negative in the vote to come, Rep. Byrnes (WI), the senior Republican on the Ways and Means Committee, offered an alternative program. Modeled after the health care plan enjoyed by federal employees, it would pay for hospitalization, nursing home care, and 80 percent of all other health care costs. Participation would be voluntary, and would be financed from general revenues and from monthly premiums paid by the elderly who had joined the plan. The political purpose of the Byrnes plan was to make the Democrats' Medicare appear limited and weak.

Mills convened his committee in closed session while he personally negotiated with Wilbur Cohen, representing the administration, over the shape of the bill. Then, stealing the thunder from both the administration and the Republicans, Mills audaciously combined all the competing plans. By doing so he simultaneously met each of his goals. First, the new bill was once again titled the "Mills bill" and that meant he would control it through Congress. Second, he had called the Republicans' bluff. They could not use the Byrnes plan to attack the Democrats. And third, he achieved his goal in separating the financing of Medicare from that of Social Security.

Specifically, the administration plan (King-Anderson) became Part A of Medicare. It paid for senior citizens' inpatient hospital services for up to 60 days, after payment of a deductible and a coinsurance fee ("copayment"). Hospital diagnostic procedures and 60 days of nursing home services, if utilized directly after a hospital stay, were also reimbursed under similar stipulations. This would be financed via a separate payroll tax, deposited into a Medicare trust fund. The Byrnes plan became Part B of Medicare. Seniors had the option of joining Part B, the "Voluntary Supplementary Insurance Plan," at a cost of $3 a month. The federal government would match this amount out of the general revenues. Under Part B, seniors would receive reimbursement for 80 percent of their outpatient health costs (i.e., visits to the doctor or home health services) and their surgeons' fees. Again, there would be a copayment and a deductible. Finally, since Medicare would make the Kerr-Mills Medical Assistance to the Aged plan largely redundant, that plan was recast. Though it would operate as before, it was now targeted at all indigent Americans, not just the aged. To reflect this change, it was renamed "Medicaid."

The Mills bill went to the floor of the House. The GOP mounted a last-ditch effort to kill the bill on the floor, but their effort to substitute the Byrnes bill for Medicare failed by a vote of 191 to 236. Medicare then passed by an overwhelming vote of 313 to 115.

Senators added several amendments, later stricken in the conference committee, before approving the bill by a vote of 68 to 21. (Senators were able to liberalize the hospital and nursing home stay limits to 90 and 100 days, respectively, in the conference committee.) Medicare was passed.

But even the bill's passage did not end the politicking. The AMA considered boycotting the new law. In late July 1965, President Johnson was forced to hold a special meeting with AMA leaders to convince them to cooperate. After the meeting he flew to Independence, Missouri, to sign Medicare into law. Former President Truman was the guest of honor.

It is difficult to overestimate the impact of Medicare. By the turn of this century, over 39 million Americans were receiving benefits under the program. It is the primary health insurance for one in seven people in the United States. The cost is staggering. From several billion dollars in the mid-60s, the price tag has grown to $210 billion in 1999. Medicaid has grown equally rapidly. Twelve percent of Americans receive health care under this program, including 37 percent of children under the age of five. Together, states and the federal government pay $169 billion for the program. Administrative costs alone near 7 billion dollars. These figures suggest that tough political choices lie ahead. But they are also proof that these programs have substantially changed life in the United States.

# 13a. The Social Security Act Amendments of 1965 "Medicare"

An Act To provide a hospital insurance program for the aged under the Social Security Act with a supplementary medical benefits program and an expanded program of medical assistance, to increase benefits under the Old-Age, Survivors, and Disability Insurance System, to improve the Federal-State public assistance programs, and for other persons.

Be it enacted by the Senate and the House of Representatives of the United States of America in Congress assembled, That this Act . . . may be cited as the "Social Security Amendments of 1965." . . .

**TITLE I—HEALTH INSURANCE FOR THE AGED AND MEDICAL ASSISTANCE**

*Part I—Health Insurance Benefits for the Aged*

. . . *Hospital Insurance Benefits and Supplementary Medical Insurance Benefits*
Sec. 102. (a) The Social Security Act is amended by adding after title XVII the following new title:

**TITLE XVIII—HOSPITAL INSURANCE FOR THE AGED**

Part A—Hospital Insurance Benefits for the Aged

Description of Program
Sec. 1811. The insurance program for which entitlement *[the right to benefits]* is established . . . provides basic protection against the costs of hospital and related post-hospital services in accordance with this part for individuals who are age 65 or over and are entitled to retirement benefits under title II of this Act or under the railroad retirement system.
*Scope of Benefits*
Sec. 1812. (a) The benefits provided to an individual by the insurance

program under this part shall consist of entitlement to have payment made on his behalf . . . for—

(1) inpatient hospital services for up to 90 days during any spell of illness;

(2) post-hospital extended care-services for up to 100 days during any spell of illness;

(3) post-hospital home health services for up to 100 visits (during the one-year period . . . ) after the beginning of one spell of illness and before the beginning of the next; and

(4) outpatient hospital diagnostic services.

*[Paragraphs (b) and (c) impose special limits on those using a psychiatric hospital or a tuberculosis hospital, and limit an individual's coverage to no more than 190 days of psychiatric hospital care over his or her entire life.]*

(d) Payment under this part may be made for post-hospital home health services furnished an individual only during the one-year period . . . following his most recent hospital discharge . . . , and only for the 100 visits in such period. . . .

*Deductibles and Coinsurance*

Sec. 1813. (a) (1) The amount payable for inpatient hospital services furnished an individual during any spell shall be reduced by a deduction equal to the inpatient hospital deductible . . . Such amount shall be further reduced by a coinsurance amount equal to one-fourth of the inpatient hospital deductible for each day (before the 91st day) on which such individual is furnished such services during such spell of illness after such services have been furnished to him for 60 days during such spell. . . . *[This section establishes the level of the deductible, the payment that individuals must make on their own before Medicare coverage begins, and the level of the coinsurance payment, the portion of the health care cost that individuals must continue to pay even after Medicare coverage begins, for the hospital portion of the medicare program.]*

*Reasonable Cost of Services*

. . . (b) The amount paid to any provider of services with respect to services for which payment may be made under this part shall . . . be the reasonable cost of such services. . . .

*Federal Hospital Insurance Trust Fund*

Sec. 1817. (a) There is hereby created on the books of the Treasury of the United States a trust fund to be known as the 'Federal Hospital Insurance Trust Fund' . . . The Trust Fund shall consist of such amounts as may be deposited in, or appropriated to, such fund as provided in this part . . . There are hereby appropriated to the Trust Fund for the fiscal year ending June 30, 1966, and for each fiscal year thereafter . . . amounts equivalent to 100 per centum of—

(1) the taxes imposed by sections 3101(b) and 3111(b) of the Internal Revenue Code of 1954 with respect to wages reported to the Secretary of the Treasury. . . .

(2) the taxes imposed by section 1401(b) of the Internal Revenue Code of 1954 with respect to self-employment income reported to the Secretary of the Treasury. . . .

*[The above section established the Medicare trust fund, to be funded by a payroll tax.]*

## Part B—Supplementary Medical Insurance Benefits for the Aged

Establishment of Supplemental Medical Insurance Program for the Aged

Sec. 1831. There is hereby established a voluntary insurance program to provide medical insurance benefits in accordance with the provisions of this part for individuals 65 years of age or over who elect to enroll under such program, to be financed from premium payments by enrollees together with contributions from funds appropriated by the Federal Government. *[This section creates the outpatient (nonhospital) portion of the Medicare program, to be funded by the monthly premiums of Americans over the age of 65, along with any general government revenues that may be necessary to pay the expenses of the program.]*

Sec. 1832. (a) The benefits provided to an individual by the insurance program established by this part shall consist of—

(1) entitlement to have payment made to him or on his behalf . . . for medical and other health services *[with certain exceptions]*; and

(2) entitlement to have payment made on his behalf . . . for—

(A) home health services for up to 100 visits during a calendar year; and

(B) medical and other health services (other than physicians' services unless furnished by a resident or intern of a hospital) furnished by a provider of services or by others under arrangements with them made by a provider of services. . . .

*Payment of Benefits*

Sec. 1833. (a) Subject to the succeeding provisions of this section, there shall be paid from the Federal Supplemental Medical Insurance Trust Fund, in the case of each individual who is covered under the insurance program established by this part and incurs expenses for services with respect to which benefits are payable under this part, amounts equal to

... 80 percent of the reasonable charges for the services. *[Eighty percent of a physician's charge for medical services will be paid to the physician out of the Supplemental Medical Insurance Trust Fund.]*

(b) Before applying subsection (a) with respect to expenses incurred by an individual during any calendar year, the total amount of the expenses incurred by such individual during such year ... shall be reduced by a deductible of $50 ... *[Medicare will not cover the first $50 of an individual's Part B—eligible health care expenses. However, several technical circumstances would lower this deductible.]*

*Eligible Individuals*

Sec. 1836. Every individual who—

(1) has attained the age of 65, and

(2) (A) is a resident of the United States, and is either (i) a citizen or (ii) an alien lawfully admitted for permanent residence who has resided in the United States continuously during the 5 years immediately preceding the month in which he applies for enrollment under this part, or (B) is entitled to hospital benefits under part A,

is eligible to enroll in the insurance program established by this part.

*... Amounts of Premiums*

Sec. 1839. (a) The monthly premium of each individual enrolled under this part before 1968 shall be $3 ...

(b) (2) The Secretary shall, between July 1 and October 1 of 1967 and of each odd-numbered year thereafter, determine ... the dollar amount which shall be applicable for premiums for months occurring in either of the two succeeding calendar years. ...

*Federal Supplementary Medical Insurance Trust Fund*

Sec. 1841 (a) There is hereby created on the books of the Treasury of the United States a trust fund to be known as the 'Federal Supplementary Medical Insurance Trust Fund ...' The Trust Fund shall consist of such amounts as may be deposited in, or appropriated to, such fund as provided in this part ...

*Changes in Tax Schedules*

Sec. 321. (a) Section 1401 of the Internal Revenue Code of 1954 ... is amended to read as follows:

Sec. 1401. Rate of Tax

... (b) Hospital Insurance.— ... there shall be imposed for each taxable year, on the self-employment income of every individual, a tax as follows: *[a schedule of tax rates from 1965 to 1986 follows. The initial rate was 0.35 per cent of self-employment income.]*

Sec. 3101 rate of tax

... (b) Hospital Insurance.— ... there is hereby imposed on the income of every individual a tax equal to the following percentages of the wages ... received by him with respect to employment ...: *[a schedule of tax rates from 1965 to 1986 follows. The initial rate was 0.35 per cent.]*

Sec. 3111 rate of tax

... (b) Hospital Insurance.— ... there is hereby imposed on every employer an excise tax, with respect to having individuals in his employ, equal to the following percentages of the wages ... paid by him with respect to employment ...: *[a schedule of tax rates from 1965 to 1986 follows. The initial rate was 0.35 per cent.]*

July 30, 1965

# 13.b The Social Security Act Amendments of 1965 "Medicaid"

Sec. 121 (a). The Social Security Act is amended by adding at the end thereof ... the following new title:

**TITLE XIX—GRANTS TO STATES FOR MEDICAL ASSISTANCE PROGRAMS**

Appropriation

Sec. 1901. For the purpose of enabling each State, as far as practicable under the conditions of such State, to furnish (1) medical assistance on behalf of families with dependent children and of aged, blind, or permanently and totally disabled individuals, whose income and resources are insufficient to meet the costs of necessary medical services, and (2) rehabilitation and other services to help such families and individuals attain or retain capability for independence or self-care, there is hereby authorized to be appropriated for each fiscal year a sum sufficient to carry out the purposes of this title. The sums made available under this section shall be used for making payments to States which have submitted, and had approved by the Secretary of Health, Education, and Welfare, State plans for medical assistance. *[This appropriation established Medicaid, a program of federal monies to support state-run health plans.]*

State Plans for Medical Assistance

Sec. 1902. (a) A State plan for medical assistance must—

(1) provide that it shall be in effect in all political subdivisions of the State, and, if administered by them, be mandatory upon them;

(2) provide for financial participation by the State equal to not less than 40 per centum of the non-Federal share of the expenditures under the plan. . . .

(10) provide for making medical assistance available to all individuals receiving aid or assistance under State plans approved under titles I,IV,X,XIV, and XVI *[These are all of the public assistance titles.]* . . .

(b) The Secretary shall approve any plan which fulfills the conditions specified in subsection (A), except that he shall not approve any plan which imposes, as a condition of eligibility for medical assistance under the plan—

(1) an age requirement of more than 65 years;

(2) effective July 1, 1967, any age requirement which excludes any individual who has not attained the age of 21 and is or would. . . . be a dependent child under title IV; or

(3) any residence requirement which excludes any individual who resides in the State; or

(4) any citizenship requirement which excludes any citizen of the United States.

(c) Notwithstanding subsection (b), the Secretary shall not approve any State plan for medical assistance if he determines that the approval and operation of the plan will result in a reduction in aid or assistance . . . provided for eligible individuals under a plan of such State approved under title I, IV, X, XIV, or XVI. *[Paragraph (c) prohibited a state from designing a Medicaid plan that reduced its expenditures on medical assistance below the amount it had previously spent under the existing Social Security Act public assistance programs.]*

July 30, 1965

## NOTES

1. Theodor R. Marmor, *The Politics of Health Care* (Chicago: Aldine Publishing Company, 1973), p. 15.

2. James L. Sundquist, *Politics and Policy: The Eisenhower, Kennedy, and Johnson Years* (Washington: The Brookings Institution Press, 1968), p. 303.

3. The vote was 52 to 48 to table. Carl Hayden (AZ) had promised to vote for the bill if he was the deciding vote; otherwise he would vote against it.

4. Sundquist, p. 315.

5. Peter A. Corning, *The Evolution of Medicare, From Idea to Law,* http://www.ssa.gov/history/corning.html (originally published, 1969).

# 14

## Employment Security Amendments of 1970

In a typical month, five to six million American workers are unemployed. Ten percent of these workers have been off the job for more than half a year. These individuals and their families rely on unemployment compensation, the program established as Title III of the Social Security Act of 1935, for their income while they seek work. Many of these workers are today able to draw these benefits only because of the Employment Security Amendments of 1970.

By 1970, the Social Security Act had been heavily amended and altered. The Title II Old-Age Benefits program was extensively revised. Eligibility and benefits levels were substantially expanded, beneficiaries' survivors were included, and a disability insurance program had been added. But Title III, the Unemployment Compensation program, had barely been touched. One can speculate why. Politically, senior citizens form a large and influential constituency for Title II programs. In contrast, the unemployed are smaller in number and far more marginalized. Most unemployed workers soon obtain another job, which prevents the formation of a permanent political interest. In addition, the unemployment program is run by the states, making it harder to reform nationally. Finally, the relatively strong economy that started at the end of the World War II dampened the concern with unemployment. In a time of high employment, plenty of other problems seemed more urgent than taking care of those who had temporarily lost their jobs.

In the 1960s, both the Kennedy and Johnson administrations believed the time had finally come to update the program. They wished to revise it in the same ways Social Security had been changed. The coverage should be expanded, the benefits increased, and the provisions of the various state programs equalized. But the issue was not a priority, and no legislation was ever passed. The most serious debate came in 1966, when Congress considered President Johnson's request to mandate that state programs pay at least 50 percent of a worker's wages for at least 26 weeks. Johnson also asked that coverage be extended to many more workers. The two houses could not agree on how to respond to the request, and the bill died in the conference committee. Just before leaving office, Johnson renewed his call for these reforms.

In 1969 the new president, Richard Nixon, asked the Department of Labor to look into the issue and surprised many by endorsing its findings that unemployment compensation reform was needed. Nixon repackaged the Johnson proposals into his own plan, offered to Congress on July 9, 1969. He called for a similar expansion in the coverage and the benefits period, and for further regulation of how state plans calculated their benefit levels. The president wished to extend the program to include farm workers and small-business employees, along with those who worked in sales, state hospitals and universities, and the nonprofit sector. This amounted to an additional 5.3 million workers. He also proposed that, in times of recession, the benefit period automatically be extended another 13 weeks. (Congress had passed temporary extensions during the previous two recessions.) To pay for these changes he asked for an increase in the wage base of the payroll tax that funded the program. Nixon wanted the tax to apply to the first $6,000 of a worker's income instead of the $3,000 under the existing law. (Because states ran their own programs, his request was for a minimum level of taxation; a state could freely impose a higher tax.)

Nixon shared the concerns of his predecessors that the unemployment compensation system was becoming increasingly inadequate. Many workers were still not covered, and state program benefits were often low and varied widely. However, Nixon was also looking to the future. The unemployment rate was rising slowly from the levels of the early 1960s. Fears of an economic slowdown were in the air. Political analysts generally believe that the Democrats are advantaged during periods of growing unemployment, a point not lost on Nixon. An outmoded unemployment compensation system would do him no favors. The program's funding was also nearing crisis. Because the wage base for the payroll tax had not changed in over 30 years, the money available with which to pay laidoff workers was increasingly scarce. (The crisis would strike in 1976, when 11 states ran out of money for their unemployment programs.)

Unfortunately for the president, nearly every revision he proposed encountered opposition. For some, he went too far in his reforms. The request to expand coverage proved just as controversial for unemployment compensation as it had been for Social Security. Small-business and agricultural interests were dead set against bringing their workers into the system. State and local governments protested the additional federal regulations, and objected bitterly to a requirement that they pay benefits equaling at least 50 percent of an unemployed worker's previous wages. The latter objections led Nixon to present his request for a 50 percent benefit level as a "recommendation." He suggested that if states voluntarily met this level, there would be no need for federal action (as of 2002 not all states have done so).

But for others, his reforms did not go far enough. The AFL-CIO believed Nixon was still too stingy. It complained that state benefits should be raised to two-thirds of an individual's wages. It also argued that Nixon's proposal to extend benefits should not be dependent upon whether there was a recession. Thirty-nine weeks of benefits should always be available, because long-term unemployment exists even when there is not a recession.[1] In addition, labor made it clear that it preferred the federal government essentially take over the program from the states, arguing that only through such a federalization of unemployment compensation could its many problems be remedied. Finally, no one liked increasing the tax base when an emergency did not seem at hand. For Nixon the only good news was the guardedly positive reception by big business.

Fortunately for Nixon, the bill went to the House Ways and Means Committee, still firmly under the control of Wilbur Mills (Dem., AR). The most controversial issue in that committee became the inclusion of farm workers. Mills' own position was ambiguous, but he bowed to a coalition of Republicans and southern Democrats and agreed to the removal of some 800,000 farm workers from the act. But otherwise, he adopted his usual strategy of navigating between the extremes. This worked to the president's advantage. On the one hand, Mills resisted the demands of liberal Democrats, supported by the labor unions, that national standards be established for the amount and duration of unemployment benefits. But he also stopped conservatives from removing small-business employees from coverage, and from eliminating the tax increase. He solved the latter dispute by splitting it down the middle. If Nixon wanted a base of $6,000 and conservatives wanted to keep it at $3,000, why not make it $4,200 along with a small rise in the tax rate?

On the floor of the House, Mills argued that these reforms were the most thorough overhaul of the unemployment compensation program since 1935 and ought to be passed. His case was made easier by the bill's consideration under a closed rule. Thus, given the stark choice of Mill's reform or no reform, the House approved the bill by a vote off 337 to 8.

The Senate did not proceed on the bill until the following year. The lack of a closed rule in the Senate ensured that, this time, the bill's opponents could not so easily be tamed. Opposition came in two forms. First was the continued debate over coverage. Advocates of farm workers geared up to reverse the House decision that these workers be excluded from unemployment compensation, while advocates of small business were just as determined to reverse the House decision that small-business employees be *included* in the program. On top of this debate was another. Liberals, led by Minnesota's two Democrat senators, Eugene McCarthy and Walter Mondale, and with the support of the AFL-CIO, prepared to fight for full federalization of America's unemployment policy.

Oddly enough, both liberals and conservatives got their wish in the bill reported out of the Senate Finance Committee. Farm workers were back in and small-business employees were out. The committee also decided to give state and local governments the option of including their employees in the system. By the time the bill reached the floor, in April 1970, a rising unemployment rate was focusing senators' attention. That very month the unemployment rate crossed the threshold that would have triggered the automatic thirteen-week extension of unemployment benefits. By the middle of the year, the unemployment rate had risen above 5 percent for the first time in five years. Politicians of every stripe believed unemployment would be a major issue in that year's congressional elections.

In such an environment, a lively debate could be expected, and the Senate did not disappoint. Walter Mondale led a charge to further expand coverage not only to farm workers, but also to migrant farm workers. He attracted just enough support from nervous Republicans to prevail. McCarthy took up the larger fight to federalize the unemployment program. First he offered an amendment for full federal financing of unemployment compensation. Southern Democrats and Republicans almost unanimously opposed him, defeating the amendment by a vote of 45 to 30. Nevertheless, McCarthy proceeded to argue for creating mandatory federal standards for all state unemployment programs. This amendment encountered the same resistance, and it, too, failed.

The conference committee's job was a difficult one, reconciling the two houses' decisions of whom to cover under the bill. (Unrelated Senate amendments that added two new classes of savings bonds did not make things easier.) Ultimately, the committee sided with the House. Farm workers were dropped. Most small-business employees were reinstated. This "compromise" outraged liberals in both houses, who vowed to kill the entire bill rather than accept this conclusion. They came the closest in the House, where Mills defended the conference report by rather weakly claiming that a lack of information about farm labor made it impossible to draft a bill covering it. The motion to recommit the bill to the conference committee with instructions to add back farm workers was supported by most Democrats, but it was defeated 219 to 170. McCarthy and Jacob Javits (Rep., NY) led the same fight in the Senate, but also lost, 50 to 19. President Nixon signed the bill into law on August 10, 1970.

The Employment Security Amendments of 1970 were the first substantial changes since the original enactment of the Title II Unemployment Compensation program. In retrospect, the 1970 act was important for four reasons. First, it began the expansion of the workforce eligible for unemployment compensation. Congress returned to this issue in the Unemployment Compensation Amendments of 1976, finally including both farm workers and employees of state and local governments. Today 97 percent of the wage and salary workforce are potentially covered under the program.[2] Second, the federal government undertook to regulate the state unemployment compensation programs on a very important issue, the duration of benefits. This initiated further moderate federal oversight of the state plans in later years. Third, the triggering mechanism was added. Congress has since altered the details of how extended benefits are triggered, but the principle remains. Fourth, the law began shoring up the financing of the program. In 1976,

Congress raised the wage base to the amount Nixon had originally sought, $6,000, and has since raised it to $7,000. The employment tax has risen in tandem. In the more than 30 years since the passage of this Act, no further significant change in the principles underlying America's Unemployment Compensation program has been made.

## 14. Employment Security Amendments of 1970

An Act To Extend and Improve the Federal-State unemployment compensation program.

*Be it enacted by the Senate and House of Representatives of the United States of America in Congress assembled,* That this Act may be cited as the "Employment Security Amendments of 1970."

**TITLE I—UNEMPLOYMENT COMPENSATION AMENDMENTS**

Part A—Coverage

Sec. 101 Definition of Employer . . .

*[This revised definition brought many small business employees into the program.]*

(a) Employer—For purposes of this chapter, the term 'employer' means . . . any person who—

(1) during any calendar quarter in the calendar year or the preceding calendar year paid wages of $1,500 or more, or

(2) on each of some 20 days during the calendar year or during the preceding calendar year, each day being in a different calendar week, employed at least one individual in employment for some portion of the day . . .

Sec. 104 State Law Coverage of Certain Employees of Non-Profit Organizations and of State Hospitals and Institutions of Higher Education.

(b) (1) . . . the Internal Revenue Code of 1954 is amended . . . by inserting . . . the following new section:

Sec. 3309. State Law Coverage of Certain Services Performed for Nonprofit Organizations and For State Hospitals and Institutions of Higher Education.

(a) State Law Requirements—

(1) . . . the services to which this paragraph applies are—

(A) service excluded from the term 'unemployment' solely by

reason of paragraph (8) of section 3306(c) *[paragraph 8 excluded employees in the nonprofit sector from unemployment compensation]*, and

(B) service performed in the employ of the State, or any instrumentality of the State or of the State and one or more other States for a hospital or institution of higher education located in the State. . . .

(2) the State law shall provide that an organization . . . which, but for the requirements of this paragraph, would be liable for contributions with respect to service to which paragraph (1)(A) applies may elect . . . to pay . . . into the State unemployment fund amounts equal to the amounts of compensation attributable under the State law to such service. . . . *[Subparagraph (2) allows employers who are exempt from contributing to their state's unemployment compensation fund because their organization is excluded from the program under Section 3309(a)(1) to contribute to the fund if they wish. This would give their employees unemployment compensation coverage.]*

(b) Section Not to Apply to Certain Service. *[Religious organizations, members of a religious order, school employees other than those in higher education, rehabilitation and worker-training employees, and working prison inmates continued to be excluded from the program.]*

(c) Nonprofit Organizations Must Employ 4 or More. . . .

### Part B—Provisions of State Law

Sec. 121. Provisions Required to be Included in State Laws.

(a) . . . the Internal Revenue Code of 1954 is amended by . . . the following new paragraphs:

(7) an individual who has received compensation during his benefit year is required to have had work since the beginning of such year in order to qualify for compensation in his next benefit year;

(8) compensation shall not be denied to an individual for any week because he is in training with the approval of the State agency . . . ;

(9) (A) compensation shall not be denied or reduced to an individual solely because he files a claim in another state . . . or because he resides in another state at the time he files a claim for unemployment compensation;

(B) the State shall participate in any arrangement for the payment of compensation on the basis of combining an individual's wages and employment covered under the State law with his wages and employment covered under the unemployment compensation law of other States . . . *[Subparagraph 9 prohibits a state from denying individuals their benefits because they now reside in another state or have also filed for benefits in another state, and mandates that the state must allow individuals to combine the wages that they may have earned in different states in determining the level of their unemployment benefits.]*

(10) compensation shall not be denied to any individual by reason of cancellation of wage credits or total reduction of his benefit rights for any cause other than discharge for misconduct connected with his work, fraud in connection with a claim for compensation, or receipt of disqualifying income. . . .

## TITLE II—FEDERAL-STATE EXTENDED UNEMPLOYMENT COMPENSATION PROGRAM

Sec. 201. This title may be cited as the "Federal-State Extended Unemployment Compensation Act of 1970."

### Payment of Extended Compensation

State Law Requirements

Sec. 202 (a) (1) . . . a State law shall provide that payment of extended compensation shall be made, for any week of unemployment which begins in the individual's eligibility period, to individuals who had exhausted all rights to regular compensation under the State law and who have no rights to regular compensation with respect to such week under such law or any other State unemployment compensation law or to compensation under any other Federal law . . . *[Individuals who have exhausted their regular unemployment compensation benefits, and cannot seek benefits from another state or the federal government, are made eligible for extended unemployment compensation.]*

Individuals' Compensation Accounts

(b) (1) The State law shall provide that the State will establish for each eligible individual who files an application therefor, an extended compensation account with respect to such individual's benefit year.

### Extended Benefit Period

Beginning and Ending

Sec. 203. (a) For purposes of this title, in the case of any State, an extended benefit period—

(1) shall begin with the third week after whichever of the following weeks first occurs:

(A) a week for which there is a national "on" indicator, or

(B) a week for which there is a State "on" indicator; and

(2) shall end with the third week after the first week for which there is both national "off" indicator and a State "off" indicator.

Special Rules

(b) (1) In the case of any State—

(A) no extended benefit period shall last for a period of less than thirteen consecutive weeks, and

(B) no extended benefit period may begin by reason of a State "on" indicator before the fourteenth week after the close of a prior extended benefit period with respect to such State . . . *[This paragraph mandates that no state may offer its extended benefit program for less than 13 weeks, nor, once the program has ended, may it offer the extended benefit program again until at least 13 more weeks have passed.]*

National "On" and "Off" Indicators

*[The following paragraphs set out the formulas for the "triggering mechanism" that automatically extends unemployment compensation benefits for an additional thirteen weeks during a period of economic recession. See the text discussion, p. 155.]*

(d) (1) There is a national "on" indicator for a week if for each of the three most recent calendar months ending before such week, the rate of insured unemployment (seasonally adjusted) for all States equaled or exceeded 4.5 per centum. . . .

(2) There is a national "off" indicator for a week if for each of the three most recent calendar months ending before such week, the rate of insured unemployment (seasonally adjusted) for all States was less than 4.5 per centum. . . .

State "On" and "Off" Indicators

(e) (1) There is a State "on" indicator for a week if the rate of insured unemployment under the State law for the period consisting of such week and the immediately preceding twelve weeks—

(A) equaled or exceeded 120 per centum of the average of such rates for the corresponding thirteen-week period ending in each of the preceding two calendar years, and

(B) equaled or exceeded 4 per centum.

(2) There is a State "off" indicator for a week if, for the period consisting of such week and the immediately preceding twelve weeks, either subparagraph (A) or subparagraph (B) of paragraph (1) was not satisfied. . . .


Payments to States

Amount Payable

Sec. 204.(a)91). There shall be paid to each State an amount equal to one-half of the sum of—

(A) the sharable extended compensation, and

(B) the sharable regular compensation,

paid to the individual under the State law. . . .

### TITLE III—FINANCING PROVISIONS

Sec. 301. Rate of Tax.

(a) . . . section 3301 of the Internal Revenue Code of 1954 is amended to read as follows:

Sec. 3301 Rate of Tax.

There is hereby imposed on every employer . . . for the calendar year 1970 and each calendar year thereafter an excise tax, with respect to having individuals in his employ, equal to 3.2 percent of the total wages . . . paid by him during the calendar year. . . .

Sec. 302. Increase in Wage Base.

Effective with respect to remuneration paid after December 31, 1971, section 3306(b) (1) of the Internal Revenue Code is amended by striking out "$3,000" each place it appears and inserting in lieu thereof "$4,200."

August 10, 1970

### NOTES

1. Technically labor leaders opposed the "triggering mechanism." Nixon had proposed that the final 13 weeks of benefits be "triggered" automatically when the unemployment rate reached 4.5 percent.

2. However, a variety of specific, nonoccupation-based regulations have reduced the number of workers eligible to receive benefits to 38%. See Michael J. Graetz and Terry L. Mashaw, *True Security: Rethinking American Social Insurance* (New Haven: Yale University Press), p. 188 ff.

# 15

# COLAs and Supplemental Security Income: The Social Security Amendments of 1972

In 1972 Congress made two fundamental changes to America's Social Security system. Each was an afterthought. Their significance was not recognized by any but a handful of legislators, nor was it understood by many in the media or among the American public. If ever the ramshackle process of constructing the American welfare state was exposed, it was through the enactment of that year's social security legislation.

The two bills, one creating a new program entitled "Supplemental Security Income," the other pegging future increases in Social Security benefits to the inflation rate, had separate legislative histories. They were linked by a common concern that the existing Social Security programs were not keeping beneficiaries from destitution, and by the political needs of the 1972 election. Supplemental Security Income (SSI) fully federalized America's three smaller Social Security poverty programs, those for the needy aged, the disabled, and the blind (Titles I, IX, and XIV of the Social Security Act of 1935), and offered recipients of these programs a guaranteed annual income. The annual cost-of-living adjustment (COLA) that was added to all Social Security benefits has ensured that beneficiaries are protected from the erosion in the real value of their monthly payments through the insidious effects of inflation, but it has also produced a massive increase in the size of the Social Security program.

Both changes emerged in the aftermath of the most ambitious attempt to reform the United States' welfare system since the original Social Security Act, President Richard Nixon's "Family Assistance Plan." Nixon's plan would have junked America's existing welfare system in favor of a simpler system of the guaranteed minimum income. Echoing a widespread feeling that the existing programs were not working, Nixon explained that "tinkering with the present welfare system is not enough. We need a complete reappraisal and re-direction of the program."[1] His plan would have accomplished this. It would not only have all but eliminated the existing welfare workhorse, the Aid to Families with Dependent Children (AFDC) program, it would have federalized the entire welfare system. The American government would have taken welfare policy from the states, and imposed the same standards across the United States. The Family Assistance Plan dominated the national debate on Social Security and welfare reform from the date of its introduction, via a nationwide Nixon television address on August 8, 1969, to its final defeat in the Senate on October 4, 1972.

Nixon's plan arose out of his perceived political need for an important domestic policy initiative, and the pressure of a number of White House aides who favored welfare reform. But the contents of the plan had been kicked around for years. Liberals had been attempting to federalize the state-run Social Security programs for a decade. The idea of a guaranteed income (also called a "negative income tax") had long been recommended by the conservative economist Milton Friedman. By 1968, it was so widely supported by economists that over one thousand signed a petition recommending it to the president.

Early in his administration, aides and advisors, led by Richard Nathan, were urging the president to nationalize the welfare system. They argued that a program that allowed the state of New York to pay an AFDC family of four $197 a month, while the same family in Mississippi received but $33, was unfair. The maze that resulted from 50 states administering four different Social Security antipoverty programs, each according to its own rules, was wasteful and inefficient. The solution was for the federal government to impose a minimum standard on all the states, and then provide the financial support to achieve it.

At the same time, other officials, this time mostly in the Department of Health, Education and Welfare, recommended that the new administration scuttle the AFDC program and replace it with a guaranteed annual income. The unpopularity of the AFDC, then America's principal welfare program, was widespread. Few could argue the program was a success, and it was exploding in size. In

1960 there were fewer than three million AFDC cases. In 10 years the number had grown to 8.4 million. Adopting in its place a guaranteed annual income was a view supported by economists, social welfare experts, and senior government officials alike.

The idea of a guaranteed annual income is simple. The federal government sets a minimum income level for all Americans. Americans who earn less than that amount receive a cash payment to bring them up to the minimum level. For example, if the minimum income level was set at $10,000 and an individual only earned $9,000 a year, that person would receive an additional $1,000 from the government.[2] Economists and social welfare experts believed such a policy would be far easier to operate. It would substantially reduce administrative overhead and inefficiencies, ensure the same treatment for all Americans, and be less degrading to recipients. However, there is one compelling argument against the idea: It could be very expensive. In 1972, bringing every American up to a guaranteed income equal to the poverty line was estimated by some experts to cost upwards of 30 or 40 billion dollars.

Cost notwithstanding, senior Nixon advisors, including the secretary of Health, Education, and Welfare, Robert Finch, and Daniel Patrick Moynihan, pushed the idea. In the spring of 1969 a welfare policy subcommittee headed by Finch put the ideas of federalizing welfare and the guaranteed annual income together into a program called the "Family Security System." The claim is that Finch thought the program would be politically popular, but its joking internal working title, the "Christian Working Man's Anti-Communist National Defense Rivers and Harbors Act of 1969," suggests that most adherents had a pretty good idea of what they would be up against.

Even within the administration the debate was fierce. Arthur Burns, Nixon's chief domestic economic advisor, vigorously fought the program. Many others joined him, including Vice President Agnew. In their view, the proposed reforms were too expensive. Moreover, to them, the idea of guaranteeing income to someone, regardless of whether he or she worked or even tried to find work, was anathema. They also shared the traditional Republican skepticism about vesting large social programs in the federal government. Their opposition forced revisions to the program, in particular the addition of strong work incentives. A portion of any income earned would be "disregarded" in computing the size of the cash payment. This raised the price tag by an estimated $10 billion. In the course of internal debate the program became renamed the Family Assistance Plan (FAP), for, in the minds of many GOP aides, the "Family Security System" sounded too much like a New Deal name.

In classic Nixon style, the president decided to support the program in June 1969, but kept the decision a secret from the anti-FAP officials in his administration before his television speech. In his national address, President Nixon startled America by proposing "that the Federal Government build a foundation under the income of every American family with dependent children that cannot care for itself, wherever in America that family may live."[3] Nixon went on to promise that his program would not lower the benefits to any welfare recipient anywhere in the United States. Welfare experts and elite opinion seemed to welcome the speech, which received many favorable newspaper editorials.

Then came the details. The guaranteed income for a family of four was to be set at $1,600 a year. The first $720 of earned income would not be counted in calculating this amount. These levels were set not because they had any particular meaning, but out of financial exigency. That's how much the administration felt it could afford to spend on the program. To honor Nixon's promise that no one's benefits would be cut, states that were already paying more than this amount through their AFDC programs were required to supplement the FAP payments up to their existing levels. All able-bodied heads of family, except for women with preschool children, were required to accept work or work training. Finally, all dependent children were guaranteed income unconditionally.

As these details emerged, huge opposition gathered. Yet, because no one could figure out if this was a liberal or a conservative reform, who was in this opposition defied easy logic. The Teamsters Union, the NAACP, and the Methodist Church, for example, lobbied against the FAP, while the League of Women Voters, the chair of the Civil Rights Commission, and Jewish and Catholic relief organizations supported it.

Three opponents were particularly powerful. The first was state governors. In their view, the FAP would not help them with their largest caseload expense, the poor who were not in, nor likely ever to enter, the workforce. Forty-two states were already paying above the FAP minimum, and these governors would not likely see their welfare expenses fall significantly. All the FAP would do was to force them to adhere to additional federal regulations. The second opponent was the AFL-CIO. Labor had two problems with the FAP. First, it appeared to undercut one the unions' critical concerns, the minimum wage. One could see the minimum wage as a sort of "guaranteed hourly income" and Nixon was proposing to replace it with a guaranteed annual income, making the former redundant. Also, FAP recipients would be entering the workforce, in all likelihood, at jobs below the minimum wage. Support for the minimum wage meant opposition to the FAP. A more selfish reason for labor opposition was the hostility of the American Federation of State, County, and Municipal Employees, a member of the AFL-CIO. The AFSCME recognized the FAP as a threat to the jobs of its social workers and thus encouraged the AFL-CIO to fight the plan.

Claiming to represent welfare recipients, the National Welfare Rights Organization also attacked the FAP. The NWRO was an organization almost entirely composed of those on the New York City welfare rolls and their political supporters. At the income levels proposed in Nixon's plan, the FAP had little to offer them. Most FAP monies would go to the working poor, and to the rural poor of the South. The NWRO at first demanded a huge increase in the guaranteed income, and, when this was not forthcoming, accused the Nixon administration of racism, and became uncompromisingly hostile to the FAP. The NWRO by itself was not a large organization, but many liberals believed that, as an authentic voice of the poor, its opposition meant that they should oppose the program as well.

These liberals found themselves strangely allied with many conservatives. For some of these conservatives, it was an issue of cost. For those in the South, where desegregation was still under way, it was yet another unwanted federal intrusion. Echoing a southern argument dating back to 1935, they remonstrated that a guaranteed income would only produce an idle poor. In the words of Rep. Phil M. Landrum (Dem., GA), "there's not going to be anybody left to roll those wheelbarrows and press those shirts."[4]

In this unpromising environment, Nixon's Family Assistance Plan was introduced in the House of Representatives. Wilbur Mills (Dem., AR), the powerful chair of the Ways and Means Committee, was once again the key legislator. Mills' recent attention to Social Security had focused on a large benefit increase that had passed in 1969 (with a second to follow in 1971). This was a product of the sense that an ever-wealthier America should be much more generous to its senior citizens. Nixon's plan arguably made the same point about America's poor. Mills, though a fiscal conservative, believed the FAP to be sound. He discovered, to his disappointment, that southern Democrats could not be budged, but once convinced that Nixon and the House Republican leaders would keep the GOP united behind the legislation, he believed that, with a little sweetening, he could find the votes to pass it. The sweetener was a federal reimbursement to the 42 states that would need to make supplementary welfare payments, dampening the revolt of the governors. His strategy for passage, as it has long been for the chair of the Ways and Means Committee, was simple. He would get the bill quickly through committee and then place it on the floor under a closed rule that sharply limited debate. This he did. Opponents were caught flat-footed, and, on April 16, 1970, the House voted 243 to 155 for the FAP.

But the FAP bill was savaged in the Senate. Special interests, aware of Mills' power, had saved their fire for the senior chamber. The Senate Finance Committee was chaired by Louisiana Senator Russell Long (Dem.). When it came to the poor this Long, unlike his uncle Huey, had no intention of sharing the wealth. Long pointedly noted that he would never vote for a bill that favored giving the poor money instead of work. His committee voted the FAP down.

While conservatives were thrashing the program inside the committee, liberals were similarly slamming it outside the committee. Sen. Eugene McCarthy (Dem., MN), at the behest of the NWRO, was holding a second set of "informal" hearings. This was just an excuse for the left publicly to berate the program, which McCarthy referred to as the "Family Annihilation Plan." This set of hearings endorsed a guaranteed income of $6,400, with no work requirement. This income level would have placed half of all Americans on the welfare rolls, and was little better than a political fantasy. A frustrated Nixon administration believed it had the votes to win on the floor, but could do nothing about McCarthy or Long. Ultimately, the Senate placed the FAP in a massive Social Security and foreign trade bill that, after a filibuster of the FAP section, died in the last days of 1970.

The following year, the administration tried again. The Family Assistance Plan floor was raised to $2,400 and other revisions were made to improve its chances in Congress. The increased FAP floor now meant that 22 states would not have to pay a dime in AFDC costs, although federal expenditures would increase. As reintroduced, the FAP would operate very simply. Using minimum national standards, the federal government would pay the stipulated benefits to a recipient family. A state could choose to have a higher level of benefits. If it did so, the federal government would pay the family the additional benefits and then bill the state.

The Ways and Means Committee liked these changes, and went even further. In consultation with the Social Security Administration and the HEW, it made similar changes to the other Social Security poverty programs, those for the blind, disabled, and needy aged. Mills and the ranking Republican committee member, John Byrnes (WI), redrafted the legislation to federalize these three programs. Mirroring the FAP reforms, the programs would be rolled into one new program, "supplemental security income," that would be completely funded and operated by the federal government. SSI recipients would be guaranteed an income of $130 a month (quickly raised to $155), at that time the size of the median monthly Old-Age and Survivors Insurance program (OASI) check. There would be no work requirement, but a portion of earned income would be excluded from an individual's reported income in calculating the size of the payment to them to reward work. States would remain free to offer higher benefits if they wished. Just as for the FAP, the federal government would bill them for the additional amount.

Making all the poverty programs consistent was one motive for this reform. But there were others. Unlike the initial FAP proposal, supplemental security income would save states money. This, in turn, might lessen their demand for "revenue sharing," a Nixon idea to return a portion of the federal general revenues back to the states that both Mills and Byrnes detested. Federal officials had also convinced the two that reform of these poverty programs was necessary to preserve the OASI program itself. Every year there were demands for sizable OASI benefit increases on the grounds that the existing benefits did not provide a livable pension. Politically, this was a difficult argument to resist. But because the OASI program is not means-tested, an across-the-board benefit increase includes all beneficiaries, no matter how wealthy they are. The result was that benefit increases were not only dubious as a matter of policy, but also very expensive. The sizable annual increases being voted in the early 1970s could sink the program. The SSI program could be used to target payment increases to the poorest Social Security recipients (those falling below the SSI-guaranteed income line) and thereby end the political demands for large Social Security benefit increases.

A second method to end demands for benefit increases was being discussed at the same time. Many Social Security experts advanced the idea of linking the growth of Social Security benefits to the growth in the cost of living. A cost-of-living adjustment (COLA) could be made annually to the Social Security benefit using the Consumer Price Index (CPI), which measures inflation. A yearly adjustment based on the CPI would be predictable, and would preserve the real purchasing power of the OASI benefit. It would also take Social Security increases out of the hands of politicians. President Nixon had asked his Department of Health, Education, and Welfare to study this plan early in his administration, and it had already been added, unsuccessfully, as an amendment to several Social Security bills. However, Arthur Burns opposed the COLA as too expensive, so the administration never supported the idea.

Mills and Byrnes far preferred the SSI approach to the COLA approach. As the senior members of the committee that had originated Social Security increases, they did not want to lose this discretionary power. So the SSI stayed in the bill; the COLA stayed out.

That June, after another 5 percent increase in Social Security benefits was added to the bill, the FAP again passed the House, this time by a vote of 234 to 187. Once more the Senate killed it. Senator Long was far more interested in the benefit increase than in the FAP. On March 12, 1971, he had offered a Senate floor amendment to raise benefits by a full 10 percent. Long, a master of the legislative process, had craftily placed this amendment onto a bill raising the debt ceiling. The national debt ceiling sets the amount of money the federal government is legally allowed to borrow. When the government is in deficit, as it was during this era, it must shut down unless Congress votes an adequate debt ceiling, as otherwise it cannot borrow the money it needs to operate. Debt ceiling bills are thus "must pass" legislation. Only the most radical members of Congress would vote to shut down the government. Therefore, amendments to these bills are almost guaranteed to become law. This was Long's strategy, and it worked. In March 1971, Social Security benefits were raised 10 percent. His benefit increase passed, Long was content to the let the FAP languish in committee.

Thus it was that a third round of the battle for the FAP began in 1972. But politics changes in an election year. Especially, if it is an election year when the chair of the Ways and Means Committee decides to run for president. Wilbur Mills' campaign for the Oval

Office was a spectacular failure, but the stances he took in the House to further his ambitions were key to the destruction of the FAP, and key to the passage of the SSI and the cost-of-living adjustment to Social Security benefits.

In early 1972, the Senate Finance Committee resumed consideration of the House welfare bill that had passed the previous year. Long again showed his preferences by rewriting the House bill to double the Social Security benefit increase it contained. But that generosity was not extended to the FAP. Long and the other nine senators who opposed the program stripped the FAP out of the bill before reporting it to the floor. The Finance Committee offered its own substitute in its place. Reflecting Long's focus on work, the committee created a program to enroll heads of AFDC families in guaranteed jobs paying $2,400 a year. Supporters of the FAP had now left but two cards they could play, a Senate floor amendment reintroducing the program or renewed action by Wilbur Mills in the House. Neither succeeded.

Mills, running for the presidency, had discovered that governors still preferred revenue sharing even to a revised FAP. Mills wanted gubernatorial support, so he reversed his opposition to revenue sharing, abandoning the FAP. The fate of the FAP thus hinged on a successful Senate floor amendment. Sen. Abraham Ribicoff (Dem., CT), who had been Kennedy's Health, Education, and Welfare secretary and was now the Senate's leading FAP supporter, was willing to try. He reached out to Nixon in an effort to fashion a compromise program that could win on the floor. But Nixon, also running for president, was no longer interested. He had reached the conclusion that it was better to run as someone who had tried to reform welfare than as a defender of the reform that passed. Ribicoff went ahead and offered his amendment to the Finance Committee's Social Security and welfare bill. It was defeated. The Senate also eliminated the Finance Committee's alternative program before passing the bill on a 68 to 5 roll call vote.

The Senate bill included the SSI. Even though it was essentially a small-scale FAP, it had been added via a friendly amendment from Senator Long. The vote was 75 to 0. Why did the SSI not share the same fate as the FAP? First, the governors liked it. It promised immediately financial relief to the states. Second, the SSI, unlike the FAP, covered individuals who were thought to be more "deserving" of assistance—the blind, the disabled, and the needy aged. This group did not arouse the political hostility often shown AFDC recipients. And third, it flew in under the radar. Politicians and special interests were so caught up in the FAP debate that no one noticed a very significant reform that was buried in it.

On October 17, Congress enacted the Social Security Amendments of 1972. On the floor of the House, Rep. Robert Price (Rep., TX) called the bill "an emasculated, mangled, and toothless shadow of the original proposal." He was right. But thanks to the little-understood SSI provisions, Rep. Mills was equally correct when he noted that "this bill contains the most far-reaching provisions of any Social Security bill since we passed Medicare in 1965."[5]

By that time Mills' run for the presidency was over. But earlier in the year, while the Senate was still debating the FAP, he had moved vastly to increase future Social Security benefits as part of his campaign. Mills, the longtime opponent of financially irresponsible benefit increases, shocked everyone that February by introducing legislation for a 20 percent across-the-board increase. Mills' power virtually guaranteed its passage, but President Nixon quickly announced his opposition because of the cost of the increase, and a veto seemed certain. Beneath the increase, Mills had, with little notice, added the COLA provision. Strong lobbying by the American Association of Retired Persons and other senior citizen groups had convinced candidate Mills to reverse his opposition to COLAs and to support ending the discretionary benefit increases that had been a major power of his own committee.

On June 30, 1972, the Senate began consideration of the benefit increase, aware of Nixon's veto threat. Having learned a trick from Senator Long, Frank Church (Dem., ID) added the 20 percent across-the-board increase as an amendment to yet another debt ceiling bill. Nixon could not veto that. Church then added a second amendment to include the COLA provision. Both easily passed. Despite its profound change to the Social Security system, placing future Social Security benefits on "automatic pilot" rather than through congressional discretion, there was virtually no debate. Nixon, anticipating the death of the FAP, and needing a different Social Security success on which to campaign, made no complaint, and signed the bill into law on July 1, 1972.

The SSI and the Social Security COLA were the two of the quietest changes to America's Social Security system. While the United States was caught up in a series of controversial benefit expansions and President Nixon's ambitious welfare reform, Congress silently passed one bill that transformed the future growth of Social Security benefits and another that remade the American welfare system for over three million recipients. Enacting the social security COLA successfully removed Social Security increases from congressional politics, and has produced a sizable growth in benefits to the 49 million Americans in the Social Security system. The present Supplemental Security Income program serves over 6 million Americans at a cost of $30 billion (with states that have more generous programs paying an additional $3 billion). Thanks to the Social Security COLA, which has virtually ended the need for a program for the needy aged, the vast majority of beneficiaries are blind or disabled. The SSI is America's first guaranteed annual income program. In 2000, the federal minimum income level for eligible individuals was set at $512 a month for someone living alone and $769 for a couple. In 2000, the average payment to these individuals to raise them to the minimum income level was $379 a month. Though the legislative process as likely appalled the democratic theorist as much as the welfare expert, the SSI and the COLA have profoundly changed the lives of those in the Social Security programs. They are the truly significant Social Security reforms that occurred while no one was looking.

## 15a. Cost-of-Living Increases in the Social Security Program*

An Act to provide for a four-month extension of the present temporary level in the public debt limitation, and for other purposes.

*Be it enacted by the Senate and House of Representatives of the United States of America in Congress Assembled . . .*

### TITLE II—AMENDMENTS TO THE SOCIAL SECURITY PROGRAM

. . . Automatic Adjustments in Benefits and in the Contribution and Benefit Base

Adjustments in Benefits

Sec. 202. (a) (1) Section 215 of the Social Security Act is amended by adding at the end thereof the following new subsection:

Cost-of-Living Increases in Benefits

(i) (1) For purposes of this subsection—

(A) the term 'base quarter' means (i) the calendar quarter ending on June 30 in each year after 1972, or (ii) any other calendar quarter in which occurs the effective month of a general benefit increase under this title *[paragraph (A) is defining a base quarter as a quarter during which social security payments were increased]*;

(B) the term 'cost-of-living computation quarter' means a base quarter . . . in which the Consumer Price Index *[the CPI is a monthly index of inflation calculated by the Department of Labor]* . . . exceeds by not less than 3 per centum, such Index in the later of (i) the last prior cost-of-living computation quarter . . . , or (ii) the most recent calendar quarter in which occurred the effective month of a general benefit increase . . . *[paragraph (B) is defining a quarter in which the CPI index is 3% higher than the most recent base quarter as a "cost-of-living computation quarter"]*.

(C) the Consumer Price Index for a base quarter, a cost-of-living computation quarter, or any other calendar quarter shall be the arithmetical mean of such index for the 3 months in such quarter *[paragraph (C) is defining the quarterly CPI as the average of the CPIs of every month in that quarter]*.

(2) (A) (i) The Secretary shall determine each year beginning with 1974 . . . whether the base quarter . . . in such year is a cost-of-living computation quarter.

(ii) If the Secretary determines that such base quarter is a cost-of-living computation quarter, he shall, effective with the month of January of the next calendar year . . . increase the benefit amount of each individual who for such month is entitled to benefits . . . , and the primary insurance amount of each other individual under this title, by an amount derived by multiplying each such amount . . . by the same percentage (rounded to the nearest one-tenth of 1 percent) as the percentage by which the Consumer Price Index for such cost-of-living computation quarter exceeds such index for the most recent prior calendar year which a base quarter . . . *[This paragraph mandates that the secretary of the Treasury shall raise Social Security payments by the increase in the CPI, to take effect in the January following the occurrence of a cost-of-living quarter.]*

July 1, 1972

*This is a portion of larger untitled bill to raise the debt ceiling.

# 15b. Social Security Amendments of 1972

An Act to Amend the Social Security Act and for other
purposes.

*Be it enacted by the Senate and House of Representatives of the United States of
America in Congress assembled,* That this Act ... may be cited as the "Social
Security Amendments of 1972."

**TITLE III—SUPPLEMENTAL SECURITY ASSISTANCE FOR THE AGED,
BLIND, AND DISABLED**

Sec. 301. Effective January 1, 1974, title XVI of the Social Security Act
is amended to read as follows:

**TITLE XVI—SUPPLEMENTAL SECURITY INCOME FOR THE AGED,
BLIND, AND DISABLED**

Purpose; Appropriations

Sec. 1601. For the purpose of establishing a national program to provide supplementary security income to individuals who have attained age
65 or are blind or disabled, there are authorized to be appropriated sums
sufficient to carry out this title.

Basic Eligibility for Benefits

Sec. 1602. Every aged, blind, or disabled individual who is determined
... to be eligible on the basis of his income and resources shall, in accordance with and subject to the provisions of this title, be paid benefits by
the Secretary of Health, Education, and Welfare.

Part A—Determination of Benefits
Definition of Eligible Individual

Sec. 1611. (a)(1) Each aged, blind, or disabled individual who does not
have an eligible spouse and—

(A) whose income ... is at a rate of not more than $1,560 for the
calendar year 1974 or any calendar year thereafter, and

(B) whose resources ... are not more than (i) in case such individual
has a spouse with whom he is living, $2,250, or (ii) in case such indi-
vidual has no spouse with whom he is living, $1,500,
shall be an eligible individual for purposes of this title.

(2) Each aged, blind, or disabled individual who has an eligible
spouse and—

(A) whose income (together with the income of such spouse) ...

is at a rate of not more than $2,340 for the calendar year 1974 or any calendar year thereafter, and

(B) whose resources (together with the resources of such spouse) . . . are not more than $2,250,

shall be an eligible individual for purposes of this title.

### Amounts of Benefits

(b) (1) The benefit under this title for an individual who does not have an eligible spouse shall be payable at the rate of $1,560 for the calendar year 1974 and any calendar year thereafter, reduced by the income . . . of such individual *[those with an eligible spouse received $2,340, reduced by their own or their spouse's income]*. . . .

### TITLE VI—GRANTS TO STATES FOR SERVICES TO THE AGED, BLIND, OR DISABLED

Sec. 601. For the purpose of encouraging each State, as far as practicable under the conditions in such State, to furnish rehabilitation and other services to help needy individuals who are 65 years of age or over, are blind, or are disabled to attain or retain capability for self-support or self-care, there is hereby authorized to be appropriated for each fiscal year . . . a sum sufficient to carry out the purposes of this title. . . .

### Payments to States

Sec. 603. (a) From the sums appropriated therefor, the Secretary shall . . . pay to each State which has a plan approved under this title, for each quarter—

(1) . . . an amount equal to the sum of the following proportions of the total amount expended during such quarter as found necessary by the Secretary of Health, Education, and Welfare for the proper and efficient administration of the State plan—

(A) 75 per centum of so much of such expenditures as are for—

(i) services which are prescribed . . . to applicants for or recipients of supplementary security income benefits under title XVI *[the Supplemental Security Assistance Program]* to help them attain or retain capability for self-support or self-care, or

(ii) other services, specified by the Secretary, as likely to prevent or reduce dependency, so provided to such applicants or recipients, or

(iii) any of the services . . . which the Secretary may specify as appropriate for individuals who . . . have been or are likely to become applicants for or recipients of supplementary secu-

rity income benefits under title XVI, if such services are requested by such individuals and are provided to such
individuals in accordance with the next sentence, or

(iv) the training of personnel employed or preparing for employment by the State agency or by the local agency administering the plan in the political subdivision; plus

(B) one-half of so much of such expenditures (not included under
subparagraph (A)) . . . as are for services provided . . . to applicants
for or recipients of supplemental security income benefits under title
XVI, and to individuals requesting such services who . . . have been
or are likely to become applicants for or recipients of such benefits;
plus

(C) one-half of the remainder of such expenditures. . . .

### REPEAL OF TITLES I, X, AND XIV OF THE SOCIAL SECURITY ACT

Sec. 303. (a) Effective January 1, 1974, titles I, X, and XIV of the Social
Security Act are repealed.

October 30, 1972

## NOTES

1. Joan Huff, *Nixon Reconsidered* (New York: Basic Books, 1994), p. 118.
2. This could also be structured so that cash payment is proportionate to how
far one falls below the "line." One could be given, for example, 80 percent of the
gap between his or her income and the guaranteed minimal level.
3. Irwin Unger, *The Best of Intentions: The Triumphs and Failures of the Great Society
Under Kennedy, Johnson and Nixon* (New York: Doubleday, 1996), p. 113.
4. Vincent J. Burke and Vee Burke, *Nixon's Good Deed: Welfare Reform* (New York:
Columbia University Press, 1974), p. 147.
5. *Congressional Quarterly Almanac* Vol. XXVIII (1972), p. 914.

# 16

# The Special Supplemental Nutrition Program for Women, Infants, and Children: The WIC Program (1972)

The Special Supplemental Nutrition Program for Women, Infants, and Children—the WIC program—is today the third largest form of food assistance in the United States. Over 7 million Americans participate in this program, at an annual cost of over 4 billion dollars. Enacted as a two-year experiment in 1972, it has become one of the most important, and by most accounts, successful of America's welfare programs.

The origins of the WIC program are to be found in a double failure. Neither the War on Poverty nor food stamps, the largest food assistance program, proved able to eliminate hunger in America. Then, efforts by liberals in Congress to create a national nutrition program for all children fell before a Richard Nixon veto in 1971. Each, in its own way, provided the impetus for a new program to grant food aid to needy mothers and their young children.

The 1960s had been marked by a number of initiatives to end poverty. In an optimistic era, their success was presumed. But in 1967, a series of dramatic reports put the lie to that belief. In the spring, a group of senators went to the Mississippi delta for a routine investigation of the War on Poverty programs. What they found was a level of hunger, even starvation, they did not know existed. At almost the same time, the Physicians' Task Force on Hunger visited Mississippi and Appalachia under the aegis of the Field Foundation. It found a rural landscape of emaciated and anemic children. Then, the CBS television network aired a series entitled "Hunger in America," which broadcast vivid images of a different, desperate America into millions of middle-class homes. Hunger became a major national issue. Whatever the merits of existing welfare programs, they did not seem to be reaching many of those most in the grip of terrible poverty.

The most important political outcome of these events was that a small group of senators determined to develop new policies to end hunger. They were led by Joseph Clark (Dem., PA) and Robert F. Kennedy (Dem., NY), both of whom had participated in the Mississippi delta investigation. Kennedy, of course, was no ordinary senator. The brother of a president, and by 1967 a major political figure in his own right, he had been particularly upset by what he had seen, and his interest in the issue ensured that it would remain at the top of America's political agenda. Policymakers recognized Kennedy's influence. A Department of Agriculture official put it bluntly: "The big change came when Bobby Kennedy got into the act."[1]

The urban rioting in 1967 and 1968 shifted the focus from rural hunger to urban poverty. Nutrition seemed a more general problem. In 1968, the Senate Select Committee on Nutrition and Human Needs was established to examine this issue. The same year, an experimental Child Care Food Program was created. It gave cash and foods to child care facilities in areas that were impoverished or had a high concentration of working mothers. Behind the scenes, officials in the Departments of Agriculture and Health, Education, and Welfare were meeting to develop a policy that would best address the problem of hunger, and meet the demands coming from the Senate.

These policymakers came to believe pregnant women and infants in low-income areas should be the primary focus of an antihunger program. Malnutrition during the first years of life irreversibly impairs both physical and mental development. A nutrition program first needed to address this critical group. Their conclusions were reinforced by the 1968 report of "A Citizen's Board of Inquiry into Hunger and Malnutrition." These outside experts too recommended a program of assistance to supplement the diets of impoverished infants and pregnant women. That year, as the Poor People's Campaign marched in the streets of Washington, Orville Freeman, the secretary of Agriculture, announced the creation of a pilot program that would donate commodities to supplement the diets of these groups, over and above that offered them through food stamps. But because the program had not been enacted by Congress, it was very small.

The assassination of Robert Kennedy in 1968 removed the issue's most important advocate, but the pressure to end hunger did not abate. In 1969, President Nixon convened the White House Conference on Food, Nutrition, and Health. The conference produced a consensus on the need for a larger program that would supplement the diet of infants and pregnant women. President Nixon himself endorsed this conclusion. But there was no agreement on how the program should operate.

To liberals, the solution was to expand the National School Lunch Act. This act, dating from 1946, set up state grant-in-aid programs to subsidize lunches for school children. The programs operated something like the public assistance programs in the Social Security Act. In 1962, it had been amended to offer special assistance to schools in low-income areas. (Today school lunches rank as the second largest food assistance program in the United States.) Liberals sought to make subsidized school lunches available to every American school child and to add a program for school breakfasts as well. The leaders in this effort were the erstwhile and future Democrat presidential candidates Hubert Humphrey (Dem., MN) and George McGovern (Dem., SD).

In 1971 such a plan was included as part of a larger child development proposal. But President Nixon vetoed the bill. Nixon opposed, first and foremost, the proposal's $2.1 billion price tag. But he, and members of Congress who had opposed the bill, also complained that there was no evidence that such a massive and complicated set of policies, benefits, and regulations would work.

The next year Humphrey returned to the fight. This time he narrowed his goals, dropping the idea of a comprehensive child development program in favor of a universal school lunch program. While he was working on this bill, he was approached by Rodney Leonard, the president of the Community Nutrition Institute, a food policy think tank that had been created in 1969. Leonard, working with a staff member of the Senate Agriculture Committee, had written a draft of a bill that would offer supplemental dietary assistance to poor pregnant women and infants at a cost of $20 million a year. The bill was influenced by Secretary Freeman's 1969 pilot program, but also by the success of local programs run by St. Jude's Hospital in Memphis and the Johns Hopkins Hospital in Baltimore. The Senate staffer, James Thornton, had encountered these programs in the course of his work. Humphrey agreed to sponsor the Leonard-Thornton plan as an amendment to the school lunch bill.

The amendment called for federal funding of a "special supplemental food program." However, the actual program would be run by the states. In other words, it would be midway between the Social Security public assistance programs and a fully federalized program. Pregnant women and infants would be eligible for assistance in obtaining specific, nutritious foods to supplement their diets, if competent professionals determined them to be at "nutritional risk."

Humphrey's amendment was not received enthusiastically. The Department of Agriculture opposed the plan. It now believed that narrowly targeted nutrition programs were not effective. Nixon was against the idea as well. The Senate Agriculture Committee struck the amendment from the bill. Yet, Humphrey pressed on. When the school lunch bill reached the floor of the Senate, Humphrey reintroduced his amendment. The legislation's floor manager made it clear that he considered the WIC program an unfriendly amendment because of its cost. But Humphrey, still the titular leader of the Democratic party, lobbied every senator, and St. Jude's Hospital had prepared a photo display of a severely malnourished little girl that Humphrey deployed with great effectiveness. On August 16, 1972, by a vote of 67 to 16, senators added the program to the bill, which then passed unanimously.

Humphrey's problem was now the House of Representatives. It had already passed its version of the bill before his amendment had been added in the Senate. Nongermane amendments are not allowed in the House, so the WIC program could not simply be added to the House version, or inserted into another piece of legislation. Instead the amendment had to be added in the House-Senate conference committee that would reconcile the two versions of the bill. But this looked nearly impossible. Under House rules, if an amendment was added in the conference committee, it must then obtain the unanimous consent of the House when it was returned for final approval. And even if the House would agree to authorize the program, there would be no funding. For the appropriations bill, too, had already been passed.

Carl Perkins (Dem., KY), the leader of the House delegation to the conference committee, solved the latter problem by finding an obscure loophole, Section 32 of the Agriculture Act of 1935, that allowed some agricultural expenditures without going through the normal congressional appropriation process. Since the WIC program would be under the Department of Agriculture, Humphrey and Perkins could make use of this provision. Next, Perkins approached Albert Quie (MN), his GOP counterpart on the delegation. If Quie could be brought on board, his fellow Republicans might follow his lead and not object to adding the program.

On September 13, 1972 the committee completed its work. Because of the rule against nongermane amendments, Perkins had to report back that the House was in "technical disagreement" with the WIC amendment. Perkins' strategy was to note that fact, but to focus upon approval for the entire bill. He would then return to the amendment and ask for unanimous consent that the House withdraw its disagreement to it. He thus opened debate by urging passage of the conference report. He was followed by Rep. Quie. Quie strongly supported Perkins, noting that the WIC program was a pilot program that included provisions for a full examination of its effectiveness. Should it prove effective, it could be expanded. Perkins had succeeded in convincing Quie of the merits of the program, and with the two party floor managers in agreement, the House voted 342 to 34 to approve the conference report. Perkins then asked that there be no objection to withdrawing the technical disagreement to including the WIC program in the National School Lunch Program amendments. Any one of the 34 members who had opposed the bill could have spoken and scuttled the program. None did so. A reluctant President Nixon signed the bill into law on September 26, 1972.

The first WIC program began in Kentucky in early 1964. By 1980, the last remaining state, Wyoming, had entered the program. In 1975, after favorable findings about its effectiveness, the WIC program was made permanent. Today the program is delivered through 10,000 sites across America. Pregnant women and children under the age of five who are in families whose income is at or below 185 percent of the federal poverty line, and who are determined to be nutritionally at risk, are eligible for benefits.[2] Beneficiaries receive coupons or checks with which to obtain a variety of high-nutrient foods to supplement their diets. These benefits amount to about $30 per month per recipient.

Though there are skeptics, the large majority of investigations have found the WIC program to be successful. One study estimates that the program averts over one billion dollars a year in medical expenses, while a number of others find genuine improvements in nutrition and health due to the program.[3] The Special Supplemental Nutrition Program for Women, Infants, and Children is today a significant component of the American welfare system.

## 16. Special Supplemental Nutrition Program for Women, Infants, and Children (Section 17 of the Children's Nutrition Act of 1966)

An Act to Amend the National School Lunch Act, as amended, to assure that adequate funds are available for the conduct of summer food service programs . . . and for other purposes related to expanding and strengthening the child nutrition programs.

*Be it enacted by the Senate and House of Representatives of the United States in Congress Assembled. . . .*

**SPECIAL SUPPLEMENTAL FOOD PROGRAM**

Sec. 17. (a) During each of the fiscal years ending June 30, 1973, and June 30, 1974, the Secretary *[of Health, Education, and Welfare]* shall make cash grants to the health department or comparable agency of each State for the purpose of providing funds to local health or welfare agencies or private non-profit agencies of such State serving local health or welfare needs to enable such agencies to carry out a program under which supplemental foods will be made available to pregnant or lactating women and to infants determined by competent professionals to be nutritional risks because of inadequate nutrition and inadequate income. Such program shall be operated for a two-year period and may be carried out in any area of the United States . . . *[P.L. 94–105, enacted October 7, 1975, established WIC as a permanent program.]*

(d) The eligibility of persons to participate in the program provided for under subsection (a) of this section shall be determined by competent professional authority. Participants shall be residents of areas served by clinics or other health facilities determined to have significant numbers of infants and pregnant and lactating women at nutritional risk.

(e) State or local agencies or groups carrying out any program under this section shall maintain adequate medical records on the participants assisted to enable the Secretary to determine and evaluate the benefits of the nutritional assistance provided under this section. . . .

(f) As used in this section—

(1) 'Pregnant and lactating women' . . . includes mothers from low-income populations who demonstrate one or more of the following characteristics: known inadequate nutritional patterns, unacceptably high incidence of anemia, high prematurity rates, or inadequate patterns of growth (underweight, obesity, or stunting). Such term . . . also

includes low-income individuals who have a history of high-risk pregnancy as evidenced by abortion, premature birth, or severe anemia.

(2)'Infants' . . . means children under four years of age who are in low-income populations which have shown a deficient pattern of growth, by minimally acceptable standards, as reflected by an excess number of children in the lower percentiles of height and weight. *[Currently, the law defines an infant as an individual under one year of age. Those under five years of age are titled "Children" and also eligible for the program.]*.

(3) 'Supplemental foods' shall mean those foods containing nutrients known to be lacking in the diets of populations at nutritional risks. . . .

(4) 'Competent professional authority' includes physicians, nutritionists, registered nurses, dieticians, or State or local medically trained health officials, or persons designated by physicians or State or local medically trained health officials as being competent professionally to evaluate nutritional risks.

September 26, 1972

## NOTES

1. Peter K. Eisinger, *Toward an End to Hunger in America* (Washington: The Brookings Institution, 1998), p. 78.

2. In 2001, the maximum income for a family of four was $32,653. Eligibility does not guarantee inclusion in the program. Clinics have caseload maximums and must prioritize among applicants.

3. Sheila Avruch and Alicia Puente Cackley, "Savings Achieved by Giving WIC Benefits to Women Prenatally," *Public Health Reports* 110 (January-February, 1995), pp. 27–34.

# 17

# The Earned Income Tax Credit

The Earned Income Tax Credit (EITC), perhaps the least controversial American antipoverty program, has also become one of its
most important. In monetary terms, it provides as much assistance
as the Food Stamp program and the Temporary Assistance for
Needy Families (TANF) program combined. While other poverty
programs remain controversial, and are always targets for budget
cuts, the EITC has kept its political popularity. Presidents as politically opposed as Ronald Reagan and Bill Clinton have been great
supporters of the program. The reason for the program's popularity is that it is explicitly directed at the "working poor." Through
the EITC, low-income workers receive a tax credit that reduces the
income tax they owe. In 2001, for example, a family that earned
less than $31,152 could receive a tax credit that reduced their in-
come tax by up to $3,888.[1] Individuals who are poor, but work, have
long received the sympathy of both the American voter and the
American politician. The EITC appears to reward personal effort,
separating it from other programs targeted at the poor. Even
though half of EITC benefits go to those below the poverty line, it
has never come to be seen as a "welfare program." The unique
popularity of the program means that efforts at welfare reform have
increasingly come to rely upon it.

The origins of the EITC lay in the collapse of Richard Nixon's
Family Assistance Plan (FAP). As may be recalled, a chief opponent
of the FAP was Louisiana Senator Russell Long (Dem.). As chair of
the Senate Finance Committee, he all but scuttled Nixon's plan.
Sen. Long's complaints were many, but they centered on his dislike

of a guaranteed income for poor people based on his belief that work should be the prerequisite for any government assistance. An early advocate of what later became called "workfare," he wanted programs that encouraged welfare recipients to gain employment. He believed Nixon's plan did just the opposite. Using his position in the Finance Committee, Long crafted an alternative to the FAP. Any employable person on welfare would be required to find a job. Otherwise, he or she would be given a government job at below the minimum wage. In either case, such a person would not be able to receive cash welfare benefits. But as an added benefit for working, Long proposed offering low-income families a cash rebate equal to 10 percent of the first $4,000 of their annual earned income. Other rebates, called tax credits, were already in the U.S. tax code to encourage various economic activities that Congress wished to promote. Long was merely proposing adding another for the working poor.

Long justified this tax credit as necessary because of the ever-increasing Social Security FICA tax. The large Social Security benefit increases of this era necessitated raising this tax, and Long argued that this placed a tremendous burden on low-income workers. California Governor Ronald Reagan made a similar argument before the Finance Committee.

Using his power as chair, Long substituted his work-incentives proposal for the Nixon plan and sent the bill to the floor of the Senate in September 1972. But the FAP died in conference committee that year, and Long's tax credit died along with it. The following year, Long added his idea to a bill amending the Social Security Act, only to see it die in committee again. Long's problem was not only the rival Nixon plan, but the strong dislike for mandatory work requirements among the liberals of his own party. Though they could not stop him in the Senate, they could wait for the conference committee and gut his legislation there. Long refused to quit, however, and next added the earned income credit portion of his workfare plan to a large social services bill in 1974. He completely rewrote the bill, the product of a careful negotiation between the Ford administration, state governors, some 40 interest groups, and members of the House Ways and Means Committee, when it reached the Senate Finance Committee. Not surprisingly, the House took its revenge in the conference committee. Using President Ford's announced opposition to the tax credit, House members successfully excised Long's plan from the final bill.

In 1975, Long finally found the legislative vehicle for his earned income tax credit. The Ford administration, eager to pull America out of a recession, was desperately pushing Congress for a large tax reduction to stimulate the economy. Tax bills must start in the House, and, when the new Ways and Means Committee chair, Al Ullman (Dem., OR), took up the administration's proposed bill, he added Long's idea. Unlike Wilbur Mills, the previous chair, Ullman shared Long's dislike of cash assistance for welfare. Picking up the argument that the credit was needed to offset the rising FICA tax, Ullman broadened the EITC to include all low-income workers, not just the heads of families. This would have made it the largest means-tested social program. To contain the cost of extending the program to 28 million Americans (four times the number in Long's plan), Ullman cut the credit from 10 to 5 percent. Even at this level it was double the cost of Long's proposal. As might be expected, when the Senate Finance Committee received the Tax Reduction Act of 1975 from the House, it simply replaced Ullman's EITC with Long's. By 1975, though, Long had slightly refined the plan slowly to "phase out" the credit from 10 percent to zero, as an individual's income grew from $4,000 to $5,600.

The Tax Reduction Act was so controversial, and the politics so intense, that no one in Congress, or among the many interest groups that lobbied it, had the time or the interest to focus on the seemingly small sideshow of the EITC. (Even though its initial projected cost was $1.7 billion!) Hence there was never any debate, in either House, over its merits. President Ford had earlier opposed the earned income credit because of its cost, but his eagerness to get the tax bill through Congress quashed his desire to quibble about the EITC.

In Wilbur Mills' day, the House version would almost certainly have triumphed in the conference committee. But Mills was gone, the casualty of a personal scandal involving public drunkenness. That, and the efforts by House Democrats to strip his committee of enough power so that no one with Mills' might would ever arise again, led to a weaker House delegation to the conference committee, and to the survival of the Senate's version of the EITC.[2] On March 29, 1975, President Ford signed the EITC into law.

Thus, the politics of the EITC was rather unusual. Given its size, it ought to have been controversial. But, as one study notes, Russell Long never had to accomplish any of the steps normally thought necessary to enact a major piece of legislation. He did not have to gain popular support, assemble interest groups, convince the administration or congressional leaders, or even strike deals with his fellow members of Congress, to pass his program. All he had to do was wait for the right bill to come along and attach the EITC to it.[3]

The EITC has become among the most politically successful programs in Washington. It has been significantly expanded five times (1978, 1986, 1990, 1993, 2001). By 2000, 18.8 million Americans used the EITC, and the combined amount of their tax credits was just under $31 billion dollars. The EITC is responsible for raising over 4 million people above the poverty line. President Clinton regarded the 1993 EITC expansion as among his most significant legislative successes. Why has it been so politically successful? Its consonance with the American work ethic must be a primary factor. The EITC seems to reward the "deserving" poor. The ease with which it operates is also important: One obtains the tax credit simply by filing one's taxes and completing the proper forms. No additional bureaucracy or government intervention is needed. The focus on the working poor has enabled the EITC to avoid being labeled a "welfare program," generally the kiss of death for anti-poverty efforts. The EITC has also had the great advantage of being included in tax or budget reconciliation bills. This has exempted each EITC expansion from the need to identify its impact on government revenues, as is now required by congressional budget procedures. Finally, the nearly 19 million Americans who use the EITC constitute a potentially considerable voting bloc, hence party competition to attract the "working poor" also makes the EITC popular. These attributes suggest that the EITC will continue its growth as a major American welfare policy for some time to come.

## 17. The Earned Income Tax Credit (Title II of the Tax Reduction Act of 1975)

An Act to amend the Internal Revenue Code of 1954 to provide for a refund of 1974 individual income taxes, to increase the low income allowance and the percentage standard deduction, to provide a credit for personal exemptions and a credit for certain earned income, to increase the investment credit and the surtax exemption, to reduce percentage depletion of oil and gas, and for other purposes.

*Be it enacted by the Senate and House of Representatives of the United States of America in Congress assembled,*
    . . . This Act may be cited as the "Tax Reduction Act of 1975."

**TITLE II—REDUCTIONS IN INDIVIDUAL INCOME TAXES**

Sec. 204 Credit for Certain Earned Income.

. . . Earned Income
    (a) Allowance of Credit.—In the case of an eligible individual, there shall be allowed as a credit against the tax imposed by this chapter for the taxable year an amount equal to 10 percent of so much of the earned income for the taxable year as does not exceed $4,000.
    (b) Limitation.—The amount of the credit allowable to a taxpayer under subsection (a) for any taxable year shall be reduced (but not below zero) by an amount equal to 10 percent of so much of the adjusted gross income (or, if greater, the earned income) of the taxpayer for the taxable year as exceeds $4,000. *[Paragraphs (a) and (b) stipulate that if a taxpayer earns less than $4,000, 10% of his or her earned income can be credited to reduce his or her income tax. But if the income is greater than $4,000, the dollar amount of this credit is reduced by 10% of the amount of the income that is over $4,000.]*
    (c) Definitions.—
        . . . Earned Income.—
    (A) The term 'earned income' means—
            (i) wages, salaries, tips, and other employee compensation, plus
            (ii) the amount of the taxpayer's net earnings from self-employment for the taxable year. . . .
March 29, 1975

**NOTES**

1. The modified adjusted gross income must also be less than this amount.
2. The EITC has since been expanded to adjust for family size and to include individuals without dependents.
3. Christopher Howard, *The Hidden Welfare State: Tax Expenditures and Social Policy in the United States* (Princeton: Princeton University Press, 1997), p. 74.

# 18

# Saving Social Security: The Social Security Amendments of 1983

With the passage of the 1972 amendments, the construction of America's old-age pension system was complete. Nearly universal coverage, expanded benefits, pensions for a beneficiary's survivors, and the inclusion of a disability insurance program concluded the aims of Franklin D. Roosevelt. The program's advocates should have been able to rest on their laurels, their victory won. Yet ironically, the same amendments that completed the program also threw it into a severe financial crisis. Just 10 years after their passage, the entire system appeared to be on the brink of collapse. Social Security suddenly needed to be "saved."

Yet participants then, and now, debated exactly what they were saving the program from. For the reforms of 1983 stemmed from two very different financial problems, a predicted shortfall in the Old-Age and Survivors Insurance (OASI) Social Security trust fund and the effects of the economic policies of the new Ronald Reagan administration.

The first of these problems was undoubtedly the result of the 1972 amendments. Recall that in that year Congress added a cost-of-living adjustment to Social Security benefits. Benefits now rise with the inflation rate, as measured by the Consumer Price Index (CPI). At the time, this was thought to improve the process for determining benefit increases. But it was based upon assumptions that turned out to be wrong. Most everyone expected that, in the years ahead, inflation rates would remain within the historical norm. This was incorrect. Inflation instead raced out of control as the 1970s progressed, and by 1980 the U.S. inflation rate was four times that of the early 1970s. As the CPI exploded, so did Social Security expenditures. Even worse, the inflation rate exceeded the rate of wage increases. This unexpected situation meant that the increase in the flow of benefits paid out of the OASI trust fund was larger than the increase in the flow of revenues coming in. (Remember that Social Security is funded through a payroll tax on wages.) The situation was serious enough so that both Gerald Ford and Jimmy Carter proposed technical adjustments to remedy the problem. However, these did not turn out to be enough.

Soon, the Social Security Administration's Office of the Actuary, charged with making long-range forecasts for the solvency of the trust funds, released a prediction that all of the trust funds might be exhausted by the mid-1980s. By 1981, the OASI trust fund was expected to be in a short-run deficit. This news was all the more alarming as the Office of the Actuary's predictions had a history of being overly optimistic. For 1980, for example, it had predicted a rise in the CPI of 4.7 percent, when in fact the rate was 13.5 percent, and it had predicted a rise in wage rates of 2.4 percent, when in fact that rate turned out to be *minus* 4.9 percent.[1] Its projected trust fund shortfall of up to $200 billion thus stunned Washington.

This short-term crisis rested atop a deeper, long-term crisis. As more Americans retired, and lived longer, the ratio of workers paying into the OASI trust fund to retirees drawing out of the trust fund was falling. This demographic shift would inevitably drain the trust fund, absent reform, unless there was far faster economic growth than most experts were expecting. Moreover, the growth of Social Security (and Medicare) was itself becoming a budget problem. From 1969 to 1980, the portion of the American federal budget devoted to income maintenance and health care rose from 20 to 40 percent. Many questioned how long this could continue.

More sober members of Congress were already attempting to address this long-term problem. They were led by J.J. (Jake) Pickle (Dem., TX), a senior member of the House Ways and Means Committee, who tried to enact legislation to raise the retirement age and end the benefit penalty on those who continued to work after reaching the age of 68.[2] Both of these changes would increase the ratio of those working to those retired. His initial efforts met with little success, for one very simple reason. Absent an immediate crisis, what congressperson wanted to vote for legislation that made Social Security less generous? The Office of the Actuary's report provided that crisis.

In the spring of 1981, as members of Congress faced the necessity of Social Security reform, unexpectedly and perhaps unwisely the Reagan administration dropped a bombshell. This, the second force behind the 1983 amendments, arose out an economic problem wholly unrelated to the trust fund crisis. "Reaganomics" is the name that has been given to the ambitious economic policy of Ronald Reagan. The Reagan administration attempted to jar the American economy out of its dismal performance of the 1970s through large-scale tax and budget cuts. It found it far easier to enact the tax cuts than the spending reductions. Nevertheless, it argued that the tax cuts would stimulate the economic growth that would, in turn, raise the additional government revenues needed to fund programs.

While it never publicly retreated from this claim, behind the scenes Reagan's budget director, David Stockman, was discovering that the administration's program was going to produce massive federal budget deficits far into the future. He desperately needed to find programs he could cut, and cut fast. Among domestic programs, only Social Security was sizable enough to make a real difference. Thus, he targeted it. In addition, he recognized that the increased deficits would mean greater reliance on borrowing from the trust funds in order to fund the current federal budget.[3] It was essential that the funds be as large as possible. He therefore proposed a series of Social Security benefit cuts, specifically delaying the cost-of-living increase, reducing benefits to those who chose early retirement (retirement at age 62), and tightening the rules on obtaining disability insurance. He also added a variety of smaller cuts, including ending what were called "windfall benefits," a sort of loophole whereby one could earn substantial income outside the Social Security system, but work just enough in the system to obtain a good pension from it. Altogether, Stockman's reforms would have cut some 30 billion dollars in benefits, and they affected nearly 60 million people. Richard Schweiker, the secretary of Health and Human Services, presented this plan to Congress on May 12, 1981.

The public outcry was deafening. Democrats, not believing their good luck, offered congressional resolutions condemning the proposals, and, with "Save Our Social Security," an umbrella lobbying organization of some 125 special interest groups, in tow, ran with its attacks on Reagan's "despicable" plan.[4] The GOP ran as well—but for cover. Republican Senate Finance Chair Bob Dole (KS) offered his own substitute resolution, that "Congress shall not precipitously and unfairly penalize early retirees,"[5] in an attempt to disassociate congressional Republicans from the White House. It passed 96 to 0. The administration quickly retreated from most of its reforms. Ultimately, it was able to attract the votes to enact only one, a proposal to eliminate the minimum Social Security benefit. But even here, the public pressure was so intense that a month later Congress reversed itself and reestablished it.

The Reagan initiative derailed further Social Security reform, and now the exhaustion of the OASI trust fund loomed. Republican legislators signaled to the president that it was imperative to get the entire issue off the political agenda lest they lose the elections of 1982. The quick fix was a bill that allowed the OASI to borrow a sufficient amount from the healthier Disability and Hospital Insurance trust funds to keep it afloat until June 1983. But what should be done then? James Baker, Reagan's chief of staff, had the answer: create a national commission to study the issue.

Historically, such commissions have seldom been effective. But, with 68 percent of Americans disapproving of Reagan's stand on Social Security, the need of the administration and the Republicans was to find a way to reform the system without being blamed for the cuts that would ensue. What is interesting is why the Democrats went along. Many Democrats preferred to stall and see the president stew in his own juices. House Speaker Tip O'Neill, the party's *de facto* leader, was tempted by this idea. But he was also pressured by those in his party who believed this was a serious issue that had to be addressed, and soon. Representative Pickle, for example, had seen his reform bill defeated in the Ways and Means Committee during the melee that followed Schweiker's announcement. He made it clear that his wing of the party would continue pressing it. There were strategic reasons as well. Democrats held the upper hand on the issue. Republican fears of making cuts before the 1982 elections might force them to agree to the Democrats' preferred solution to the crisis: reforms that would increase the revenues flowing into the trust fund. If they didn't, the GOP could be blamed for the cuts. Finally, and perhaps most important, the expiration of the authority to continue borrowing from the other trust funds hemmed in O'Neill just as much as the president. Neither could see Social Security collapse.

In December 1981 the 15 members of the National Commission on Social Security Reform were appointed. Five were chosen by congressional Republicans, five by congressional Democrats, and five by the administration. Alan Greenspan, the future head of the Federal Reserve Bank, was made the chair. Throughout 1982, members of the commission attempted to negotiate a bipartisan package of Social Security reforms to save the system. Parallel negotiations took place between President Reagan, Speaker O'Neill, and their emissaries. Both sets of discussions nearly ended in failure.

The essential difference between each party's approach to saving Social Security was simple. Republicans saw the solution as reducing expenditures (cutting benefits) while the Democrats saw the solution as increasing revenues (raising taxes). Neither, however, was so bold as to clearly state these preferences.

Work ground to a halt as the election neared and partisanship took hold. "Save Social Security—Vote Democratic" was the Democratic slogan for the 1982 campaign. Most observers felt the issue did indeed produce Democratic gains in both houses of Congress. Senator Dole, a member of the national commission, blamed the loss of 13 Republican House seats on the issue and wondered aloud about the cost to the party in 1984.

Thus emboldened, the Democrats went on the offensive. Among the commission, where power had by now devolved upon a rump of members who could actually work together, Robert Ball, the Democrat leader, offered a package deal to the Republicans shortly after the election. Conceding Republican demands for a one-time delay in the cost-of-living adjustment and a small decrease in benefits for early retirees, he added a variety of revenue provisions to shore up the trust fund. But the more liberal Democrats called his concessions "premature" and, when Baker told Chairman Greenspan that the administration would not accept Ball's package, the commission deadlocked.

So action moved to the White House negotiations. Hard bargaining between Ball, a second Democrat commission member, Senator Daniel Patrick Moynihan (NY), and Stockman who, with other senior presidential aides, represented the White House, began the following January. The Democrats kept in close touch with the party's real powers, Speaker O'Neill and the House Ways and Means Committee chair, Chicago's Daniel Rostenkowski. Both sides accepted a key compromise that made a deal possible. Shoring up the trust fund must be based equally on benefit cuts and revenue increases. Still, they could not find enough mutually acceptable reforms that would both close the trust fund deficit and maintain the 50–50 formula. A series of secret meetings were arranged at James Baker's house.

The break came with an idea to tax the Social Security benefits of high-income recipients. Such a tax would bring an additional $30 billion into the OASI trust fund. This reform could be touted either as a cut or an increase in revenue and so kept the 50–50 ratio. Though it came from Democrats, President Reagan liked the idea and accepted it.

With this reform added, the negotiators had closed over $160 billion of the $200 billion shortfall in the OASI trust fund. Republicans suggested raising the retirement age to accomplish the rest. Democrats countered by arguing for a payroll tax increase to begin in 2010 if the trust fund needed it. Neither side would budge, so they decided to forward the package, still short of the $200 billion, without either of these reforms.[6]

As these politicians knew, the real problem was who was going to be blamed for the reforms. How would they be sold to Congress and the American public? O'Neill and Reagan promised they would not attack each other, and would both fight for the plan in Congress. The reforms were drawn deliberately to be opaque, complex, and confusing. Would-be critics would have to wade through a mind-numbing sheaf of complicated details just to figure out what was happening.

The next step was to return to the national commission and secure its approval of the deal. This would be the bipartisan stamp of approval needed to drive the bill through Congress. Negotiators were worried. Though a number of the commission members had at least been informed of the negotiations, the most conservative and liberal members had purposely been excluded. Now their votes were needed. The GOP right wanted, and got, a "stabilizer" added to the reforms. This was a provision to ensure that, should the trust fund fall below a set amount, the cost-of-living adjustment would be based not upon the CPI, but upon the lower of the CPI or the rate of wage increases. Commission member Lane Kirkland, head of the AFL-CIO, wanted, and got, a credit on the future payroll tax increase that led to workers being taxed slightly less than employers. After these compromises, the two parties convinced 12 commission members to vote for the final report. The Republicans were never able to get their most conservative members on board, and three voted against it.

Upon its release, numerous interest groups swung into action. The most threatening was an alliance between the 14-million-member American Association of Retired Persons and the American Federation of Independent Business. The combined opposition of retirees and small-business interests could be lethal to the bill. The latter hated a proposed increase in the self-employed payroll tax, while the former was dead set against any benefit reductions. Congressional leaders realized the bill must move through Congress fast, and must be protected from amendments. To that end Rostenkowski shoved the bill through his Ways and Means Committee with only two weeks of hearings. He would have preferred the closed rule prohibiting alterations of the bill on the House floor that had so often helped Social Security reformers in the past. But he had a problem. Perhaps the most liberal national commission member had been Claude Pepper (Dem., FL), the self-appointed congressional champion of senior citizens. Pepper had reluctantly signed onto the commission report, disappointed that the 2010 payroll tax increase had not been adopted. This would have been of no consequence except that Pepper was also chair of the House Rules Committee, and he made it clear that he was determined there would be a floor vote to impose that tax.

A compromise was fashioned. Would Pepper go along with a rule to allow only two amendments on the floor? One would be Pepper's amendment and the other Pickle's proposal, now supported by the GOP, to raise the retirement age to 67. Pepper disliked the idea of raising the retirement age, but certain that his amendment would easily pass, he offered a rule whereby the floor would vote on the two amendments, but only the amendment with the largest vote would be added to the bill.

On the floor, the Pickle amendment passed 228 to 202. Virtually the entire Ways and Means Committee, Republican and Democrat members alike, voted for it. Pepper was astonished; then angry. He could only attract half of his own party to his amendment, which went down to defeat. He then joined Bill Archer, the Texan GOP congressman and one of the three national committee members who had opposed the report, to fight the entire bill. Together they failed, as the amended Social Security reforms passed by a vote of 282 to 148.

The Senate, which could not so easily control debate, waited for the House to complete action. Its Finance Committee then took up the bill, and savaged it. Among other changes, the powerful Russell

Long (Dem., LA) forced a stronger "fail-safe" mechanism onto the bill. That is, if the trust fund amounts fell too much, benefits would automatically be cut. On the floor, 24 other amendments were debated as well.

Though the bill passed the Senate, there were fears that a conference committee would be unable to resolve the now substantial differences between the two houses. And the conference committee did stall over Long's "fail-safe" provision. Senators finally agreed to drop it if the House would allow a change in the "stabilizer" provision. House conference committee members agreed to change the stabilizer to take effect when the ratio of the total amount in the trust funds to a given year's expected payout to beneficiaries fell to below 15 percent. On every other issue, the senators deferred to their House colleagues.

The weak performance of the senators on the conference committee led to the bill's final difficulty. An annoyed Senate refused to approve a bill so weakly negotiated by its members, and Senator Dole was afraid to even bring it to a vote. It took the personal efforts of Senate Majority Leader Howard Baker (TN), Moynihan, and various lobbyists to smooth ruffled feathers and obtain final approval by a 58 to 14 vote.

The 1983 reforms were difficult to negotiate, but they did succeed in stabilizing the Social Security system. Not only was the OASI trust fund "saved," reformers thought they had closed anywhere from one half to two-thirds of the long-run Social Security deficit. In 1983 the Social Security Administration's Office of the Actuary predicted that the trust funds would last until 2063. Unfortunately, this has turned out to be an optimistic guess. By the turn of the millennium actuaries had shaved nearly thirty years off of that forecast. As a result, most experts now see a renewed crisis in the program's finances in the generation ahead. Undoubtedly, as that date approaches, we will see a reenactment of the politics and passions that surrounded the 1983 amendments to the Social Security Act.

## APPENDIX: THE MAJOR 1983 SOCIAL SECURITY REFORMS[7]

1. One-time 6-month delay in the cost-of-living adjustment
2. Addition of a "stabilizer" to the OASI trust fund
3. New federal employees and nonprofit sector employees added to the system

4. State and local governments cannot withdraw their employees from the system

5. Taxation of higher-income retirees social security benefits (one half of the benefit to be taxed for retirees with annual incomes over $25,000 if single and $32,000 if married)

6. Payroll tax for the self-employed is increased to its full level (the level equivalent to the combined employer plus employee rates of other workers)

7. Acceleration of the schedule of future payroll tax increases

8. $18 billion transferred from general revenues to the OASI trust fund to pay for benefits granted to retired military personnel

9. The "Deferred Retirement Credit" changed to favor individuals who delayed retirement to age 72

10. Increase in the retirement age to 67 by the year 2027 [this was added by Congress to the national commission's proposals]

# 18. The Social Security Amendments of 1983

An Act to assure the solvency of the Social Security Trust Funds, to reform the medicare reimbursement of hospitals, to extend the Federal supplemental compensation program, and for other purposes.

*Be it enacted by the Senate and House of Representatives of the United States of America in Congress assembled,*

## Short Title

Section 1. This Act . . . may be cited as the "Social Security Amendments of 1983."

## TITLE I—PROVISIONS AFFECTING THE FINANCING OF THE SOCIAL SECURITY SYSTEM

### Part A—Coverage
### Coverage of Newly Hired Federal Employees

Sec. 101. (a)(1) . . . the Social Security Act is amended *[by striking out the subsections excluding federal workers from the program, with the exceptions below]* . . .

(5) Service performed in the employ of the United States or any instrumentality of the United States, if such service—

(A) would be excluded from the term 'employment' for purposes of this title if the *[previous law]* had remained in effect, and

(B) is performed by an individual who (i) has been continuously in the employ of the United States or an instrumentality thereof since December 31, 1983 . . . or (ii) is receiving an annuity from the Civil Service Retirement and Disability Fund, or benefits . . . under another retirement system established by a law of the United States for employees of the Federal Government (other than for members of the uniformed services);

except . . . *[future presidents, presidential appointees, senior political executives, federal judges, and those working in the legislative branch remain excluded from social security].*

(6) Service performed in the employ of the United States or any instrumentality of the United States, if such service is performed—

(A) in a penal institution of the United States by an inmate thereof;

(B) by *[interns and student employees]*;

(C) by *[temporary employees].*

### Coverage of Employees of Nonprofit Organizations

Sec. 102. (a) *[The Social Security Act is amended to include most nonprofit employees.]*

### Duration of Agreements for Coverage of State and Local Employees

Sec. 103. (a) . . . the Social Security Act is amended to read as follows:
"Duration of Agreement

(g) No agreement under this section may be terminated, either in its entirety or with respect to any coverage group, on or after the date of the enactment of the Social Security Amendments of 1983. . . ."

### Part B—Computation of Benefit Amounts
### Shift of Cost-of-Living Adjustments to Calendar Year Basis

Sec. 111. (a) (1) Section 215(i)(2)(A)(ii) of the Social Security Act is amended by striking out "June" and inserting in lieu thereof "December." . . .

. . . (8) The amendments made by this subsection shall apply with respect to cost-of-living increases . . . after 1983. . . .

Cost-of-Living Increases to Be Based on Either Wages or Prices (whichever is lower) When Balance in OASDI Trust Funds Falls Below Specified Level.

Sec. 112 (a) Section 215(i)(1) of the Social Security Act is amended—
... (4) by inserting after subparagraph (B) *[which contains the formula to calculate the cost-of-living increases]* the following new subparagraphs:

(C) the term 'applicable increase percentage' means—

(i) with respect to a base quarter or cost-of-living computation quarter in any calendar year before 1984, or in any calendar year after 1983 and before 1989 for which the OASDI fund ratio is 15.0 or more, or in any calendar year after 1988 for which the OASDI fund ratio is 20.0 percent or more, the CPI increase percentage; and

(ii) with respect to a base quarter or cost-of-living computation quarter in any calendar year after 1983 and before 1989 for which the OASDI fund ratio is less than 15.0 percent, or in any calendar year after 1988 for which the OASDI fund ratio is less than 20.0 percent, the CPI increase or the wage increase percentage, whichever ... is the lower; ...

*[Section 112 is the "stabilizer" that mandates that when amounts in the Social Security trust fund fall below the levels specified in (i) and (ii), the cost-of-living adjustments will be made using an index of wage increases rather than by using the consumer price index.]*

Elimination of Windfall Benefits for Individuals Receiving Pensions From Noncovered Employment

Sec. 113(a) Section 215(a) of the Social Security Act is amended by adding at the end thereof the following new paragraph:

(7)(a) In the case of an individual ... who first becomes eligible after 1985 for a monthly periodic payment ... which is based in whole or in part upon his or her earnings for service which did not constitute 'employment' as defined *[under the Social Security Act]* ... the primary insurance amount of that individual ... shall be computed or recomputed. ...

*[according to a complicated computation schedule for such individual. Its effect is to lower the Social Security benefit of that individual.]*

Increase in Old-Age Insurance Benefit Amounts on Account of Delayed Retirement

Sec. 114.(a) Section 202(w)(1)(A) of the Social Security Act is amended. ...

*[with a complicated computation schedule for calculating increased monthly benefits for workers who retire after the age of 70]*

## Part C—Revenue Provisions
### Sec. 121 Taxation of social security and tier 1 railroad retirement benefits

. . . the Internal Revenue Code of 1954 . . . is amended by . . . inserting . . . the following new section:

Sec. 86 . . .

(a) In General—Gross income for the taxable year of any taxpayer . . . includes social security benefits in an amount equal to the lesser of—

>    (1) one-half of the social security benefits received during the taxable year, or

>    (2) one-half of the excess described in subsection (b)(1).

*[One half of a taxpayer's Social Security benefits will count as taxable gross income, subject to the restrictions in the following paragraphs.]*

(b) Taxpayers to Whom Subsection (A) applies—

>    (1) In General—A taxpayer is described in this subsection if—

>>        (A) the sum of—

>>>            (i) the modified adjusted gross income of this taxpayer for the taxable year, plus

>>>            (ii) one-half of the social security benefits received during the taxable year, exceeds

>>        (B) the base amount . . .

(c) Base Amount . . . means—

>    (1) except as otherwise provided in this subsection, $25,000.

>    (2) $32,000, in the case of a joint return, and

>    (3) zero, in the case of a taxpayer who—

>>        (A) is married at the close of the taxable year . . . but does not file a joint return for such year, and

>>        (B) does not live apart from spouse at all times during the taxable year. . . .

*[Paragraphs (b) and (c) restrict the requirement that taxpayers must include one half of his or her Social Security benefits as taxable income to just those taxpayers who earn more than $25,000 (this amount is increased to more than $32,000 for a married couple filing jointly, but lowered to zero for all taxpayers who are married, live apart, and don't file a joint return.]*

### Sec. 123. Acceleration of Increases in FICA Taxes . . .

*[Paragraphs (a)(1) and (a)(2) set out new dates for the imposition of higher FICA taxes on employers and employees.]*

Sec. 124 Taxes on Self-Employment Income; . . .

(a) Increase in Rates. . . . *[The Internal Revenue Code is revised to impose a Social Security payroll tax upon the self-employed equal to the combined rate of the employer and employee FICA tax, to begin after December 31, 1983.]*

## Part F—Other Financing Amendments
## Financing of Noncontributory Military Wage Credits

Sec. 151 . . . Appropriation to Trust Funds

(g)(1) Within thirty days after the date of the enactment of the Social Security Amendments of 1983, the Secretary shall determine the amount equal to the excess of . . . (A) the actuarial present value of past and future payments from *[the Social Security trust funds]* . . . , over (B) any amounts previously transferred from the Treasury to such Trust Funds pursuant to the provisions of this subsection. . . . Within thirty days after the enactment of the Social Security Amendments of 1983, the Secretary of the Treasury shall transfer the amount determined under this paragraph with respect to each such Trust Fund to such Trust Fund from amounts in the general fund of the Treasury not otherwise appropriated. *[The paragraph requires that the Treasury Department deposit monies from the general revenues into the trust funds to pay for Social Security benefits that were granted to retired military personnel.]*

(2) The Secretary shall revise the amount determined under paragraph (1) with respect to each such Trust Fund in 1985 and each fifth year thereafter. . . . Within 30 days after any such revision, the Secretary of the Treasury . . . shall transfer to such Trust Fund, from amounts in the general fund of the Treasury not otherwise appropriated, or from such Trust Fund to the general fund of the Treasury, such amounts as the Secretary of the Treasury determines necessary to take into account such revision. *[This paragraph indicates that the calculation and financial transfers required in paragraph (g)(1) must be performed annually.]*

## Accounting for Certain Unnegotiated Checks For Benefits Under the Social Security Program

Sec. 152. . . . (m)(1) The Secretary of the Treasury shall implement procedures to permit the identification of each check issued for benefits under this title that has not been presented for payment by the close of the sixth month following the month of its issuance.

(2) The Secretary of the Treasury shall, on a monthly basis, credit each of the Trust Funds for the amount of all benefit checks (including interest

thereon) drawn on such Trust fund more than 6 months previously but not presented for payment and not previously credited to such Trust Fund. . . .

*[Section 152 indicates that if a Social Security benefit check has not been cashed within six months of its issue, the amount of the check shall be restored to the trust fund from which it was issued.]*

## TITLE II—ADDITIONAL PROVISIONS RELATING TO LONG-TERM FINANCING OF THE SOCIAL SECURITY SYSTEM

### Increase in retirement age

Sec. 201. (a) Section 216 of the Social Security Act is amended by adding at the end thereof the following new subsection:

Retirement Age

(1)(1) The term 'retirement age' means—

(A) with respect to an individual who attains early retirement age *[the earliest age at which one can retire and begin Social Security benefits, currently age 62]* . . . before January 1, 2000, 65 years of age;

(B) with respect to an individual who attains early retirement age after December 31, 1999, and before January 1, 2005, 65 years of age plus the number of months in the age increase factor (as determined in paragraph (3)) for the calendar year in which such individual attains early retirement age;

(C) with respect to an individual who attains early retirement age after December 31, 2004, and before January 1, 2017, 66 years of age;

(D) with respect to an individual who attains early retirement age after December 31, 2016, and before January 1, 2022, 66 years of age plus the number of months in the age increase factor (as determined in paragraph (3)) for the calendar year in which such individual attains early retirement age;

(E) with respect to an individual who attains early retirement age after December 31, 2021, 67 years of age.

(3) The age increase factor for any individual . . . shall be determined as follows:

(A) With respect to an individual who attains early retirement age in . . . the years 2000 through 2004, the age increase factor shall be equal to two-twelfths of the number of months in the period beginning with January 2000 and ending with December of the year in which the individual attains early retirement age. *[The number of months one has worked between January 2000 and December of the year in which he or she retires multiplied by one sixth is the "age increase factor" for those who reach age 62 between 2000 and 2004. This number, which will be in months, is added to the age of 65 to determine the age at which one can retire with full benefits.]*

(B) With respect to an individual who attains early retirement age in . . . the years 2017 through 2021, the age increase factor shall be equal to two-twelfths of the number of months in the period beginning with January 2017 and ending with December of the year in which the individual attains early retirement age. *[This is the same calculation as (A), but for individuals who turn 62 between 2017 and 2021.]*

(b)(1) Section 202(q)(9) of such Act is amended to read as follows:

(9) The amount of the reduction for early retirement specified in paragraph (1)—

(A) for old-age insurance benefits, wife's insurance benefits, and husband's insurance benefits, shall be the amount specified in such paragraph for the first 36 months of the reduction period . . . and five-twelfths of 1 percent for any additional months included in such periods. . . . *[This amount constitutes a reduction of the amounts stipulated before the Amendments of 1983.]*

April 20, 1983

## NOTES

1. Sylvester J. Schieber and John B. Shoven, *The Real Deal: The History and Future of Social Security* (New Haven: Yale University Press, 1999), p. 184.

2. The benefit penalty was later repealed through the Senior Citizen's Freedom to Work Act of 2000, see below.

3. The federal government is able to borrow funds from the Social Security trust fund for current operating expenses. This is simply an accounting transaction, and does not reduce the size or security of the fund. It has lately become a controversial practice, and is at the heart of debates over a Social Security "lockbox."

4. The description is that of then House Speaker Tip O'Neill (Dem., MA).

5. Paul Light, Artful Work: *The Politics of Social Security Reform* (New York: Random House, 1985), p. 125.

6. The appendix lists the major components of the package.

7. The following are only the most important of the 17 reforms. Those endorsed by the National Commission on Social Security Reform can be found in detail at http://www.ssa.gov/history/1983amend2.html.

# 19

## The Family Support Act of 1988

Welfare reform has reappeared with disappointing regularity atop the American political agenda. The problem has been that nothing seemed to work. By the 1980, the poverty rate was only slightly lower than at the start of the War on Poverty. The welfare caseload had grown by millions and, by 1988, the AFDC program alone was costing the federal government $8.1 billion a year. We have seen President Nixon's failed effort at reform. In 1977 Jimmy Carter offered yet another solution, only to see it, too, go down to defeat. In 1981–1982 Ronald Reagan attempted to change the welfare system through restricting eligibility. One half of a million families were taken off the AFDC rolls, and another one million lost their eligibility for food stamps. He also eliminated several old War on Poverty programs.

Reagan's changes neither solved the problem, nor removed the issue from the agenda. By 1986, the president was again highlighting welfare reform in his state of the union address. He told the Congress that "we must revise or replace programs enacted in the name of compassion that degrade the moral worth of work, encourage family breakups, and drive entire communities into a bleak and heartless dependency."[1] He announced he was ordering the White House Domestic Council to develop a new welfare strategy. He repeated the message the following year.

Reagan's renewed interest reflected a heightened debate over the effect of America's welfare system on its recipients. Reagan's emphasis on welfare "dependency" echoed that debate. There was a growing consensus that, for at least some of its recipients, the American welfare system was inadvertently producing a long-term dependence on public assistance and encouraging the breakup of families. Welfare had become a vicious cycle that reproduced behaviors that made it difficult for recipients to find and hold work, thus entrapping them in the system. However, the Reagan speech also reflected a second concern. In an era of massive deficits, the U.S. government was coming under increasing pressure to reduce welfare spending.

Liberals and conservatives took distinct stances in this new welfare debate. Both agreed on the need to end welfare dependence, but disagreed over how to do it. Liberals believed the best approach was to provide welfare recipients the resources and support they would need to enter the workforce. So they focused upon issues such as job training, child care, health coverage, and a more generous "disregard" of earned income when calculating AFDC support. Conservatives agreed on the need to get welfare recipients into the workforce, but they were skeptical that increasing resources would be successful. They preferred a tougher policy of mandatory work requirements as a condition for welfare benefits.

President Reagan's White House Domestic Council never articulated a new welfare strategy. Stumped, it could only recommend that the federal government give increased latitude to the states to experiment with new approaches to welfare. For the first time since passage of the Social Security Act in 1935, the federal government had to ask the states what to do. This was made easier by the fact that, also for the first time since 1935, the states had an answer. In the 1980s, the National Governors' Association had come up with its own welfare plan, and several states had already been trying new measures to get individuals on AFDC into the workforce. Massachusetts had a program called "ETC," Employment and Training Choices, and Illinois had "Project Choice," to take two examples. The common thread was combining public assistance with job training, followed by help in finding employment. The National Governors' Association drafted a program based on these state models, essentially changing welfare into a jobs program. This program, endorsed by every governor but one, offered the appealing slogan of "a contract, not a check." Welfare recipients would enter into contracts with the state welfare agency. They would promise to engage in the education or job training needed to obtain a job, and the state would give them the support and resources they needed to move into the workforce. The most controversial portion of the plan was a guaranteed minimum payment, set to the local standard of living, to be given to welfare families as they progressed through their contract. Washington's role in this new program was simply to pick up the cost, estimated by the governors at around one billion dollars. The chair of the National Governors' Association, Bill Clinton of Arkansas, announced the plan on February 24, 1987.

Legislation containing some of these proposals was already in Congress. But it was a month later that Harold Ford (Dem., TN) introduced an $11.8 billion program with the purpose of moving individuals from welfare to work. Ford's plan was more liberal, and more expensive, than that of the governors. It called for the creation of an education and job training program for AFDC recipients and for the provision of resources to help them overcome obstacles to joining the workforce, such as child care and health benefits. The centerpiece of the legislation was a job program called NET-Work, set to replace the old Work Incentive Program that had been added to the AFDC through amendments in 1967. NETWork made it mandatory for AFDC recipients whose children were over age six to enroll in an education or job training program (states could lower the age limit by providing child care). Ford's bill also imposed new requirements on states. They would be forced to institute the AFDC-UP (AFDC-Unemployed Parent) program. AFDC-UP, enacted as a voluntary program in the 1962 reforms, made two-parent families in which the principal wage earner was unemployed eligible for AFDC benefits. States also would have to offer eligible families a minimum welfare benefit equal to at least 15 percent of the state's median income. And they would have to target their NETWork program at long-term welfare dependents.

Ford's program was in fact the Democrat party program. The House majority leader and majority whips were among its cosponsors. Governors were not keen on the additional requirements, even though the bill called for additional matching grants for the states. The Reagan administration did not like the bill either. The bill's price tag, and then Ford's indictment for personal financial irregularities, slowed its legislative progress. Worried, Democrats reduced the program's cost by one half, and then rammed the bill through the Ways and Means Committee on a series of party-line votes. Money was saved by reducing Medicaid health benefits and by eliminating the state minimum welfare benefit.

Though Democrat leaders kept close watch on the bill in the Ways and Means Committee, they lost control of the legislation as it wended its way through two other House committees. The Education and Labor Committee and the Energy and Commerce Committee each also examined the bill. Both are historically more liberal than the Ways and Means Committee, and senior Democrats in each redrafted the bill to reflect their more liberal viewpoints. Augustus F. Hawkins (Dem., CA), the head of the Education and Labor Committee, would have raised the job training exemption to recipients with children under the age of 15. Critics noted this would exclude the lion's share of AFDC recipients. His plan also prohibited a state from requiring that a recipient perform work to remain eligible for welfare payments. In the Energy and Commerce Committee, the Medicaid subcommittee redrafted the bill to include not six, but 42 months of Medicaid coverage after an AFDC recipient entered the workforce. By the time the committees had finished, the bill was significantly more expensive than that drafted in the Ways and Means Committee.

The legislation emerged at about the same time as Speaker James Wright (Dem., TX) and President Reagan were negotiating the budget. House Democrat leaders tried to fold the bill into the "reconciliation" budget measure that the two were hammering out. Doing so would protect Democrats from a potentially unpopular welfare vote, as well as disguise the bill's final cost. As important, it would protect the bill from a Reagan veto. But 48 Democrats abandoned their leadership and voted with Republicans to reject the rule for debate on the reconciliation bill, and leaders had to strip the welfare bill from the reconciliation measure.

The vote demonstrated that conservative Democrats did not like their party's welfare plan. It took six weeks of lobbying by party leaders to secure their support. Finally, the House leadership allowed conservative Democrats one floor amendment that would cut $500 million from the program. (The Republicans were also allowed one substitute.) This allowed them to show their concern over the cost, and protected them from public hostility over the bill. Even so, the rule to debate the bill barely passed, 213 to 206.

While activity buzzed in the House, the Senate moved more deliberately. There, the debate was dominated by Sen. Daniel Patrick Moynihan (Dem., NY). Moynihan had a long-standing academic interest in welfare policy and had been a progenitor both of the War on Poverty program and Nixon's Family Assistance Plan. In July 1987, Moynihan introduced his own bill for welfare reform. Moynihan's approach differed in two important respects from the

House legislation. First, he was disturbed by what he saw as the decline of the American family. Increasing numbers of children were being raised in single-parent households, and children whose parents had never been married had grown sixfold since 1970. Fewer than one third of poor women received any child support from the child's absent father. He believed the welfare system needed to focus upon encouraging stable families and responsible parenting. In his rather blunt words, "if you can't support your kids, don't have them."[2] Thus his legislation included strict provisions to determine paternity and enforce child support payments. To reflect his emphasis, he wished to change the name of the AFDC to "Child Support Supplements."

These measures did not attract much controversy. But he also wanted a job training program. Unlike Democrats in the House, he wanted a program that would not provoke a Reagan veto. That meant defusing the administration's hostility and bringing Republicans on board. Thus, he proceeded cautiously. His bill did not raise welfare benefits or impose minimum benefit standards. He called his work program JOBS ("Job Opportunity and Basic Skills Training Program"). JOBS cost $400 million less than NETWork. The aim was to keep the cost at a level that would obtain bipartisan support. However, by the end of 1987, he had yet to gain either Reagan's or Republican Senate Minority Leader Robert Dole's (KS) approval, so he did not bring his bill up for consideration that year.

At the beginning of 1988, the governors descended upon Washington, determined to rebuild interest in their welfare plan. They found Reagan supporting a GOP alternative to the Ford and Moynihan bills. Offered in the House the previous year, it authorized $500 million a year to be given to the states to allow them to experiment on new approaches to welfare. It also required every AFDC recipient to work or to participate in a job training program, unless she was a mother with a child under the age of six months. This alternative would cost about one fifth of the Democrats' bill.

The governors were able to convince Senate Finance Committee Chair Lloyd Bentsen (Dem., TX) to hold hearings on the welfare bill passed by the House by presenting him with a petition signed by 48 governors. The committee preferred to consider Moynihan's version. With a little prodding from Bentsen, Moynihan cut another $300 million from his proposal and the Finance Committee voted to approve it, 17 to 3. Included in the majority was Robert Dole, whom the New York senator had convinced to support his bill.

Senators claimed that, unlike the House bill, their welfare bill was "revenue-neutral." A variety of technical measures were included purportedly to bring in new revenues equal to its five-year $2.8 billion cost. But that did not protect it from a threatened Reagan veto. Reagan remained adamant that states not be required to join the AFDC-UP program. Not all states had adopted the program, and Reagan was hostile to anything that would force them to do so. In his view, the mandate would raise the number of Americans on the welfare rolls, expanding rather than reforming the program. As a compromise, Dole offered an amendment to require individuals in AFDC-UP to work at least 16 hours a week in a community work experience program, during which they would "earn" their welfare payments. Senators approved Dole's amendment. In so doing, Congress had for the first time imposed a requirement that welfare recipients must work to receive welfare benefits. As might be expected, this aroused fierce controversy. It came not only from welfare advocates, but from state welfare administrators as well. Implementing this "workfare" could be very expensive for states, without necessarily training welfare recipients for real jobs.

Dole's amendment led to a logjam. Moynihan would not accept a bill with the amendment, and the president would not accept a bill without it. Bentsen and the Finance Committee decided to redraft the bill in as administration-friendly manner as possible, and let the chips fall where they may. To placate Reagan, states were mandated to include two activities from among job search, community work experience, or subsidized employment, in their AFDC programs. The AFDC-UP work requirement was included. States were also required to enroll at least 22 percent of their welfare caseloads into their JOBS programs by 1994. With these changes, the Senate passed the Family Support Act.

The opposition of Reagan, and clear differences between liberals and conservatives, as well as between the houses, guaranteed a difficult conference committee for the bill. Oddly, neither the child support provisions nor the JOBS program, the cornerstone programs of the legislation, turned out to be the problem. Instead, it was the expense of the respective versions (the Senate's programs were to cost $2.8 billion over the next five years, the House's $7 billion), and whether work ought to be mandatory in order for welfare recipients to obtain their benefits. It was House Democrats who most itched for a conference fight. The House GOP indicated it would accept the Senate bill, but Speaker Wright was determined to pull the legislation closer to the more liberal House version. A split within his own caucus fatally undercut his plans. Sixty-five moderate and conservative Democrats crossed the aisle to vote with Republicans to instruct the House conference delegates to support the Senate's bill.

In spite of entering the conference committee with this weak hand, House leaders still demanded the removal of the work requirement in exchange for reducing the bill's cost. This dispute appeared insolvable until the 1988 presidential race became a factor. Massachusetts Governor Michael Dukakis, the Democrats' choice for president that year, had picked Lloyd Bentsen to be the party's vice presidential nominee. Dukakis publicly praised Sen. Bentsen for his work on the welfare bill, an implicit message to House leaders to yield on the work requirement and successfully conclude the conference committee. As the governor of a state with a heralded welfare-job training program, a similar national bill would be a feather in his cap for the fall campaign.

A last-ditch negotiation was scheduled for September 26, 1988. Bentsen canceled campaign appearances to attend. A deal was finally struck. The work requirement was kept. Welfare recipients would have to work 16 hours in community service to obtain benefits. In exchange, liberals would get a larger program than the Senate had desired. Conferees kept the provision mandating the AFDC-UP program on the states, as well as the expanded child care and Medicaid benefits. The job training program would be called JOBS, as in the Senate version.

With this compromise, Congress enacted what the *Congressional Quarterly* called "the most significant overhaul of the welfare system in half a century."[3] Reagan accepted the compromise, signing the Family Support Act on October 13, 1988.

Though the Family Support Act did not entail vast expenditures, it marked a significant reorientation in the American welfare system. The purpose of welfare was explicitly recast as that of moving recipients into the workforce as quickly as possible. The government's role was to provide the resources necessary to do so. Strengthening family obligations, especially through child support, and ending long-term dependence upon the welfare system, were added to welfare's goals. Thus, the aims of the 1988 act were quite bold. But the numerous compromises, and, given the ambitions of the JOBS program, inadequate funding, that were necessary to pass the Family Support Act produced an act that ultimately did not revolutionize America's welfare system. Contrary to the beliefs of the time, the Family Support Act of 1988 turned out to be one more incremental step in the evolution of a very complicated policy rather than a radical new solution to America's welfare problem.

## 19. The Family Support Act of 1988

An Act to revise the AFDC program to emphasize work, child support, and family benefits, to amend Title IV of the Social Security Act to encourage and assist needy children and parents under the new program to obtain the education, training, and employment needed to avoid long-term welfare dependence, and to make other necessary improvements to assure that the new program will be more effective in achieving its objectives.

*Be it enacted by the Senate and House of Representatives of the United States of America in Congress assembled . . .* this Act may be cited as the 'Family Support Act of 1988.' *[The Act contains seven titles. Title I establishes provisions to assist the collection of child support and the establishment of paternity. Title II creates the JOBS training program. Title III mandates additional supportive services for families. Title IV makes changes in the AFDC program, while Title V authorizes money for innovative welfare demonstration projects undertaken by the states. Title VI includes a variety of miscellaneous provisions, and Title VII contains funding provisions for the legislation. Below are the most important of elements of the Family Support Act of 1988.]*

### TITLE I—CHILD SUPPORT AND ESTABLISHMENT OF PATERNITY

#### Subtitle A—Child Support

Sec. 101. Immediate Income Withholding

(A)(3)(a) . . . The wages of an absent parent shall be subject to *[automatic]* withholding *[out of his or her paycheck]* . . . except that such wages shall not be subject to such withholding . . . in any case where (i) one of the parties demonstrates, and the court . . . finds, that there is good cause not to require immediate income withholding, or (ii) a written agreement is reached between both parties which provides for an alternative arrangement . . .

#### Subtitle B—Establishment of Paternity

Sec. 111. Performance Standards for State Paternity Establishment Programs.

*[Section 111 requires a State Paternity Establishment Program to successfully establish paternity for at least 50 percent of its cases, to increase its success rate by 3 percentage points a year, or to meet the national average of state success rates, otherwise the state program will found to be in noncompliance. Further, the state program may compel genetic testing to establish paternity, may charge non-AFDC individuals for such testing, and is* "encouraged to develop a civil process for voluntarily acknowledging paternity and a civil procedure for establishing paternity in contested cases."]

## Subtitle C—Improved Procedures for Child Support Enforcement and Establishment of Paternity

Sec. 121. Requirement of Prompt State Response to Requests for Child Support Assistance.

... The *[state welfare program]* standards ... shall include standards establishing time limits governing the period or periods within which a State must accept and respond to requests ... for assistance in establishing and enforcing support orders, including requests to locate absent parents, establish paternity, and initiate proceedings to establish and collect child support awards.

## TITLE II—JOB OPPORTUNITIES AND BASIC SKILLS TRAINING PROGRAM

Sec. 201. Establishment and Operation of Program

(a) State Plan Requirement—the Social Security Act is amended to read as follows:

... (A) that the State has in effect and operation a job opportunities and basic skills training program ... ;

(B) that—

(i) ... will ... —

(I) require all recipients of aid to families with dependent children ... to participate in the program; and

(II) allow applicants for and recipients of aid to families with dependent children who are not required ... to participate in the program to do so on a voluntary basis. ...

(C) that an individual may not be required to participate in the program if such individual ...

(i) is ill, incapacitated, or of advanced age,

(ii) is needed in the home because of the illness or incapacity of another member of the household

(iii) subject to paragraph (D)—

(I) is the parent or other relative of a Child under 3 years of age. . . .

(II) is the parent or other relative personally providing care for a child under 6 years of age, unless the State assures . . . that child care . . . will be guaranteed or that participation in the program . . . will not be required for more than 20 hours a week;

(iv) works 30 or more hours a week;

(v) is a child who is under 16 or attends, full-time, an elementary, secondary, or vocational . . . school;

(vi) is pregnant if it is has been medically verified that the child is expected to be born in the month in which such participation would otherwise be required or within the 6-month period immediately following such month; or

(vii) resides in an area of the State where the program is not available;

(E) that—

(i) . . . in the case of a custodial parent who has not attained 20 years of age, has not successfully completed a high-school education (or its equivalent) . . . and is required to participate in the program . . . , the State agency . . . will require such parent to participate in an educational activity; and

(ii) the State agency may—

(I) require a parent described in clause (i) . . . to participate in educational activities directed toward the attainment of a high school diploma or its equivalent on a full-time . . . basis,

(II) establish criteria . . . under which custodial parents . . . who have not attained 18 years of age may be exempted from the school attendance requirement . . .

(III) require a parent described in clause (i) who is age 18 or 19 to participate in training or work activities . . . if such parent fails to make good progress in successfully completing such educational activities. . . .

(F) that—

(1) if an individual who is required to participate . . . fails without good cause to participate in the program or refuses without good cause to accept employment . . . *[the needs of that individual, and that individual's spouse, should the spouse also not be participating]* . . . shall not be taken into account in making the determination with respect to his or her family *[of the amount of the AFDC support to be given the family]*. . . .

(b) *[The Social Security]* Act is further amended by adding at the end the following new part:

Part F—Job Opportunities and Basic Skills Training Program

Purpose and Definitions

Sec. 481. (a) Purpose—It is the purpose of this part to assure that needy families with children obtain the education, training, and employment that will help them avoid long-term welfare dependence. . . .

Establishment and Operation of State Programs

. . . each State shall establish and operate a Job Opportunities and Basic Skills Training Program . . . under a plan approved by the Secretary . . .

*[The JOBS training program must assess the service needs, skills, and employability of each program participant and then develop an* "employability plan" *for the participant. This plan explains the services to be provided and the activities in which the participant must engage, with the purpose of attaining employment for that participant. States are required to offer a range of services, such as educational activities, job skills training, and job placement assistance. The state is allowed to include a* work supplementation program, *a* community work experience program, *and a* job search program, *among the activities in which participants engage.]*

**TITLE III—SUPPORTIVE SERVICES FOR FAMILIES**

Sec. 301. Child Care During Participation in Employment, Education, and Training.

. . . Each State agency must guarantee child care . . .

(i) for each family with a dependent child requiring such care . . . necessary for an individual in the family to accept employment or remain employed; and

(ii) for each individual participating in an education and training activity. . . .

Sec. 302. Extended Eligibility for Child Care.

. . . Each State agency must guarantee child care . . . necessary for an individual's employment in any case where a family has ceased to receive aid to families with dependent children as a result of increased hours of, or increased income from, such employment. . . .

Sec. 303. Extended Eligibility for Medical Assistance.

(a) . . . each State Plan . . . must provide that each family which was receiving aid . . . in at least 3 of the 6 months immediately preceding the month in which such family becomes ineligible for such aid, because of hours of, or income from, employment . . . shall . . . remain eligible for assistance . . . during the immediately succeeding 6-month period. . . .

(b) *Additional 6-month Extension*—each State plan . . . shall provide that the State shall offer to each family . . . in the last month of the period the option of extending coverage . . . for the succeeding 6-month period. . . .

### TITLE IV—RELATED AFDC AMENDMENTS

Sec. 401.(b) State Flexibility in Structuring Two-Parent Family Program—

(2)(A) . . . a State may design its programs to reflect the individual needs of the State . . .

(B)(i) . . . a State may, its option, limit the number of months with respect to which a family receives aid to families with dependent children to the extent determined appropriate by the State . . .

(ii)(I) A State may not limit the number of months under clause (i) . . . unless it provides in its plan . . . a program for providing education, training, and employment services . . . in order to assist parents of the children . . . in preparing for and obtaining employment.

(II) a State plan may not provide for the denial of aid . . . unless the family has received such aid . . . in at least 6 of the preceding 12 months. . . .

(C) a State may, at its option—

(i) except as otherwise provided . . . require that any parent participating in such program engage in program activities up to 40 hours per week; and

(ii) provide for the payment of aid to families with dependent children . . . after the performance of assigned program activities.

Sec. 403. Households Headed by Minor Parents.

. . . at the option of the State . . . in the case of any individual who is under the age of 18 and has never married, and who has a dependent child in his or her care (or is pregnant and is eligible for aid to families with dependent children . . . ) . . . Such individual may receive aid . . . only if such individual and child . . . reside in a place of residence maintained by a parent, legal guardian, or other adult relative . . . , or reside in a foster home, maternity home, or other adult-supervised supportive living arrangement; and . . . such aid . . . shall be provided to the parent, legal guardian, or adult relative on behalf of such individual and child . . . *[This stipulates that parents who are unmarried and legal minors may receive public assistance only if they live with an adult or in adult-supervised home, and that their assistance payments will be given directly to that adult or home.]*

### TITLE V—DEMONSTRATION PROJECTS

*[This Title provided federal money for state-run experimental programs in the following areas. States were encouraged to compete for monies with which to develop*

*new programs that would introduce new methods to accomplish the goals indicated
in the section title.]*

Sec. 501. Family Support Demonstration Projects.

Sec. 502. Demonstration Projects to Encourage States to Employ Parents
Receiving AFDC as Paid Child Care Providers.

Sec. 503. Demonstration Projects to Test Alternative Definitions of Unemployment.

Sec. 504. Demonstration Projects to Address Child Access Problems.

Sec. 505. Demonstration Projects to Expand the Number of Job Opportunities Available to Certain Low-Income Individuals.

Sec. 506. Demonstration Projects to Provide Counseling and Services to
High-Risk Teenagers.

## NOTES

1. Ronald Reagan, State of the Union Address, February 4, 1986, Public Papers
of the Presidents of the United States, Ronald Reagan, 1986, Volume I.

2. Julie Kosterlitz, "Fading Fathers," *The National Journal* 19, no. 38 (Sept. 19,
1987): 2337.

3. "After Years of Debate, Welfare Reform Clears," *Congressional Quarterly Almanac* (Washington: CQ Press, 1988), XLV, p. 349.

# 20

# The Personal Responsibility and Work Opportunity Reconciliation Act of 1996

The Personal Responsibility Act (PRWORA) was the most significant change in U.S. welfare policy since the passage of the Social
Security Act. It toughened work requirements for welfare recipients. Specifically, it ended the entitlement aspect of welfare, placing
time limits on how long an individual can obtain welfare benefits.
It also ended the AFDC program, replacing it with a program of
block grants to the states called Temporary Assistance for Needy
Families (TANF). It was a radical reform that reversed the approach
to welfare that had been developed in the 1960s.

The PRWORA developed out of a double crisis. The Family Support Act of 1988 had been followed not by the amelioration of
America's welfare problem, but by its deepening. In the three years
after its enactment, the welfare caseload grew by almost one third.
By 1994, a record 14.2 million Americans were on AFDC, costing
states and the federal government more than $20 billion a year.[1]
By anyone's reckoning, the welfare system appeared to have broken
down. To make matters worse, the escalating cost of welfare directly
collided with America's other great domestic problem of that era,
a massive budget deficit. The U.S. budget appeared to be out of
control. Severe spending measures were being urged on Congress
to somehow end this deficit.

In 1992, the Democrat presidential candidate, Bill Clinton, made
a political issue of the welfare mess. George H.W. Bush was the
president first since Eisenhower not to initiate any substantial welfare reform. Clinton attacked the president for this failure, prom-
ising, if elected, to "end welfare as we know it." Clinton's victory

laid the groundwork for the PRWORA. Unfortunately for Clinton, however, the actual legislation was as much the result of the stunning Republican congressional victory of 1994.

Clinton had been an active welfare reformer as governor and was a key drafter of the National Governors' Association plan that had led to the Family Support Act. Two academics most influenced his thinking. One was Lawrence Mead, who argued that the great failure of American welfare policy was to ignore the behavioral problems of the poor. A "culture of poverty" had been created, and federal programs needed to break it. The antithesis of this culture was the work ethic, and welfare should explicitly inculcate the latter through mandatory work requirements.[2] The second was David Ellwood, who subsequently joined the administration. Ellwood argued that the way to end welfare dependence was to make long-term AFDC recipients work at the minimum wage in exchange for public assistance and to limit the time period during which they could receive AFDC benefits.[3] Neither was a typically liberal view.

Mead, Ellwood, and Clinton did, however, share the liberal view that welfare policies could work only if the poor were given adequate resources to make a transition into the workforce. They must be given sufficient child care and health insurance support, job training resources, and work incentives. This would not be cheap. Ellwood estimated that such a program might cost $30 billion. Their view was that this short-term expense would produce long-term savings as people left the welfare rolls. But there was no getting around the political problem of that initial expenditure. Clinton created a 32-member interagency task force to surmount this problem and pull these ideas together into a coherent, new welfare initiative that he could take to Congress and the American public.

The Clinton team drafted a program, but stumbled badly over its politics. A lack of presidential attention and infighting, especially between the centrist and liberal wings of the administration, made its development difficult. But the bigger mistake was to place welfare reform behind national health care on the administration's list of priorities. There is a good argument to be made that a national health care system is an important part of poverty reform, as health care costs are thought to be a major obstacle in moving welfare recipients into the workplace. But it was impossible to push two major pieces of legislation at the same time, and the eventual failure of Clinton's health plan not only exhausted the administration, it also depleted its political capital. After this defeat, how would the administration summon the energy and public support to launch another major legislative effort? To compound the mistake, the delay in launching Clinton's plan let the GOP take the initiative on welfare. Republicans, too, had created a welfare task force, and they unveiled their plan before Clinton could announce his.

Clinton did offer his welfare package to Congress in 1994. It was based on the contract idea that the National Governors' Association had endorsed in 1987. Clinton summarized his plan in a speech that June. "We propose to offer people on welfare a simple contract. We will help you get the skills you need, but after two years, anyone who can go to work must go to work—in the private sector if possible, in a subsidized job if necessary . . . And it must be enforced."[4] The key ideas of the plan were time limits, mandatory work, and expanded assistance in finding a job. Certainly, the biggest break with the past was the proposal that most welfare recipients could receive no more than two years of cash assistance. The work requirements built on those of the Family Support Act, but were much tougher. All AFDC recipients would have to find a job within 12 weeks or they would automatically be placed in an education or job training program. All who did not comply with their "contract" would lose their pay and a portion of their AFDC benefits.

To assist individuals as they pursued their contract, the government would provide health care, child care, and job resources. The Earned Income Tax Credit would be increased, allowing the working poor a larger tax rebate, and those in job programs would be guaranteed the minimum wage. The plan was not inexpensive. It was expected to cost $9.3 billion over five years. New budget laws made it imperative to cover this added expense. The administration suggested restricting the eligibility of noncitizens to all welfare programs, including food stamps and SSI, ending the eligibility of alcoholics and drug addicts, capping state AFDC expenditures, and extending a tax that funded a hazardous waste cleanup program, as well as a variety of smaller measures.

But the Clinton plan, the most ambitious presidential welfare proposal in 20 years, was dead on arrival. Part of this was timing. The plan was released five months before congressional elections, and in the wake of the politically disastrous health care fight. Another part was bad luck. Key to guiding the bill through Congress would be the House Ways and Means Committee chair. That chair,

Daniel Rostenkowski (Dem., IL) had just been indicted on federal charges and had to resign. The committee's Human Resources subcommittee chair was Harold Ford (Dem., TN), who had just returned to his chairmanship following the resolution of his own indictment. In the Senate, the Finance Committee would play the key role. Its chair was Daniel Patrick Moynihan (Dem., NY), the author of the 1988 act, and still devoted to it. Disparaging Clinton's commitment to the issue, Moynihan characterized the president's plan as "boob bait for Bubbas."[5] In other words, congressional leadership was absent. Finally, Clinton's bill split his own party. Liberals did not like the work requirements or the time limits. Knowing they had allies inside the administration, they were not prepared to accept the plan as Clinton's final offer. The Hispanic caucus opposed the restrictions on aid to noncitizens. Democratic governors feared the state AFDC caps meant the states would wind up paying for the program. And public sector unions worried that the plan would take jobs from their members. In this environment, Democrats on the Ways and Means Committee, who first saw the plan, killed it.

Had they known what was coming, they may have rethought that strategy. For in November 1994, the Republicans won their most resounding congressional victory since 1946. Running under the "Contract with America," they took control of both houses. As a result, the future of welfare reform passed to Republican hands.

One of the "Contract with America's" 10 planks had pledged an end to welfare. The Republican bill went even further than Clinton in calling not just for time limits, but for a lifetime limit on public assistance. No one could draw benefits for more than five years of his or her entire life. Eligibility requirements for welfare programs would be stiffened to reduce the welfare rolls. Clinton's restrictions on noncitizens were kept. Eligibility for Supplemental Security Income was virtually ended for alcoholics, drug addicts, and children with behavioral disorders. Children born to teenage unwed mothers would be excluded from AFDC benefits, as would children whose paternity had not been established and children born to women already on AFDC. The latter was called the "family cap." For those who remained eligible, work was made mandatory or the recipient would lose all his or her welfare benefits. Finally, the federal government would get out of the welfare business. Instead of federal programs, the government would transfer funds to the states in a block grant, called Temporary Assistance to Needy Families

(TANF), and the states could create their own programs. The GOP trumpeted savings of some $40 billion over five years.

Child advocacy and other liberal public interest groups were aghast, but, with little influence in the Republican party, they could only watch the congressional debate from the sidelines. Ironically, the Republicans' biggest problem came from other Republicans. Before the election, the most conservative wing of the party had sponsored a bill entitled "The Real Welfare Reform Act." Written by an analyst at the Heritage Foundation, a conservative Washington think tank, it called for much faster implementation of the work requirement as well as monies for orphanages and group homes that presumably would be needed once ineligible women could no longer obtain AFDC benefits. This wing continued to favor this more stringent approach. A second group of GOP congresspersons feared that the AFDC benefit exclusions could trigger abortions among mothers who recognized they would not be able to support their children. And GOP governors were worried that "block grants" were really code words for shifting welfare's costs onto the states. House Speaker Newt Gingrich (Rep., GA), in charge of getting the "Contract with America" through the Congress in 100 days, had to negotiate with them all.

Once it became clear that Gingrich would be able to keep the Republicans united, the Democrats faced a dilemma. Lacking the votes to stop the reform, and able to unify only behind a remarkably conservative alternative (drafted by a representative who then defected to the Republican party), what should they do? They were not helped by Clinton's retreat to a sphinx-like silence. Would he veto the GOP bill or sign it?

Republicans did not know Clinton's intentions either. But they decided that no matter what he did, the GOP would win. A veto would place the onus for the failure to reform welfare fully on the president in the 1996 election. Thus, they made no efforts at bipartisanship. As it turned out, Gingrich had to overcome a minirevolt of antiabortion Republicans as well as the nearly unanimous opposition of the Democrats, but he eked out a 217 to 211 victory on the floor.

His promise fulfilled, Gingrich turned the bill over to Robert Dole (Rep., KS), the new Senate majority leader. Dole was no fan of the "Contract with America," and he had a much larger group of moderate Republicans to worry about. He wanted a more centrist bill, a preference shared by Bob Packwood (Rep., OR), chair of the Finance Committee. Packwood had his own problems, notably Senator Moynihan, reduced to being the committee's ranking minority member, but still the bill's most vituperous opponent. Packwood wanted, and needed, to tack to the left in order to get the bill through his committee. Packwood endorsed the House's TANF block grant program, but he did not like the eligibility exclusions that went with it. He excised them.

Packwood got his bill out of committee only to face a united front of 20 conservative GOP senators, led by future majority leader Trent Lott (MS), who wished to reinstall the exclusions. Sen. Dole was afraid to put the bill on the floor while the dispute lingered. While he waited for a more opportune time, Bob Packwood became snared in sexual harassment allegations, so Dole had to take personal control of the bill. He announced that the Senate would not go into recess until the bill was done, and then went to work rewriting it to appease the conservatives, while still keeping the moderates happy. His key compromise was to bring back the eligibility exclusions, but to make them optional at the states' choice. He also changed the state funding formulas to help states with high population growth rates, ending the complaints of sunbelt senators that across-the-board spending caps disproportionately harmed them.

Once again Democrats did not have the votes for their own alternatives, but unlike in the House, they were able to join with the band of moderate Republicans to take control of the bill on the Senate floor. This coalition stopped the most significant eligibility exclusions, hiked the bill's child care funding, and insisted that states be required to spend at least 80 percent of the amount of their old AFDC programs in their new TANF programs. The result was a bill that, while still radical, was substantially moderated from the House version. Its most bitter opponent was still Moynihan, who, claiming the bill utterly abandoned America's dependent children, urged a presidential veto.

In a huge conference committee that lasted three months, House and Senate Republicans resolved their differences. Republican leaders then attempted to insert the Personal Responsibility Act within the tortuously complicated 1995 budget reconciliation bill, only to see Clinton veto the reconciliation measure because of other provisions within it. Forced on its own, the bill passed both houses on close votes just before the end of the year. Clinton allowed outside pressure from public interest groups to gather, and then on January

9, 1996 vetoed the bill. He said that he could have signed the Senate version but that the sacrifices made to the House in the conference committee had cost the bill his support.

So, in the following session of Congress, reformers had to begin their efforts anew. Clinton called for a bipartisan welfare plan in his 1996 state of the union address, but it was really the National Governors' Association (NGA) that kick-started the year's legislation. In February, governors, facing ever more severe state budget difficulties, proposed a compromise plan to reform welfare. Similar to the 1995 Senate bill, it called for more federal spending on job training, child care, and other resources, and for fewer eligibility exclusions. The "family cap," for example, would be made optional. They claimed the bill would save $44 billion over seven years (the Congressional Budget Office estimated the 1995 House bill to save $64 billion).

That May, House Republicans introduced their 1996 version of the Personal Responsibility Act. Taking a page from Senate Republicans and the NGA, the act had been moderated to include more money for the states and to make the eligibility exclusions optional. But it kept the TANF, the lifetime benefit limits (with states allowed to make some exceptions), and very stiff work requirements. Several weeks earlier, Sen. Dole had surprised Washington by resigning from the Senate to devote all his efforts to the 1996 presidential campaign. With Dole gone, the Republican strategy reverted to that of the previous year: pass their bill and dare Clinton to veto it. They knew Clinton badly needed a bill to satisfy his campaign promise of 1992.

The first confrontation came over a side issue: medicaid reform. Republicans had decided to include in the 1996 bill a reform of Medicaid along the same lines as the AFDC, and this Clinton vowed to veto. It was only when internal polls began predicting a disappointing Republican showing in the coming election that GOP leaders decided to drop this demand. Junior GOP representatives, preparing for their first reelection battle, wanted a welfare bill upon which to run, and did not want the dispute over Medicaid to cost them a victory. Leaders felt they had to accede.

With the GOP yielding, it was now the Democrats who had to decide how hard they would fight the rest of the bill. Leadership did not come from Clinton, who once more remained mum. Though liberals continued to oppose the entire tenor of the reform effort, many moderate and conservative Democrats liked some of the changes and disliked the idea of publicly opposing the rest just before an election. In the House, stern Republican control over the rules of debate did not give Democrats a chance to vent their views one way or the other. With only two amendments allowed, the bill passed 256 to 170. Thirty Democrats voted with the Republican majority.

The bill's cost savings ($61 billion over five years) had been used to designate the bill a deficit-reducing budget reconciliation measure. In the Senate, this technical distinction was actually a strategic move to disallow a filibuster. (Budget bills may not be filibustered.) But reelection worries had split the Democrat opposition anyway. Half of the Senate's Democrats (23) ultimately voted for the bill. Only one Democrat seeking reelection in 1996 voted no. Thus, on an overwhelming 74 to 24 vote, the bill went to the conference committee in early August. All eyes now turned to Clinton. Would he veto the bill? Liberals, led by Moynihan, begged him to stop a disastrous bill. Moderate Democrats were just as insistent that he sign it. They did not want the president and themselves to campaign without having fulfilled his major promise of four years earlier.

Liberal activists attempted to generate outside pressure via a march on Washington. It fizzled. Far more damaging to their cause, though they did not know it, was the private advice of presidential pollster Dick Morris that a veto could turn a 15-percentage point Clinton triumph into a 3-percentage point Dole victory.[6] On August 22, 1996, President Clinton signed the Personal Responsibility and Work Opportunity Reconciliation Act into law.

A full evaluation of the effects of the PRWORA awaits its reauthorization in 2002. However, there is little doubt about the scope of its changes to America's welfare system. The Aid to Families with Dependent Children program, the backbone of the old system, is gone. No state has yet initiated a program radically different, but each is reforming in its own direction. Some have tightened eligibility far beyond the old federal rules. Idaho, for example, has reduced its welfare caseloads by 79 percent. Public assistance is no longer a right, subject to income requirements. No American can receive more than five years of cash benefits over their entire life, and never for more than two years at any one time. By 2002, at least half of those on welfare must be participating in a work activity. Anyone who refuses to work may see a part or all his or her benefits end.

Did these reforms make a difference? The coincidence of a booming economy with the enactment of the PRWORA makes it too early to tell. From 1996 to 2000 the number of families receiving welfare has dropped by one half. Half of unemployed, single mothers on welfare have found jobs.[7] Advocates claim this shows the success of the new policy. However, the caseload actually began falling in 1994, two years before the new legislation, and many experts, including David Ellwood, credit changes in the Earned Income Tax Credit and child support laws more than the PRWORA for this dramatic improvement in welfare. The definitive test of the PRWORA will not come until an economic downturn. Then we shall see if improving the incentive to work is sufficient to keep Americans off of public assistance, or whether Congress will turn to yet another welfare reform.

## 20. The Personal Responsibility and Work Opportunity Reconciliation Act of 1996

An Act to provide for reconciliation pursuant to section 201(a)(1) of the concurrent resolution on the budget for fiscal year 1997

*Be it enacted by the Senate and House of Representatives of the United States of America in Congress assembled,* . . . this Act may be cited as the "Personal Responsibility and Work Opportunity Reconciliation Act of 1996."

*[This large statute has nine separate titles. The first creates the TANF block grant program to replace the AFDC program. Title II imposes new eligibility restrictions for Supplemental Security Income payments and redefines the category of disabled children. Title III strengthens child support collection and paternity establishment, including penalties for the failure to cooperate in either. Title IV restricts welfare and other public benefits for aliens. Title V bolsters child protection by granting authority for state foster care payments, kinship care, and the creation of child welfare information systems. Title VI creates the Child Care and Development Block Grant program. Title VII amends child nutrition programs, generally by tightening eligibility and expenditures. Title VIII revises the food stamp and commodity distribution programs by imposing work requirements upon recipients and tightening eligibility standards. Title IX contains miscellaneous provisions, including several "senses of the Senate" concerning the act's implementation. Below are the key provisions of the act.]*

## TITLE I—BLOCK GRANTS FOR TEMPORARY ASSISTANCE FOR NEEDY FAMILIES

SEC. 401. PURPOSE.

(a) . . . The purpose of this part is to increase the flexibility of States . . . *[in providing public assistance programs that promote job preparation, work, and marriage.]*

SEC. 402. ELIGIBLE STATES; STATE PLAN.

(a) . . . the term 'eligible State' means . . . a State that . . . has submitted to the Secretary a plan that the Secretary has found includes the following:

(1) OUTLINE OF FAMILY ASSISTANCE PROGRAM-

(A) GENERAL PROVISIONS—A written document that outlines how the State intends to do the following:

(i) Conduct a program . . . that provides assistance to needy families with (or expecting) children and provides parents with job preparation, work, and support services to enable them to leave the program and become self-sufficient.

(ii) Require a parent or caretaker receiving assistance under the program to engage in work . . . once the State determines the parent or caretaker is ready to engage in work, or once the parent or caretaker has received assistance under the program for 24 months (whether or not consecutive), whichever is earlier.

(iii) Ensure that parents and caretakers receiving assistance under the program engage in work activities. . . .

(v) Establish goals and take action to prevent and reduce the incidence of out-of-wedlock pregnancies, with special emphasis on teenage pregnancies, and establish numerical goals for reducing the illegitimacy ratio of the State . . . for calendar years 1996 through 2005.

(vi) Conduct a program . . . that provides education and training on the problem of statutory rape so that teenage pregnancy prevention programs may be expanded in scope to include men. . . .

SEC. 403. GRANTS TO STATES.

(1) FAMILY ASSISTANCE GRANT—

(A) IN GENERAL—Each eligible State shall be entitled to receive from the Secretary, for each of fiscal years 1996, 1997, 1998, 1999,

2000, 2001, and 2002, a grant in an amount equal to the State family assistance grant.

(2) BONUS TO REWARD DECREASE IN ILLEGITIMACY—

(A) IN GENERAL—Each eligible State shall be entitled to receive from the Secretary a grant for each bonus year for which the State demonstrates a net decrease in out-of-wedlock births.

(3) SUPPLEMENTAL GRANT FOR POPULATION INCREASES IN CERTAIN STATES—

*[This paragraph sets out the formula of extra payments for states with higher than average population growth.]*

SEC. 407. MANDATORY WORK REQUIREMENTS.

(a) PARTICIPATION RATE REQUIREMENTS—

(1) A State . . . shall achieve the minimum participation rate specified in the following table for the fiscal year with respect to all families receiving assistance under the State program funded under this part:

1997—25 [*percent*] 1998—30 1999—35 2000—40 2001—45 2002 or thereafter—50.

(2) . . . A State . . . shall achieve the minimum participation rate specified in the following table for the fiscal year with respect to 2-parent families receiving assistance under the State program funded under this part:

1997—75 [*percent*] 1998—75 1999 or thereafter—90 . . .

(d) WORK ACTIVITIES DEFINED— . . . the term 'work activities' means—

(1) unsubsidized employment;

(2) subsidized private sector employment;

(3) subsidized public sector employment;

(4) work experience (including work associated with the refurbishing of publicly assisted housing) if sufficient private sector employment is not available;

(5) on-the-job training;

(6) job search and job readiness assistance;

(7) community service programs;

(8) vocational educational training (not to exceed 12 months with respect to any individual);

(9) job skills training directly related to employment;

(10) education directly related to employment, in the case of a recipient who has not received a high school diploma or a certificate of high school equivalency;

(11) satisfactory attendance at secondary school or in a course of study leading to a certificate of general equivalence, in the case of a recipient who has not completed secondary school or received such a certificate; and

(12) the provision of child care services to an individual who is participating in a community service program.

(e) PENALTIES AGAINST INDIVIDUALS—

(1) IN GENERAL— . . . if an individual in a family receiving assistance under the State program funded under this part refuses to engage in work required in accordance with this section, the State shall—

(A) reduce the amount of assistance otherwise payable to the family pro rata (or more, at the option of the State) with respect to any period during a month in which the individual so refuses; or

(B) terminate such assistance,

subject to such good cause and other exceptions as the State may establish.

SEC. 408. PROHIBITIONS; REQUIREMENTS.

(a) IN GENERAL—

(1) NO ASSISTANCE FOR FAMILIES WITHOUT A MINOR CHILD—

(2) REDUCTION OR ELIMINATION OF ASSISTANCE FOR NONCOOPERATION IN ESTABLISHING PATERNITY OR OBTAINING CHILD SUPPORT— . . .

(4) NO ASSISTANCE FOR TEENAGE PARENTS WHO DO NOT ATTEND HIGH SCHOOL OR OTHER EQUIVALENT TRAINING PROGRAM—

(5) NO ASSISTANCE FOR TEENAGE PARENTS NOT LIVING IN ADULT-SUPERVISED SETTINGS— . . .

(7) NO ASSISTANCE FOR MORE THAN 5 YEARS—

(C) HARDSHIP EXCEPTION—

(i) IN GENERAL—The State may exempt a family from the application of *[the five-year limit]* by reason of hardship or if the family includes an individual who has been battered or subjected to extreme cruelty.

(ii) LIMITATION—The number of families with respect to which an exemption made by a State under clause (i) is in effect for a fiscal year shall not exceed 20 percent of the average monthly number of families to which assistance is provided under the State program funded under this part . . .

...DENIAL OF ASSISATANCE AND BENEFITS FOR CERTAIN DRUG-RELATED CONVICTIONS.

(a) ...An individual convicted...of any...felony...which has as an element the possession, use, or distribution of a controlled substance...shall not be eligible for—

(1) assistance under any State program funded under part A of title IV of the Social Security Act, or

(2) benefits under the food stamp program or any State program carried out under the Food Stamp Act of 1977.

## TITLE II—SUPPLEMENTAL SECURITY INCOME

SEC. 211. DEFINITION AND ELIGIBILITY RULES.

(a) DEFINITION OF CHILDHOOD DISABILITY

...(i) An individual under the age of 18 shall be considered disabled for the purposes of this title if that individual has a medically determinable physical or mental impairment, which results in marked and severe functional limitations, and which can be expected to result in death or which has lasted or can be expected to last for a continuous period of not less than 12 months.

(ii) Notwithstanding clause (i), no individual under the age of 18 who engages in substantial gainful activity...may be considered to be disabled....

## TITLE III—CHILD SUPPORT

SEC. 301. STATE OBLIGATION TO PROVIDE CHILD SUPPORT ENFORCEMENT SERVICES.

(a) STATE PLAN REQUIREMENTS—*[states are required to . . . ]*—

(A) provide services relating to the establishment of paternity or the establishment, modification, or enforcement of child support. obligations, as appropriate....

(B) enforce any support obligation established...

SEC. 331. STATE LAWS CONCERNING PATERNITY ESTABLISHMENT.

*[States are required to have procedures for establishing the paternity of a child at any time before the child attains 18 years of age.]*

## TITLE IV—RESTRICTING WELFARE AND PUBLIC BENEFITS FOR ALIENS

SEC. 401. ALIENS WHO ARE NOT QUALIFIED ALIENS INELIGIBLE FOR FEDERAL PUBLIC BENEFITS.

(a) ...Notwithstanding any other provision of law...an alien who is not a qualified alien...is not eligible for any Federal public benefit

*. . . [Subsection (b) creates some exceptions to the above for things such as emergency medical care, disaster relief, public health assistance, and subsidized housing.]*

SEC. 402. LIMITED ELIGIBILITY OF QUALIFIED ALIENS FOR CERTAIN FEDERAL PROGRAMS.

. . . an alien who is a qualified alien . . . is not eligible for any specified Federal program. . . . *[Again, there are exceptions to (a)(1), including an exception for refugees and asylum seekers, lawfully admitted aliens with a significant work history in the United States and aliens who have served in the U.S. armed forces.]*

SEC. 411. ALIENS WHO ARE NOT QUALIFIED ALIENS OR NONIMMIGRANTS INELIGIBLE FOR STATE AND LOCAL PUBLIC BENEFITS.

**TITLE VI—CHILD CARE**

. . . This title may be cited as the 'Child Care and Development Block Grant Amendments of 1996.'

SEC. 602. GOALS.

(1) to allow each State maximum flexibility in developing child care programs and policies that best suit the needs of children and parents within such State;

(2) to promote parental choice to empower working parents to make their own decisions on the child care that best suits their family's needs;

(3) to encourage States to provide consumer education information to help parents make informed choices about child care;

(4) to assist States to provide child care to parents trying to achieve independence from public assistance; and

(5) to assist States in implementing the health, safety, licensing, and registration standards established in State regulations.

. . . GENERAL CHILD CARE ENTITLEMENT—

. . . each State shall, for the purpose of providing child care assistance, be entitled to payments under a grant under this subsection. . . .

**TITLE VIII—FOOD STAMPS AND COMMODITY DISTRIBUTION**

SEC. 823. DISQUALIFICATION RELATING TO CHILD SUPPORT ARREARS.

. . . At the option of a State agency, no individual shall be eligible to participate in the food stamp program as a member of any household during any month that the individual is delinquent in any payment due under a court order for the support of a child of the individual.

SEC. 824. WORK REQUIREMENT.

... Subject to the other provisions of this subsection, no individual shall be eligible to participate in the food stamp program as a member of any household if, during the preceding 36-month period, the individual received food stamp benefits for not less than 3 months (consecutive or otherwise) during which the individual did not—

(A) work 20 hours or more per week, averaged monthly;

(B) participate in and comply with the requirements of a work program for 20 hours or more per week, as determined by the State agency;

(C) participate in and comply with the requirements of a program under section 20 or a comparable program established by a State or political subdivision of a State ...

(3) EXCEPTION—Paragraph (2) shall not apply to an individual if the individual is—

(A) under 18 or over 50 years of age;

(B) medically certified as physically or mentally unfit for employment;

(C) a parent or other member of a household with responsibility for a dependent child;

(D) otherwise exempt ... ; or

(E) a pregnant woman ...

## TITLE IX—MISCELLANEOUS

SEC. 902. SANCTIONING FOR TESTING POSITIVE FOR CONTROLLED SUBSTANCES.

... States shall not be prohibited by the Federal Government from testing welfare recipients for use of controlled substances nor from sanctioning welfare recipients who test positive for use of controlled substances.

August 22, 1996

## NOTES

1. R. Kent Weaver, *Ending Welfare as We Know It* (Washington: Brookings Institutions Press, 2000), p. 103ff.

2. Lawrence Mead, *Beyond Entitlement: The Social Obligations of Citizenship* (New York: The Free Press, 1985).

3. David T. Ellwood, *Poor Support: Poverty in the American Family* (New York: Basic Books, 1988).

4. "Welfare Reform Takes a Back Seat," *Congressional Quarterly Almanac,* Volume L, p. 364.

5. Weaver, p. 232.

6. Weaver, p. 328.

7. Martin Feldstein and Kathleen Feldstein, "Welfare-to-Work Success Story," *The Boston Globe*, July 17, 2001, p. D4.

# 21

## Senior Citizens' Freedom to Work Act of 2000

The new century began amidst increasing worries about America's Social Security system. With many projecting the Social Security trust fund would be exhausted within 40 years, for how long would our retirement system be able to support the increasing numbers of Americans who relied upon it? Yet, because of the political risks involved in tackling this problem, it was not this worry but the good news brought by the economic expansion of the 1990s that led to the next revision of the U.S. social insurance system. The boom years had enticed and enabled many senior citizens to reenter the workforce. Once there, many of them encountered a unexpected twist: a reduction in their Social Security benefits.

The original Social Security Act contained an all-or-nothing "earnings test." Otherwise eligible seniors who continued working did not receive a Social Security check. In 1940, the act was amended to allow retirees to earn up to $14.99 a month and still receive their check. This amendment itself was changed many times over the years, as Congress continually tinkered with the earnings test. In 1950, seniors over the age of 75 were exempted from the test. In 1960, Congress decided that seniors above the earning test limit would see their benefits reduced by only one dollar for every two dollars earned, rather than completely cut off. This was expanded to a dollar for every three earned for those who delayed retirement to age 65. In 1972 the dollar amount of the earnings test was changed to increase with the cost of living. In 1983, the age for the earnings test was reduced to 70. And finally, in 1996, a far more liberal earnings test was imposed: By the year 2003 senior citizens would be able to earn $30,000 before they would see their benefits reduced. However, even under these relatively lenient terms, by 1999 1.2 million retirees were affected by this law. Retiree interest groups, led by the influential AARP (the American Association for Retired Persons), thus pressured for its end.

At least some of this pressure was based on a misunderstanding. Under the law, working seniors were not having their benefits taken away from them. Instead, so long as they worked, they were receiving Delayed Retirement Credits in lieu of their full benefits. When they finally fully retired, or reached the age at which the earnings test no longer applied, they or their survivors would receive their credits as additional payments to their regular benefits, thus eventually returning to them all their benefits that had been earlier reduced. This complicated system, not surprisingly, was not widely known or appreciated by retirees.

Together with the booming economy, the existence of the Delayed Retirement Credits made the debate over the end of the earnings test uncontroversial. There would be only a very small cost to the government or the Social Security system in changing the law, and even some savings in no longer having to administer such a cumbersome system. Historically, low unemployment rates meant that the issue that had initially produced the law, the fear of older workers displacing younger ones, was not of concern. Thus, when Sam Johnson (Rep., TX), along with 203 cosponsors in the House, introduced the bill, it encountered little resistance. The White House, the Social Security Administration, and all testifying interest groups supported the bill in congressional hearings.

Only one real problem arose. Recall that individuals have a choice of when to retire, one can retire at the "normal" retirement age of 65, or at the early age of 62. In the latter case, one receives smaller monthly benefits. Today about 60 percent of retirees choose the early option. The worry was that anything that encouraged these individuals to retire early would lead them, and their surviving spouses, to live on a smaller level of benefits for the remainder of their lives. This would increase the levels of poverty and hardship for these individuals after they, or their spouses, could no longer work. Since all parties, including the AARP, shared this concern, it was agreed to end the earnings test only for those retiring at the normal age. The test was kept for those retiring at age 62 to discourage them from this choice.

The House of Representatives by an overwhelming 422 to 0 vote passed the bill. The Senate followed with its own 100 to 0 vote. On April 7, 2000 President Clinton signed the Senior Citizens' Freedom to Work Act into law. Is it a sign of the future that one of the very first U.S. laws of the new century dealt with America's social insurance system?

# 21. The Senior Citizen's Freedom to Work Act of 2000

An Act to amend title II of the Social Security Act to eliminate the earnings test for individuals who have attained retirement age.

Be it enacted by the Senate and House of Representatives of the United States of America in Congress assembled,

**SECTION 1. SHORT TITLE.**

This Act may be cited as the 'Senior Citizens' Freedom to Work Act of 2000.'

**SEC. 2. ELIMINATION OF EARNINGS TEST FOR INDIVIDUALS WHO HAVE ATTAINED RETIREMENT AGE.**

*[This section revises Section 203 of the Social Security Act of 1935, the section that includes the "earnings test," by lowering the age at which one is exempt from this test from 70 to the current full retirement age. The Social Security Amendments of 1983 created, in Section 216(1), a schedule by which this age will slowly rise from 65 to 67. This complication is why Section 2 of this act must refer to Section 216(1).]*

Section 203 of the Social Security Act (42 U.S.C. 403) is amended—

(1) in subsection (c)(1), by striking "the age of seventy" and inserting "retirement age (as defined in section 216(l))";*[etc., through the entirety of the Section.]*

**SEC. 3. NONAPPLICATION OF RULES FOR COMPUTATION OF EXEMPT AMOUNT FOR INDIVIDUALS WHO HAVE ATTAINED RETIREMENT AGE.**

(a) . . . the Social Security Act . . . is amended by adding at the end the following new subparagraph:

"(E) . . . no deductions in benefits shall be made . . . with respect to the earnings of any individual in any month beginning with the month in which the individual attains retirement age (as defined in section 216(l))."

The amendments made by this Act shall apply with respect to taxable years ending after December 31, 1999.

April 7, 2000.

# Glossary

**AFDC (Aid to Families with Dependent Children).** Originally called Aid to Dependent Children (Title IV of the Social Security Act of 1935), AFDC was the primary American low-income welfare program until Congress terminated it in 1996. It has been replaced by the TANF (Temporary Assistance for Needy Families) program.

**Appropriations (appropriation bill).** A congressional act to designate a specified sum of money from a fund of the United States Treasury to pay for an authorized public program. All government programs that need federal funds with which to operate must have funds appropriated for them.

**Authorization (authorization bill).** A congressional act that establishes or continues an agency or program, and provides it with the legal authority to operate.

**Block Grant.** Monies distributed by the federal government to the states under broad policy categories. The states then use the monies, largely as they see fit, to advance the designated policy.

**COLA (Cost-of-Living Adjustment).** An annual increase made in the benefits of many social security and welfare programs to counter the effects of inflation. Generally the Consumer Price Index (CPI) is used to make this adjustment.

**Conference Committee.** A congressional committee composed of senators and representatives who resolve the differences between legislation as it was passed in the Senate and in the House. The resulting bill is then returned to both houses of Congress for their approval.

**CPI (Consumer Price Index).** Compiled by the U.S. Department of Labor, the CPI is a compilation of the cost of a "basket" of goods and services purchased by a typical urban resident. It is used as a measure of the inflation rate in the United States. Many programs with COLAs rely on the CPI.

**Early Retirement.** Under the Social Security Act, qualified individuals may currently elect to begin receiving benefits at the age of sixty-two. However, individuals who choose early retirement receive smaller monthly benefits than if they had continued to work until their full retirement age.

**Entitlement Programs**. Social security and welfare programs available to any American who has met the criteria for eligibility.

**FICA (Federal Insurance Contributions Act)**. The law that sets the rate of taxes on earned income to pay for Social Security and Medicare.

**Finance Committee**. The committee of the Senate that has jurisdiction over tax and revenue measures. Most social security and welfare legislation is under the jurisdiction of this committee.

**Grant-In-Aid**. Also called a categorical grant. Money distributed by the federal government to another government, institution, or person, for a specific program or policy. Typically, for social security and welfare policies, state or local governments must match the federal money with additional money of their own. This form of federal assistance places far more restrictions on the use of the money than do Block Grants.

**HEW (Department of Health, Education, and Welfare)**. A cabinet-level department created by Dwight Eisenhower in 1953. It was active in formulating and managing federal welfare policies. In 1980, a separate Department of Education was established, and the HEW became the Department of Health and Human Services.

**HHS (Department of Health and Human Services)**. The successor to the HEW, it houses most of the federal agencies responsible for managing welfare and income security programs.

**Income Tax Credit**. A tax offset which a taxpayer may subtract from the taxes he or she otherwise would owe. A credit differs from a tax deduction, which is subtracted from an individual's income before the tax is computed.

**Means-Tested Programs**. Social security and welfare programs available only to those who demonstrate that their incomes fall below the level of need designated by the program.

**OASDI (Old-Age, Survivors, and Disability Insurance)**. Though it is commonly called "social security," the OASDI is actually but one part of the Social Security Act. It is composed of two programs, the OASI (Old-Age and Survivors Insurance) and the DI (Disability Insurance), each with its own trust fund. The OASDI is managed by the Social Security Administration (SSA).

**Pay-as-you-go**. A form of program financing in which current benefits are paid from current revenues. This may be contrasted with programs that are funded through reserve accounts or trust funds.

**Social Insurance**. A comprehensive welfare plan that is universal in its coverage and based on a program that spreads the cost of the benefits among the entire population rather than upon individual recipients. Social Security is the primary American social insurance program.

**SSA (Social Security Administration)**. Under the direction of the Commissioner of Social Security, it administers the Social Security (OASDI) and Supplemental Security Income (SSI) programs established under the Social Security Act. The SSA has been an independent agency since 1995.

**SSI (Supplemental Security Income)**. The primary welfare program for aged, blind, and disabled individuals. It provides cash assistance to these individuals from the general revenues. SSI was established in 1974, replacing earlier programs created in the Social Security Act of 1935.

**Title**. The heading or introductory clause of a statute that indicates the subject of the statute. A complicated piece of legislation may contain multiple titles. Each specific program in the Social Security Act of 1935, for example, was placed under a different title.

**Trigger Mechanism**. A formula or indicator that, upon reaching a predetermined level, initiates specific actions within a program. Economic indicators, such as the unemployment or inflation rates, are often used as triggers of such actions as increased benefits or extended eligibility within the program.

**Trust Fund**. Money set aside for the benefit of eligible recipients and managed by a trustee. Social security (OASDI) and Medicare both are financed in part through the use of trust funds.

**Unemployment Rate**. The Department of Labor estimates the number of unemployed workers in the United States by conducting a monthly survey of households. From the figures gained through this survey, the unemployment rate is estimated as:

[(number unemployed Americans seeking work)/(number in the labor force)] X 100.

**Ways and Means Committee**. The committee of the House of Representatives that has jurisdiction over tax and revenue measures. Most social security and welfare legislation is under the jurisdiction of this committee.

**Work Incentives**. Since 1967, many income support programs have contained provisions to encourage beneficiaries to enter the workforce. Incentives may include tax credits or more generous benefits. More recent programs have contained provisions mandating work as a condition to receive, or continue to receive, benefits.

# Bibliography

Achenbaum, W. Andrew. *Social Security: Visions and Revisions* (New York: Cambridge University Press, 1986).

Altmeyer, Arthur J. *The Formative Years of Social Security* (Madison: University of Wisconsin Press, 1966).

Amenta, Edward, and Skocpol, Theda. "Redefining the New Deal: World War II and the Development of Social Provision in the United States," in Margaret Weir, Ann Shola Orloff, and Theda Skocpol eds., *The Politics of Social Policy in the United States* (Princeton: Princeton University Press, 1988).

Amenta, Edwin, and Parikh, Sunita. "Capitalists Did Not Want the Social Security Act." *American Sociological Review* 56, no. 1 (Feb. 1981): 124–29.

Avruch, Sheila, and Cackley, Alicia Puente. "Savings Achieved by Giving WIC Benefits to Women Prenatally." *Public Health Reports* 110 (January-February, 1995), pp. 27–34.

Bennett, Michael J. *When Dreams Come True: The G.I. Bill and the Making of Modern America* (Washington: Brassey's, 1996).

Berkowitz, Edward. *America's Welfare State: From Roosevelt to Reagan* (Baltimore: Johns Hopkins, 1991).

Berkowitz, Edward, and McQuaid, Kim. *Creating the Welfare State: The Political Economy of Twentieth Century Reform* (New York: Praeger, 1988).

Bernstein, Irving. *The Lean Years: A History of the American Worker: 1920–1933* (Baltimore: Penguin Books, 1970).

Bernstein, Merton C., and Bernstein, Joan Brodshaug. *Social Security: The System That Works* (New York: Basic Books, 1988).

Berry, Jeffrey M. *Feeding Hungry People: Rulemaking in the Food Stamp Program* (New Brunswick: Rutgers University Press, 1984).

Blaustein, Saul J. *Unemployment Insurance in the United States: The First Half Century* (Kalamazoo: W.E. Upjohn Institute, 1993).

Burke, Vincent J., and Burke, Vee. *Nixon's Good Deed: Welfare Reform* (New York: Columbia University Press, 1974).

Cammisa, Anne Marie. *From Rhetoric to Reform? Welfare Policy in American Politics* (Boulder: Westview Press, 1998).

Cohen, Wilbur J., and Myers, Robert J. "Social Security Act Amendments of 1950: A Summary and Legislative History." *Social Security Bulletin* (October 1950), pp. 3–14.

*Congressional Quarterly Almanac*, Vol. XX (1964) (Washington: CQ Press, 1964).

*Congressional Quarterly Almanac*, Vol. XXVIII (1972) (Washington: CQ Press, 1972).

*Congressional Quarterly Almanac*, Vol. XLIV (1987) (Washington: CQ Press, 1987).

*Congressional Quarterly Almanac*, Vol. XLV (1988) (Washington: CQ Press, 1988).

*Congressional Quarterly Almanac*, Volume L (1994) (Washington: CQ Press, 1994).

*Congressional Quarterly Almanac*, Volume LI (1996) (Washington: CQ Press, 1996).

*Congressional Quarterly Weekly Report*, Vol. 27, No. 47 November 21, 1969 (Washington: CQ Press, 1969).

*Congressional Quarterly Weekly Report*, Vol. 32, No. 52 December 28, 1974 (Washington: CQ Press, 1974).

Corning, Peter A. *The Evolution of Medicare, From Idea to Law.* http://www.ssa.gov/history/corning.html (originally published, 1969).

Curry, Leonard P. *Blueprint for Modern America: Nonmilitary Legislation of the First Civil War Congress* (Nashville: Vanderbilt University Press, 1968).

Davies, Wallace Evan. *Patriotism on Parade: The Story of Veterans' and Hereditary Organizations in America 1783–1900* (Cambridge: Harvard University Press, 1955).

Derthick, Martha. *Policymaking for Social Security* (Washington: The Brookings Institution Press, 1979).

Du Bois, James T., and Matthews, Gertrude S. *Galusha A. Grow: Father of the Homestead Law* (New York: Houghton Mifflin, 1917).

Eisinger, Peter K. *Toward an End to Hunger in America* (Washington: The Brookings Institution, 1998).

Ellwood, David T. *Poor Support: Poverty in the American Family* (New York: Basic Books, 1988).

Feingold, Eugene. *Medicare: Policy and Politics* (San Francisco: Chandler Publishing Company, 1966).

Feldstein, Martin, and Feldstein, Kathleen. "Welfare-to-Work Success Story." *The Boston Globe*, July 17, 2001.

Finegold, Kenneth, "Agriculture and the Politics of U.S. Social Provision: Social Insurance and Food Stamps," in Margaret Weir, Ann Shola Orloff, and Theda Skocpol, eds., *The Politics of Social Policy in the United States* (Princeton: Princeton University Press, 1988).

Foner, Eric. *Free Soil, Free Labor, Free Men: The Ideology of the Republican Party Before the Civil War* (New York: Oxford University Press, 1970).

Glasson, William H. *Federal Military Pensions in the United States* (Oxford: Oxford University Press, 1918).

Gordon, Colin. "New Deal, Old Deck: Business and the Origins of Social Security." Politics and Society, 19, no. 2 (June 1981): 165–208.

Graetz, Michael J., and Mashaw, Jerry L. *True Security: Rethinking American Social Insurance* (New Haven: Yale University Press, 1999).

Gregg, Phillip M. "The Food Stamp Program: Is It a State or Federal Problem?" *Illinois Issues*, August 17, 1977, pp. 16–19.

Hacker, Jacob S., and Pierson, Paul. "Business Power and Social Policy: Employers and the Formation of the American Welfare State," Paper Prepared for the 2000 Annual Meeting of the American Political Science Association.

Harrington, Michael. *The Other America* (New York: Macmillan Press, 1962).

Hernandez-Murillo, Ruben. "The Earned Income Tax Credit at Work." *National Economic Trends* (Federal Reserve Bank of St. Louis), April 2001, p. 1.

Hibbard Benjamin. *A History of the Public Land Policies* (New York: Peter Smith, 1939).

Howard, Christopher. *The Hidden Welfare State: Tax Expenditures and Social Policy in the United States* (Princeton: Princeton University Press, 1997).

Huff, Joan. *Nixon Reconsidered* (New York: Basic Books, 1994).

Ingersoll, Lurton D. *Life of Horace Greeley: American Newspaperman* (New York: Beekman Publishers, 1974 [originally 1873]).

Jackson, Kenneth T. *Crabgrass Frontier: The Suburbanization of the United States* (New York: Oxford University Press, 1985).

Johnson, James. "The Role of Women in the Founding of the United States' Children's Bureau," in Carol V.R. George, ed., *Remember the Ladies: New Perspectives on Women in American History: Essays in Honor of Nelson Manfred Blake* (Syracuse: Syracuse University Press, 1975).

King, Ronald. *Budgeting Entitlements: The Politics of Food Stamps* (Washington: Georgetown University Press, 2000).

Klein, Philip Shriver. *President James Buchanan: A Biography* (University Park: Pennsylvania State University Press, 1962).

Kosterlitz, Julie "Fading Fathers." *The National Journal*, 19, no. 38 (Sept. 19, 1987), pp. 2337–39.

Leff, Mark H. "Taxing the Forgotten Man: The Politics of Social Security Financing in the New Deal." *Journal of American History* 70, no. 3 (1983): 359–81.

Leman, Christopher. *The Collapse of Welfare Reform: Political Institutions, Policy and the Poor in Canada and the United States* (Cambridge: MIT Press, 1980).

Leman, Stanley J. *The Woman Citizen: Social Feminism in the 1920s* (Urbana: University of Illinois Press, 1973).

Levenstein, Lisa. "From Innocent Children to Unwanted Migrants and Unwed Moms: Two Chapters in the Public Discourse on Welfare in the United States, 1960–1961." *Journal of Women's History*, 11, no. 4 (Winter 2000): 10–33.

Light, Paul. *Artful Work: The Politics of Social Security Reform* (New York: Random House, 1985).

MacDonald, Maurice. "Food Stamps: An Analytical History." *Social Service Review* 51, no. 4 (December 1977):

Marmor, Theodor R. *The Politics of Health Care* (Chicago: Aldine Publishing Company, 1973.)

Mason, Jr., Herbert M. "Rallying the Home Front: The VFW and the G.I. Bill." *The VFW Magazine*, June 1999, pp. 12–19.

Mead, Lawrence. *Beyond Entitlement: The Social Obligations of Citizenship* (New York: The Free Press, 1985).

Moynihan, Daniel Patrick. *Maximum Feasible Misunderstanding: Community Action and the War on Poverty* (New York: The Free Press, 1969).

Murray, Charles. *Losing Ground: America's Social Policy* (New York: Basic Books, 1984).

Nelson, Daniel. *Unemployment Insurance: The American Experience 1915–1935* (Madison: University of Wisconsin Press, 1969).

Nevins, Allan. *The Emergence of Lincoln, Volume 1* (New York: Charles Scribners, 1950).

Olasky, Marvin. *The Tragedy of American Compassion* (Lanham, MD: Regnery Gateway, 1992).

O'Neill, June. "Welfare Reform Worked." *The Wall Street Journal,* August 1, 2001, p. A14.

Patterson, James T. *America's Struggle Against Poverty: 1900–1980* (Cambridge: Harvard University Press, 1981).

Perrett, Geoffrey. *Days of Sadness, Years of Triumph: The American People 1939–1945* (New York: Coward, McCann, and Geoghagan, 1973).

Peters, B. Guy. *American Public Policy: Promise and Performance, 5th edition* (New York: Chatham House Publishers, 1999).

Pierce, Neal R. "Governors' Breakthrough on Welfare Reform." *The National Journal* 19, no. 11 (March 14, 1987), p. 637.

Quadagno, Jill. *The Transformation of Old-Age Security: Class and Politics in the American Welfare State* (Chicago: University of Chicago Press, 1988).

———. "From Old Age Assistance to Supplemental Security Income: The Political Economy of Relief in the South, 1935–1972," in Margaret Weir, Ann Shola Orloff, and Theda Skocpol, eds., *The Politics of Social Policy in the United States* (Princeton: Princeton University Press, 1988).

Ripley, Randall. "Legislative Bargaining and the Food Stamp Act, 1964," in Frederick N. Cleveland, ed., *Congress and Urban Problems* (Washington: The Brookings Institution Press, 1969).

Ross, Davis R.B. *Preparing for Ulysses: Politics and Veterans During World War II* (New York: Columbia, 1969).

Rotham, Sheila. *Woman's Proper Place: A History of Changing Ideals and Practices, 1870 to the Present* (New York: Basic Books, 1978).

Rubinow, I.M. *Social Insurance* (New York: Henry Holt, 1913).

Schieber, Sylvester J., and Shoven, John B. *The Real Deal: The History and Future of Social Security* (New Haven: Yale University Press, 1999).

Schlesinger, Arthur M., Jr. *The Age of Roosevelt: The Coming of the New Deal* (New York: Houghton Mifflin, 1988).

Schottland, Charles I. *The Social Security Program in the United States* (New York: Appleton-Century-Crofts, 1963).

Skocpol, Theda. *Protecting Soldiers and Mothers* (Cambridge: Harvard University Press, 1992).

Solomon, Carmen D. "Major Decisions in the House and Senate Chambers on Social Security." *CRS Report for Congress. Congressional Research Service,* December 29, 1986.

Steiner, Gilbert Y. *Social Insecurity: The Politics of Welfare* (Chicago: Rand McNally, 1966).

Stevens, Robert B., ed. *Statutory History of the United States: Income Security* (New York: Chelsea House Publishers, 1970).

Sundquist, James L. *Politics and Policy: The Eisenhower, Kennedy, and Johnson Years* (Washington: The Brookings Institution Press, 1968).

Unger, Irwin. *The Best of Intentions: The Triumphs and Failures of the Great Society Under Kennedy, Johnson and Nixon* (New York: Doubleday, 1996).

United States Government. Department of Agriculture, Food and Nutrition

Service. *History of WIC: 1974–1999, 25th Anniversary.* http://www.fns.usda.gov/wic/MENU/NEW/wic25.htm.

United States Government. Department of Agriculture. *Food Stamp Program FAQs.* http://www.fns.usda.gov/fsp/menu/faqs/faqs.htm.

United States Government. Department of Health and Human Services. Office of the Assistant Secretary for Planning and Evaluation, Human Services Policy. *AFDC: The Baseline* (June 1998).

United States Government. Department of Health, Education, and Welfare. *Report of the Committee on Public Welfare* (September 1961).

United States Government. Public Papers of the Presidents, John F. Kennedy, 1962.

United States Government. Public Papers of the Presidents, Lyndon Baines Johnson, 1963–64, volume 1.

United States Government. Public Papers of the Presidents, Ronald Reagan, 1986, volume 1.

United States Government. Public Papers and Addresses of Franklin D. Roosevelt, 1934.

United States Government. Social Security Administration, Office of the Commissioner. *The Supplemental Security Program at the Millennium* (nd.). http://www.ssa.gov/policy/programs/ssi/millenium/index.html.

United States Government. United States House of Representatives. *Economic Security Act.* Hearings on HR 4120 before the House Ways and Means Committee, 74 Congress, 1st Session (1935).

United States House of Representative, Committee on Ways and Means, Staff Report. "Committee Staff Report on the Disability Insurance Program," 93rd Congress, Second Session, (July 1974.)

Weaver, R. Kent. *Ending Welfare As We Know It* (Washington: Brookings Institution Press, 2000).

Witte, Edwin. *Development of the Social Security Act* (Madison: University of Wisconsin Press, 1963).

# Index

**About the Author**

STEVEN G. LIVINGSTON is Associate Professor of Political Science at Middle Tennessee State University. He is also a Research Associate with the Business and Economic Research Center located on the MTSU campus.